Management Accounting for Decision Makers

Management Accounting for Decision Makers

Graham Mott

PITMAN
PUBLISHING

To Valerie, Catherine, Judith and Elizabeth

Pitman Publishing
128 Long Acre, London WC2E 9AN
A Division of Pearson Professional Limited

First published in 1987

Second edition 1991

© Graham Mott 1987, 1991

British Library Cataloguing in Publication Data
Mott, Graham *1938–*
    Management accounting for decision makers
    1. Management accounting
    I. Title
    658.1511

ISBN 0 273 03318 2

10 9 8 7

Printed in England by Clays Ltd, St Ives plc

Contents

Preface

This book is written primarily for practising managers who need a working knowledge of costing and management accounting techniques. The explanations given are as non-technical as possible and numerous examples are used to illustrate both the principles and their application.

Accounting has a language of its own and many accounting terms, like 'contribution' or 'profit', have a precise meaning which is not always understood. Whether communicating with colleagues or subordinates, managers need to know both the language and the ways that detailed financial information can be used or misused.

Three of the key functions performed by management are planning, control and decision making. It is no exaggeration to suggest that many plans and decisions are founded on, or influenced by, financial considerations.

This book is in three parts. Part I looks at the origins of costs and their various classifications, leading to the costing of the firm's output, be that a product, a process or a service. Such costing is necessary for valuing stocks and determining company profits, for cost control and for pricing purposes.

Part II of the book takes planning and control as its theme. These two management functions are interwoven in the sense that planned or standard costs, budgets, divisional objectives, etc. all need to be monitored and controlled to become effective. The techniques of marginal costing, budgetary control and accounting ratios allow this to be done.

Finally, Part III explains the financial aspects of decision making and draws heavily on the principles of marginal costing. Some decisions are short term, concerning the best or most profitable use of a firm's existing resources. Other decisions involve capital expenditure which may have a life span of many years.

Managers provide the information for these decisions and they need to know how it is used in discounted cash flow techniques. They should also know which factors influence the acceptance or rejection of new investments so that they can more easily identify worthwhile opportunities.

Most of the material in this book applies to any form of business organization, both large and small, in both public and private sectors. Some government departments, for example health, education and social services are not commercial activities. The goods or services they provide are not directly paid for by their clients. Even so, many costing techniques have relevance to the costing, budgeting and decision-making roles of public service managers. Nationalized industries are of course now virtually indistinguishable from private sector companies and in many cases have joined their ranks.

To supplement the text, you will find at the end of each chapter some questions on which to practise, with the answers provided in Appendix 4. Other questions are included for class use and a Lecturer's Guide, with answers, is available free to lecturers from the publishers. Some suggestions for work-based activities are also included at the end of each chapter. This is to encourage you as managers to find out more about management accounting practices in your own organization. Lastly, a list of further reading references is provided in case you want to go a bit deeper.

I hope you find this new edition of the book both interesting and useful. If you are a manager you will certainly find the examples given have practical application to your everyday work. I hope my efforts help you to increase your competence in the field of management accounting.

Acknowledgements

I would like to thank the following professional bodies for permission to use samples of their past examination questions throughout the text.

The relevant body for each question is denoted in brackets as indicated below. The suggested solutions are my own and not those of the body concerned, except where indicated in the case of AAT.

Association of Accounting Technicians (AAT)

The Chartered Association of Certified Accountants (Certified Diploma)

The Institute of Marketing (IOM)

The Royal Institution of Chartered Surveyors (RICS)

In addition I would like to thank the Northern Regional Management Centre for permission to use some of the work-based assignment ideas, generated when I was seconded there.

Finally, I wish to thank the various colleges who provided the questions relating to the Diploma in Management Studies (DMS).

Part I
Costing and pricing

Overview

Broadly speaking there are two main types of accounting: they are normally referred to as 'Financial Accounting' and 'Management Accounting', which also embraces costing.

Financial accounting concentrates on the recording of all financial transactions, the receipt and payment of cash, and keeping track of monies owed and owing. This all culminates in the preparation of global financial statements such as the profit and loss account, the balance sheet, value added and the sources and applications of funds. Such statements are global in the sense that they refer either to the whole company, or to some semi-autonomous unit within it.

Costing and management accounting, however, is concerned with a more detailed analysis of the costs and incomes going into the profit and loss account. This detailed analysis is used to facilitate the planning, controlling and decision-making roles of managers with respect to resources, departments, products and activities.

It must be stressed immediately that the costs and incomes making up a profit and loss account are the same costs and incomes that are analyzed in detail for costing purposes. For example, a profit and loss account may have one global figure for wages paid to the operations staff. What cost analysis does is to break down that total wage bill to identify the departments concerned, the operations performed and the products or services involved.

All financial information originates from the same basic documents. These include:

- Timesheets or timecards for wage and salary costs
- Stores issue notes or requisitions for material costs
- Invoices for purchases of materials, goods and services
- Invoices for charges to customers
- Budgets and standards for planned activities

The way this information is handled is by the use of a cost-coding system that is capable of describing every aspect of each transaction. Cost codes are structured and designed to suit the requirements of individual firms, but basically they consist of a series of numbers that identify costs and income in detail. In some ways a cost code can be likened to the UK telephone numbering system.

As both the value and description of any transaction can be expressed in numerical form, the input of cost information to computerized systems is the norm these days. The term 'Management Information System' is used to describe any planned system of collecting, storing, processing and subsequent presentation of information to management so that effective decision making and control can take place. This term suggests one complete system when in reality it is composed of a number of sub-systems and even sub-sub-systems. Financial information is one such sub-system, comprising many sub-sub-systems dealing with trading performance, overhead recovery, product costs and cost control via standards or budgets.

One of the prime tasks of any management information system is to be able to cost out the products or services provided to a firm's customers. This entails the evaluation of labour, material and overhead costs attributable to that output, whether it is a one-off product, a mass produced article, a process or a service. In this way the value of work-in-progress and stocks of finished goods (if applicable) can be determined; this valuation is essential to the determination of profit in a given period of time.

The objective of any profit-seeking organization will be to recover the total costs of the outputs and to make sufficient profit to satisfy the providers of its capital. This can be achieved either by adding a percentage oncost to total costs as a profit margin, or by aiming for an average percentage contribution from sales sufficient to recover general overheads and to leave the required profit.

These topics are now explored in detail in the following four chapters.

1 Cost analysis and classification

If you have read or studied any branch of accounting before, you may have thought you were studying a foreign language at times. The whole subject is riddled with terms and jargon that often leave the layman confused. This is not helped by the fact that occasionally we have more than one name for the same thing, and we do not always agree precisely on the same definition.

Although this book is not about bookkeeping, the story comes to mind of the accountant who was not allowed to join the top management team. So to get his own back and make sure he was indispensable, he invented a language and system of recording called 'double entry bookkeeping' that only he could understand!

I hope you will not feel this way about this book, but it is essential that we start by introducing some of the terms and definitions in costing, before going on to put them to use in other chapters. The terms we particularly need to grasp are:

- Cost unit
- Cost centre
- Direct and indirect cost
- Cost allocation
- Cost apportionment
- Overhead recovery and absorption
- Cost classification
- Cost coding

Cost Units and Cost Centres

A 'cost' is any expenditure that can be attributed to a particular item or activity and may be related to past events or to budgeted activities. The term 'cost' may apply to one individual item but is more often a function of price multiplied by quantity.

A 'cost unit' is a product or service to which costs can be charged. The term is not restricted to the final product or service supplied to clients, but includes intermediate products and services transferred internally.

In a polytechnic, for example, cost units might include a course, a refectory meal, or a library issue. In an advertising agency, examples of cost units are a specific promotion or a market research survey. Finally, in a manufacturing firm, cost units are the end-product or the cost of an internal service, for example a computer hour or a purchase order.

A 'cost centre', on the other hand, is not a unit of output but a physical location within an organization, namely a department or a section or even a piece of equipment. These locations are identified by having a unique number as part of the coding system described later.

Again in a polytechnic, examples of cost centres are an academic department, an administrative department, a computer unit and a careers service. In a leisure complex, cost centres will include a pool, squash courts, a gymnasium, a hall or other separate activities. In a manufacturing firm, cost centres will include each functional department or service activity.

Cost centres and cost units eventually come together in that the costs in cost centres are all somehow charged to cost units for control, pricing and decision-making purposes.

Direct and Indirect Costs

As the term implies, 'direct costs' are those which can be specifically identified with the output of the firm, be that a product or a service. We might also use the term when relating costs to intermediate products or services within the firm, so we need to watch the context in which it is used. For the moment we will concentrate on the former definition. All costs can be classified as either labour, materials or expenses, so we can classify direct costs in this way:

- Direct labour is the cost of wages and/or salaries of those personnel specifically working on the provision of the product or service to the customer.
- Direct materials are materials, parts and components forming part of the product or provided in the service to the customer.
- Direct expenses include other bought-in services that are specific to the product or service provided to a customer. They embrace royalties, design fees, hire charges, contract labour and similar items.

The distinctive nature of direct costs, therefore, is that their whole cost can be charged or allocated to the end product sold to the customer, without first having to be channelled through intermediate stages.

Indirect costs, however, are different. As their name implies, they are the exact opposite to direct costs. The easy definition of indirect costs is to say they are all costs which cannot be identified as direct costs! Although true, this begs the question somewhat, so we shall define them as costs which cannot be immediately identified with the end product going to customers, but which first must go through some intermediate channelling process.

As with direct costs, we can classify indirect costs by their elements as follows:

- Indirect labour includes the wages/salaries of all supervisory, maintenance, cleaning, administrative, sales, distribution and management staff. In effect it includes the pay of any employee not engaged on the product or service supplied to the customer.
- Indirect materials may often be relatively insignificant in total value, but will include stationery, cleaning materials and maintenance parts.
- Indirect expenses include power, insurance, depreciation, rent and rates, and any other general expense that is neither labour nor material.

The name often given to the total cost of all the indirects is that of 'overheads' whilst the total of all direct costs is referred to as 'prime cost'. To summarize, so far we can say:

Prime Cost = Direct Labour + Direct Materials + Direct Expenses

Overheads = Indirect Labour + Indirect Materials + Indirect Expenses

Total Cost = Prime Cost + Overheads

As one purpose of costing is concerned with the determination of profit or selling price, we can go a stage further and show the build-up of costs and profit to a final selling price in the way illustrated in Figure 1.

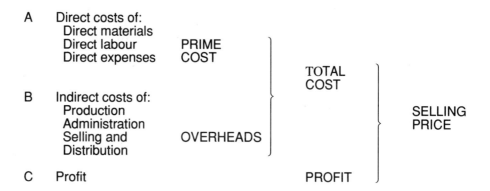

Figure 1 Build-up of costs

The ascertainment of the prime cost of any cost unit seldom causes a problem. This is because the very nature of direct costs specifically relates them to particular cost units. Much more problematical is the ascertainment of the amount of the various overheads to charge to cost units. If these indirect costs are general in nature, rather than specific to one cost unit, then they need to be allocated or apportioned to cost units as best they can.

Example

Take the case of a local garage doing car service and repair work. The mechanics' time and the material parts expended on any one job will be easily ascertained as they are written down on the customer's job sheet and are valued by a clerk in the office.

The question now remaining is how much to add for overheads and profit. Should it be the same amount for a car service taking two hours to complete as for a more tricky repair taking seven hours to do?

You are probably all too familiar with garage procedure if you run your own car! Although the mechanics might get paid say £4 per hour, this is pushed up to say £14 per hour when overheads and profit are included. The £10 per hour for overheads will have been calculated by dividing the total budgeted overheads for the year (say £200,000) by the estimated total mechanics' hours (say 20,000).

The two-hour service will be charged out at £28 plus parts whilst the seven-hour repair will be charged out at £98 plus parts. In this way the time taken to do a job is used as a basis for charging to that job a small proportion of the total overheads incurred by the garage.

Provided the garage achieves the estimated workload for its mechanics and the budgeted overheads turn out to be reasonably correct, then during the year these small amounts of overheads recovered on each job will pay for all the overhead bills incurred.

Cost Allocation and Apportionment

When a cost can be charged in total to either a cost unit or a cost centre, without first being divided into smaller parts, we say it is allocated. One example would be the material components of a microcomputer being allocated to the cost unit for that particular model.

Another example of cost allocation would be the purchase cost of invoice sets from a printing firm being allocated to the user cost centre, namely the sales department. All direct costs can be allocated to cost units, but some indirect costs may not be allocatable to cost centres without first being split into smaller parts and spread over a number of centres. This process is known as cost apportionment. A typical example is the rent paid for a building which can be apportioned to the different departments within it on a floor area basis.

There are a number of generally agreed guidelines, or bases, for overhead apportionment to user cost centres. Each individual firm, however, must determine what is appropriate in the light of its own circumstances.

Some typical examples of apportionment bases are:

Cost to be apportioned to centres	Basis
Establishment charges, e.g. rent, rates	Floor area
Stores handling and storage	Number/value of issues
Canteen subsidy	Number of employees
Depreciation	Value of assets
Administration	Number of employees

Overhead Recovery and Absorption

Whatever the output of a firm happens to be, the total cost of each product line needs ascertaining:

- for stock valuation purposes to determine company profit
- for control purposes to compare with a standard cost or an estimate and, possibly,
- for pricing purposes if prices are cost-based

By definition, direct costs are easily identifiable with individual products, but indirect costs, or overheads, have no such direct link. They are therefore allocated or apportioned to cost centres first, and from there are later shared out among the different cost units/products going through those cost centres.

Products are said to absorb overheads which are charged to them from cost centres by way of either one global or a number of individual overhead recovery rates. Typical overhead recovery rates are expressed as '£x per hour' or '£x per £1 of prime cost'.

We can summarize our knowledge of the costing process so far in the diagram in Figure 2.

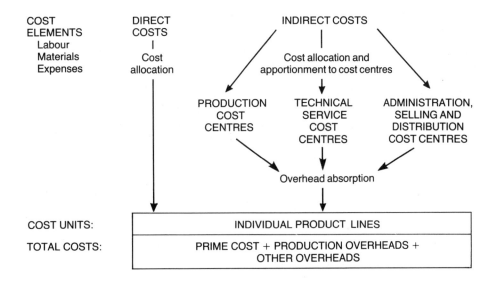

Figure 2 The costing process

Cost Classification

We have already seen that costs can be classified into the two broad categories, direct or indirect. In order to allocate and apportion costs in a logical way we need to group them in much more detail. The groupings, or classifications, to be used will vary from firm to firm as they are determined both by their origin and by their destination in the costing system.

Grouping costs by their origin is a subjective classification based on the nature of the cost concerned. For example, labour costs can be classed together according to the work carried out:

- Direct labour   Wages   Forming
     Wiring
     Assembling
     Testing

- Indirect labour   Wages   Packing
     Despatch
     Driving
     Maintenance

     Salaries   Administration
     Personnel
     Sales
     Accounting

The other main requirement is for an objective classification of costs which means that we group costs according to the cost centre and/or cost unit to which they are to be charged. All these classifications will find expression in the cost coding system but there are other classifications outside the coding system as we shall see later.

Cost Coding

A cost code is like a system of shorthand consisting of a series of numbers and/or letters used to describe both the nature and destination of costs. It facilitates the input of financial data to computerized accounting systems which cannot sort information described in words.

The following characteristics are present in a well-designed cost code:

- Clarity   The structure of the coding system and the logic of the classifications used should be clear to all users. Codes should be grouped in short blocks of about three digits with only one code possible for any one item of cost. Letters like 'O' and 'I' which can be mistaken for numbers should be avoided.
- Brevity   The number of digits should be kept to a minimum consistent with the need for information. Nothing can be retrieved that is not separately coded at the input stage.

- Flexibility   There should be enough spare capacity in the system to allow further codes to be allocated as the need arises, without destroying the original logic of the structure.

Most coding systems are composite systems where the codes are expressed in two or three blocks or sections. Typically the first block will relate to the cost centre which initiated the cost, the second block will describe the nature of the expenditure and the third block will allow appropriate costs to be charged to cost units.

Example

An example of this kind of structure would be 50 – 963 – 374 where the number 50 identified the originating department; the number 963 described the work carried out and the number 374 identified the cost unit to which it was charged:

Cost centre	*Description*	*Cost unit*
50	963	374
Location number of dept/section where cost incurred	Nature of the expense	Batch, job or customer order

---

Although cost codes have been described as a system that allows the complete analysis of costs it should not be thought that they cater only for costs. Coding numbers are also allocated to sales receipts, stocks and work-in-progress, capital receipts and capital expenditure, although most of these codes will be reserved for accountants' use only.

The branch of accounting called financial accounting is concerned solely with the subjective classification of costs denoted by the describing number. However, the other main branch, called management accounting, is concerned with all three classifications. Here, much use is made of the objective classification of costs in terms of cost centres and cost units for overhead recovery, pricing and cost control purposes.

Other Classifications

So far we have grouped costs subjectively into direct and indirect categories by the elements of labour, materials and expenses. We have also grouped them objectively by cost centre and by cost unit. All of these classifications are built into the cost coding system.

There are, however, other classifications of cost which normally do not fit into the cost coding system, but nevertheless have very important applications in costing.

The first of these is the classification of costs by behaviour, aspects of which appear continuously throughout this book as it permeates all management decision making. By behaviour we mean the relationship of cost to the level of activity or output.

Costs can be classified according to whether they remain a constant total sum irrespective of fluctuations in short-term activity levels, or whether they vary in a roughly *pro rata* manner. The former constant costs are called 'fixed' whilst the latter *pro rata* costs are called 'variable'. It is also possible to have an in-between category of costs composed of both elements and suitably described as 'semi-fixed' or 'semi-variable'.

The reason why this analysis is not built into the cost coding system is that it is not a constant classification over time. In the very short term of a week or two it is correct to describe direct labour as a fixed cost, although we normally regard it as a variable cost. Conversely, rent and rates which we regard as a fixed cost in the short term become a variable cost if we extend our time horizon enough. This is because in the long term firms can reduce the size of premises from which they operate and hence reduce the fixed cost of rent and rates.

Other classifications of costs appearing elsewhere in the text include 'opportunity cost' which is the cost of a resource in its alternative use; 'sunk cost' which is a cost already incurred, and 'controllable' or 'non-controllable' cost, which relates to the authority of the manager receiving such information.

Summary

This chapter has very much set the scene for the first part of the book, which deals with costing and pricing. We have introduced some of the key terms used in the costing process that allow costs to be charged to the end-products/ services.

Fundamental to this process is the classification of costs in both a subjective and an objective way. The subjective classification is based on the nature and description of the cost whilst the objective classification is concerned with the cost unit (product/service) or cost centre to which it is charged.

Direct costs can be allocated directly to cost units whilst indirect costs have to be allocated or apportioned to cost centres and then absorbed by products in some suitable way.

Much of the classification of costs is designed into the cost coding system, which is a kind of shorthand that allows cost information to be uniquely described and input to computer systems.

The next chapter examines the costing and pricing of labour, materials and overheads.

Further reading	**Books** Drury, C. *Management and Cost Accounting*, 2nd edn (VNR). Lucey, T. *Costing*, 3rd edn (DPP). Pizzey, A. *Principles of Cost Accountancy*, 5th edn (Cassell).

Work-based assignment	Ascertain the cost code structure of your organization, identifying the subjective and objective groupings used. If you can, obtain a detailed listing of codes and identify the coding applicable to any items of income and expenditure relating to your department.

Question with answer (see Appendix 4)	1 (a) Explain what is meant by 'subjective' and 'objective' classification of costs. (b) What are the advantages derived from the use of coding? <div align="right">(DMS)</div>

Questions for class use	1 Cost must be classified to facilitate its arrangement in as flexible a manner as possible. Required: (a) Explain the meaning of the 'classification of cost' and give some practical examples of the ways cost is classified. (b) Design a code number series for use in a costing system integrated with a financial accounting system. Detail some practical examples of the code numbers. (c) Detail four advantages of using code numbers for stock materials. <div align="right">(AAT)</div> 2 Briefly outline the cost code structure you would adopt for a boat-building company, building to customers' own design specifications. Each boat requires work in some of the six production departments which are supported by centralized technical services and administrative departments. <div align="right">(DMS)</div>

2 Costing labour, materials and overheads

The three main elements of cost are labour, materials and overheads, which in the final analysis are all charged to the end-product or service sold to customers. The amount of direct costs to charge to any cost unit is easy to identify but the amount of indirect costs is less certain.

This chapter looks at each of these cost elements in turn as there are a number of issues that need clarifying before we can understand how total costs are built up.

Labour Costs and Remuneration Systems

If we go back in time, labour costs used to form a large proportion of total costs and their analysis and control were therefore very important to the financial health of a firm. This was particularly true when output was related to the effort put in, leading to remuneration systems designed to reflect that effort and to increase motivation.

This preoccupation with labour costs has lessened with the increase in automated processes and the substitution of capital equipment for labour in manufacturing and commercial activities. In some cases, the rate of output is machine-paced rather than labour-paced, but in other industries labour may be the key controllable cost and the factor on which a profitable level of output depends.

All organizations need to keep records of employee attendance for holiday, sickness and other personnel functions. In addition, the remuneration of the employee is related to attendance and also possibly to performance. Finally, the destination of the cost of labour to cost centres and cost units needs recording to enable the input of labour cost details into the accounting system.

For all these reasons there is a need for one or more documents to record employee attendance and performance. The attendance document takes the form of either a timecard or a timesheet. A timecard can be clocked into a time-recording machine to record working hours for a week. Subject to security safeguards it is a cheap and efficient system to operate.

Timesheets can be used simply to record working hours when they are certified by a supervisor. More often, they are used in conjunction with timecards to record details of work performed during each day. In this case timecards are used to confirm attendance hours, which should reconcile with those on the timesheet. This latter document, however, contains details of work done and the codes of cost units and cost centres to be charged.

Where remuneration is to be based on output, some kind of piecework ticket will be required to record and certify the good production qualifying for payment. A further document which may be required is a job card. As the title suggests, this relates more to the job or batch being produced than to any one individual. Labour times for many workers over the whole length of the production cycle will be entered on such documents.

The costing section of a firm will use all of these documents – job cards, piecework tickets and timesheets – to charge labour costs to the appropriate cost centres and cost units. Direct labour, including bonuses and premiums, can readily be charged to the cost units involved. Indirect labour must first be channelled to a cost centre and absorbed into cost units by an overhead recovery rate.

The remuneration of employees can take two main forms. It can either be based on time attendance, or on output achieved, with many variations on the theme.

Time-based systems pay a basic rate per hour up to the normal weekly hours, say 38 hours, and enhanced rates in excess of that. Bonuses can be paid in addition to basic time rates for shift work or other unsocial hours. Such systems are easy to administer and understand but do little to provide motivation and incentive.

'Measured day work' is a variety of time-based system where relatively high basic time rates are paid in return for high output/quality. Production line operations, as in car assembly, is a typical situation for this payment method, where group rather than individual performance is measured. The title derives from the use of industrial engineers in applying work study and work measurement techniques to set agreed output rates.

The other main payment system relates wages to output in some kind of incentive scheme. This can be of benefit to both parties as employees earn more for their extra effort whilst their employer reduces his unit cost by spreading overheads over a greater output. Arguments against incentives are that they may be complex and costly to administer leading to disputes and jealousy among workers. Most systems allow for a minimum guaranteed or fall-back wage should incentive earnings not suffice through no fault of the operative.

The simplest form of incentive is 'straight piecework', where operatives are paid a constant rate or amount of time for each unit produced. To increase incentive at higher levels of production a 'differential piecework' system may be used, where higher and higher rates are paid for successive chunks of output.

A hybrid of a time base and an incentive base is the 'premium bonus system', which pays normal hourly or daily rates plus a bonus depending on the time taken relative to the time allowed.

It is also possible to provide incentives on a group rather than on an individual basis. This may be more appropriate where production is group-based, as in coalface working, or where a process cannot be identified with one individual.

An extreme example of group incentives is where all a firm's employees are rewarded on a profit-sharing or value-added basis. This allows employees to share in the general prosperity of the company but has the disadvantages of being remote and capable of being affected by external influences.

Sometimes there is confusion between the terms 'production' and 'productivity'. Production is an absolute measure of the physical quantity or value of the amount produced. Productivity is a relative measure of the output for a resource input. We might talk of production as 1,000 units but we would describe productivity as, say, 100 units per direct labour hour. The following example demonstrates this difference.

Example

You are at present considering the following results from one of your production divisions for an accounting period:

Production costs:	£
Direct material	6,000
Direct labour (rate of £3 per hour)	3,000
Variable overheads	1,200
Fixed overheads	4,500
Cost of production	£14,700

The number of units that were produced in the period was 5,000.

The cost per unit was £2.94

You have been asked to investigate a form of productivity bonus, and to explain the difference between production and productivity with specific reference to:

(a) the effect on the above figures of a 15% increase in production without any increase in productivity.
(b) the effect of the same 15% increase in production with an increase in labour productivity of 15%.
(c) the other considerations, other than labour, that should be taken into account when considering productivity bonuses. (Certified Diploma)

The production level is initially 5,000 units which would rise to 5,750 units if increased by 15%. Provided the rate of labour productivity remained constant, then the labour, material and variable overhead costs will rise by 15% in line with the increase in production. Fixed overheads, by definition, remain constant.

Should labour productivity rise by 15% also, then there will be no increase in the total labour cost for the extra output. Material and variable overhead costs will still increase *pro rata*. The total and unit costs can be set out as follows:

| | Existing situation | Increased production | |
		Same rate of productivity	Increased rate of productivity
Production level (units)	5,000	5,750	5,750
Production Costs:			
Direct material	£6,000	£6,900	£6,900
Direct labour	£3,000	£3,450	£3,000
Variable overheads	£1,200	£1,380	£1,380
Fixed overheads	£4,500	£4,500	£4,500
Cost of Production	£14,700	£16,230	£15,780
Cost per unit produced	£2.94	£2.83	£2.74
Cost reduction due to increased production		11p	11p
Cost reduction due to labour productivity		—	9p
		11p	20p

The 15% increase in the production level has brought about a reduction of 11p per unit in the cost because the fixed overheads are now spread over 5,750 units instead of the previous 5,000 units. When labour productivity increases by 15% in addition to the 15% increase in the production level, then the unit cost falls by a further 9p because the labour cost per unit is less.

Although we talk of labour productivity, this can be misleading in that it may result from the introduction of more equipment or new technology, in many instances making the job easier than before. In this case the gain in labour productivity needs to be offset by the running costs of the equipment to gauge the net overall benefit. This point should be borne in mind in any negotiations on remuneration systems that are output-based. We now turn our attention to the costing of materials.

Material Costs and Stores Pricing

When a firm holds materials or parts in stores for subsequent issue, the final profit or loss of the company can be very much influenced by the management of those stores and the cost assigned both to material issues and to the stocks remaining at each period end.

There are a number of sequential stages in the acquisition, issue and holding of stores which require their own documentation for use in the costing system:

- A 'purchase requisition' is raised internally, specifying the quantity and quality of materials required as soon as the re-order level is reached.
- A 'purchase order' for an 'economic order quantity' is then sent to the selected supplier which offers the best combination of price, quality and delivery.
- In some industries these stages may form part of a 'materials requirement planning' system based on computerized information needs to meet future orders.
- Materials received are checked for quantity/quality and a 'goods received note' is raised after matching with the purchase order. A 'goods returned note' is issued in respect of any materials returned to suppliers.
- The invoice from the supplier is matched with the goods received note before payment is made.
- Stores issues are only allowed when authorized by a 'stores requisition'.
- Annual stocktaking, or preferably continuous stocktaking on a rotating basis throughout the year, confirms stores values in the books.

All of this documentation plays a part in the bookkeeping and costing for materials. The former deals with the correct payment to suppliers for materials received but it is the latter with which we are primarily interested as managers.

If a material is purchased for a specific purpose and the specific invoice is chargeable in full immediately, without the materials being held in store for some time, then the cost unit or cost centre can be charged accordingly. It is by no means so straightforward when materials are stored for future issue on a piecemeal basis.

There are two key and interlocking aspects when we price materials. We need to value those materials remaining in store at any moment in time and we need to value each issue of materials as it takes place. If the purchase cost of materials never varied, these valuations would cause no problems, but costs do vary over time and the value we place on issues from stores affects the value of the items remaining in store.

The choice of stores pricing method rests between four main contenders which we shall examine in turn.

- First in first out method (FIFO)
- Last in first out method (LIFO)
- Weighted average method
- Standard price method

FIFO Method

The FIFO method prices stores issues in the strict order in which they were taken into stock. The oldest stock is issued first at its purchase price, then the next oldest, and so on. This could result in one issue of stores being composed of more than one price. Although materials are priced in order of receipt it is possible that they may not be issued in that same order, particularly if they are not identifiable in this way.

One effect of FIFO practice is that it will tend to understate product costs in times of rising material prices if the materials are held in stock for any great length of time. The boost this gives to profits is illusory, and positively dangerous if all profits are distributed as dividends. The reason is that some of the profit is needed to be retained in the business to buy new replacement stock at the now higher prices.

However, the balance sheet value of materials stocks, when FIFO is used, will reflect the more up-to-date prices of recent purchases. Stock values are therefore more realistic under FIFO than when the opposite LIFO system mentioned below is used.

FIFO is one of the methods approved by the accounting profession in its Statement of Standard Accounting Practice (SSAP) No.9 and is also allowed by the Inland Revenue in the computation of profit for tax purposes.

We will take a few sample transactions in one month to illustrate the principle of FIFO.

Example

A firm starts the month of July with 50 kg of Material X in stock which it bought at £2 per kg and has further receipts and issues during the next few weeks:

1 July	Opening stock 50 kg at £2
6 July	Issued 10 kg
17 July	Received 50 kg at £2.40
20 July	Issued 60 kg
31 July	Closing stock 30 kg

Using the FIFO system we can price the issues of materials and value the stock of Material X remaining at the month end as follows:

The first in first out (FIFO) method

Date	Receipts			Issues			Balance		
	Qty	Price	Value	Qty	Price	Value	Qty	Price	Value
1 Jul.	50	£2.00	£100.00				50	£2.00	£100.00
6 Jul.				10	£2.00	£20.00	40	£2.00	£ 80.00
17 Jul.	50	£2.40	£120.00				{ 40	£2.00	£ 80.00
							50	£2.40	£120.00
20 Jul.				{ 40	£2.00	£80.00			
				20	£2.40	£48.00	30	£2.40	£ 72.00
31 Jul.							30	£2.40	£ 72.00

It can be seen that any issue or receipt relates the quantity concerned to the specific price at which it is held in stock, with materials being issued in strict rotation. For example, the issue of 60kg that took place on 20 July uses up all the 40kg oldest stock at £2 before issuing the 20kg balance at the later price of £2.40 per kg. The stock in hand at the month end is valued at the most recent price at which Material X has been purchased.

LIFO Method

The LIFO method prices stores issues in the reverse order to the FIFO system by saying that the last materials to be received are the first to be issued. This has the effect that materials are always issued at, or near, their current prices, but the value of stock remaining in stores is always out of date.

LIFO is more popular in America although its use in the UK is allowed by the Companies Act 1985 along with the FIFO and weighted average methods. The use of LIFO in the UK may, however, conflict with SSAP 9 and Inland Revenue requirements.

Whichever method is used, it is impossible to get both entries in the profit and loss account and balance sheet correct. With FIFO, profits are overstated but stock values in the balance sheet are more correct. With LIFO, profits are more correct but stock values are understated in the balance sheet.

Using the same example as we did for FIFO we can price the issues and value the stock on a LIFO basis and draw conclusions.

The last in first out (LIFO) method

Date	Receipts			Issues			Balance		
	Qty	Price	Value	Qty	Price	Value	Qty	Price	Value
1 Jul.	50	£2.00	£100.00				50	£2.00	£100.00
6 Jul.				10	£2.00	£20.00	40	£2.00	£ 80.00
17 Jul.	50	£2.40	£120.00				{ 40	£2.00	£ 80.00
							50	£2.40	£120.00

20 Jul.	{	50	£2.40	£120.00					
		10	£2.00	£ 20.00	30	£2.00	£ 60.00		
31 Jul.							30	£2.00	£ 60.00

The essential differences between LIFO and FIFO centre around the pricing of the issue of materials on 20 July and the valuation of the remaining stock at the month end. LIFO values the 60kg issued at £140, which is £12 more when compared with FIFO's £128, but this is compensated by LIFO valuing remaining stock at only £60 which is £12 less than FIFO's £72 value.

Weighted Average Method

Without the use of computers both FIFO and LIFO systems would be cumbersome as they entail the recording of the same stock item at various prices.

One way round this problem is to value all items at a single price, which can best be described as a weighted average. This method also has the effect of smoothing out material price changes rather than implementing them in one jump. It also has the advantage of being acceptable to statutory, tax and accountancy authorities.

The weighted average price at any particular time is the total value of a material held divided by the number of units of that stock item. Issues of materials do not affect the weighted unit price but every time the stock is replenished a new weighted average price must be calculated. This can be illustrated by using the same example that was used above to demonstrate the LIFO and FIFO methods.

The weighted average method

Date	Receipts			Issues			Balance		
	Qty	Price	Value	Qty	Price	Value	Qty	Price	Value
1 Jul.	50	£2.00	£100.00				50	£2.00	£100.00
6 Jul.				10	£2.00	£20.00	40	£2.00	£ 80.00
17 Jul.	50	£2.40	£120.00				90	£2.22	£200.00
20 Jul.				60	£2.22	£133.33	30	£2.22	£ 66.67
31 Jul.							30	£2.22	£ 66.67

The only time the average price changes is when new materials are purchased on 17 July at a higher price than that reigning at the time. This purchase brings the previous average of £2 per unit up to approximately £2.22 per unit, which may need to be calculated to more decimal places in practice.

Standard Price Method

The final method of stores pricing occurs when a firm uses the standard costing system described in Chapter 6. In this case all materials are given a standard price and all stock and any subsequent issues are priced at this rate. Any variations of purchase prices from standard are transferred to the profit and loss account at the time of purchase.

Example

Referring back to the original example let us now assume that the standard price of Material X was set at £2 per kg. In a standard costing system all receipts are put into stock at £2 and all issues priced at the same rate. The balance of stock will also be priced at £2 per kg at any time until the standard is revised. The purchase on 17 July, however, was executed at £2.40 per kg so the excess £20 (i.e. 50kg × 40p) is written off as a loss to the profit and loss account immediately.

Four methods of stores pricing have now been discussed, each of which will give different values for the materials issued on 17 July and differing stock valuations at the month end. Over the whole life of a company there is no difference between the methods as to the total profit made, as the cost of the materials will be allowed in full on each method.

However, when looking at the performance over a discrete period of one month or one year, then the method chosen will affect the profit or loss made. This is because the cost of materials used, and hence the residual stock value, varies from method to method when purchase prices change.

We have now examined the two principal direct costs of labour and materials. Any remaining direct expenses should never cause any pricing or costing problems as the cost is chargeable immediately to a specific cost unit. Would that we could say the same about indirect costs or overheads, to which we turn our attention next!

Overhead Recovery and Apportionment

'Overheads' is the collective term for indirect costs which include every cost other than direct labour, direct materials and direct expenses. Direct costs pose no problem in the costing process because of their specific link with the end-product/service sold to customers. Unfortunately this is not the case with overheads as there is no such link with individual products for many general administrative costs.

We therefore need to examine the ways in which overheads are absorbed by products, recognizing that by the very nature of overheads this process may be somewhat arbitrary at times.

Let us take a very small firm as a first example. Such a firm may decide to lump all overheads together and absorb them by reference to some element of the direct cost going into products. (An alternative would be to relate the overhead charge to the time taken to carry out the work.)

Example

A television repair company has total overheads of £50,000 per annum, comprising rent, rates, heating, lighting and office salaries, etc.

The direct labour bill for the year amounts to £40,000 and the company decides to recover its overheads by reference to the labour cost of each repair. We can therefore calculate the overhead recovery rate as:

$$\text{Overhead recovery rate} = \frac{\text{Total overheads p.a.}}{\text{Direct labour cost p.a.}} \%$$

$$= \frac{£50,000}{£40,000} \% = 125\%$$

This overhead recovery rate states, in effect, that £1.25 overheads will be added for every £1 of direct labour cost incurred on a repair. If a certain repair required £15 of new components and took 1½ hours to complete by an engineer paid £4 per hour, then the total cost of the repair would be:

Materials	£15.00	
Labour	£ 6.00	
Overheads	£ 7.50	(£6.00 × 125%)
Total cost	£28.50	

In this way the total overheads will be apportioned over all repair work carried out and recovered in the total cost charged to customers, together with an element of profit. Under this method, products are said to absorb the overhead costs, leading to the obvious title of absorption costing.

The overhead recovery rate illustrated above should be based on forward estimates for the coming year for both overheads and labour costs. Should either, or both, of these estimates turn out to be incorrect, as is likely to happen in practice, then an under- or over-recovery of overheads will occur. An under-recovery results in a lower profit than was anticipated whilst an over-recovery results in more profit than expected.

Referring back to the example above, let us assume the estimate of £50,000 overheads was more or less correct but the direct labour cost amounted to only £35,000 for the year due to the loss of an engineer. If the 125% recovery rate remained unaltered then only £43,750 of the £50,000 overheads would have been recovered in customer charges during the year.

Although direct labour cost was chosen as a basis on which to illustrate how overheads are recovered in a small firm, there are a number of other suitable candidates. These include:

Basis	*Overhead recovery rate*
• Direct labour hours	£ overheads per labour hour
• Machine hours	£ overheads per machine hour
• Direct material cost	% of direct material cost
• Prime cost	% of prime cost
• Volume of products	£ per unit

The choice of an appropriate basis rests with an individual firm and depends on the nature of the product or service provided for customers. Where only one product is made, overheads can be recovered at £x per unit – and likewise when a number of similar products are made taking similar times and with similar direct costs. Should one product have double the direct cost of another then it is patently unfair to charge them equal amounts of overheads, and another basis must be used.

Many overheads such as rent, rates and salaries relate to the passing of time and many popular overhead recovery rates reflect this by charging £x overheads per labour or machine hour. The other main approach is to base overhead recovery on the direct costs of the product concerned using direct labour cost or direct material cost or prime cost. If either labour or material cost predominates, then it will be chosen.

The above system of lumping all overheads into one pot and absorbing them into products by means of one global overhead recovery rate may work quite satisfactorily in small firms. It will be much less satisfactory the more diverse the products and processes become, when some products would be charged for services from which they had no benefit.

This makes it necessary for overheads to be identified with specific cost centres and absorbed in the most appropriate way for that centre. At this stage, it is worth repeating part of the diagram we met in Chapter 1 when describing the costing process. As shown in Figure 3, overheads are seen to be allocated and apportioned to individual cost centres and then absorbed into products by the most appropriate overhead absorption rate for each centre.

Overheads incurred in production cost centres will be absorbed into product costs using one of the overhead recovery rates mentioned above in the context of small firms. Technical services such as maintenance, storekeeping and purchasing are all overhead costs and are apportioned to production or other cost centres on a suitable basis, for example:

Cost centre	Suitable basis
• Maintenance	Value of equipment
• Storekeeping	Number/value of issues
• Purchasing	Number of orders placed

Production overheads and technical service overheads can now be absorbed by individual product lines passing through each production cost centre. When these overhead costs are added to prime cost, we arrive at the 'production cost', but there are many general overheads remaining.

These other overheads include the cost of all administrative departments, research and development, selling and distribution. By their very nature most of these overheads have no identifiable link with individual product lines. They are therefore usually recovered by an overhead absorption rate based on production costs.

An example of overhead recovery and absorption leading up to the pricing of products is given in the section on full cost pricing contained in Chapter 4.

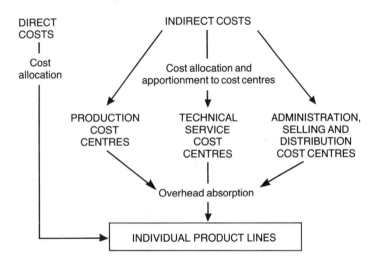

Figure 3 Allocation and absorption of overheads

A problem sometimes arises in the apportionment of service cost centre overheads to production cost centres. One or more of these service cost centres may carry out work for other service or administrative cost centres in addition to servicing production needs. The maintenance and stores departments are typical cases in point, where requests for repairs and servicing or stores issues may be initiated from anywhere in the firm.

This leads to the situation where one service cost centre may be apportioning its costs partly to other service cost centres who in turn may be apportioning costs to the first cost centre. Such a process could be never-ending but there are a number of ways to resolve this interlocking situation.

A manual method is to carry out the service cost centre apportionments in the way described and to keep repeating the process until the amounts become small enough to ignore. A variation on this theme is to place the service cost centres in some order of priority and not to allow further apportionments in, once the apportionment out has been completed. Other methods of resolving the problem of interlocking service departments involve the use of mathematical formulae which is most easily performed by computer.

Activity-Based Costing

This is a relatively new approach to the perennial problem of how to apportion overhead costs to individual product lines in absorption costing. Direct costs, by definition, can be charged immediately to the relevant product line. The absorption of overheads into total product costs is essentially a two-stage process. Indirect or overhead costs must first be charged to cost centres and at a later stage are absorbed into products.

This absorption may often be by use of a single global overhead recovery rate, commonly using direct labour hours, or their cost, as a base. Although satisfactory in some cases, it will prove more unsatisfactory when firms are highly automated, when production methods and product volumes differ widely, and when labour costs are no longer very significant relative to the fixed overhead costs.

'Activity-based costing' seeks to address this problem of inequitable overhead absorption and its consequential dangers of under- or over-pricing different product lines. It suggests that a more valid approach is to accumulate overheads not on a departmental basis but on an activity basis. This approach regards activities as incurring costs and products as consuming those activities.

In any firm, so-called 'cost drivers' need to be identified as these are the main determinants of the cost of activities. Activities will vary from firm to firm, but could include the number of production runs, the number of purchase orders placed, the number of customer orders received, etc.

When costs are accumulated by activity cost centres then the average cost per transaction can be calculated by dividing the total cost of an activity by the number of transactions performed. This average cost is then used to charge each product line for the amount of service demanded from each activity centre.

In this way, products receive a more equitable share of whatever overheads they have required the firm to incur. Product costs and product profitabilty will be more accurate than before, leading to better management decisions concerning product offerings and acceptable prices. (Articles by Drury, and by Jeans & Morrow, refer to activity-based costing; see 'Further reading'.)

Summary

In this chapter we have examined the recording and costing of the three key costs – materials, direct labour and overheads. The aim is to charge the appropriate amounts to each product or service provided to customers as a basis for pricing and control.

Methods of remuneration for direct labour fall into one of two camps. Workers are either rewarded on a time basis or on the volume of output they achieve, with a number of possible variations around these themes.

Materials to be held in stores for subsequent issue are not as straightforward to deal with as might be supposed. It is possible to price stores issues in four main ways, but whichever method is chosen affects the value of the remaining stock differently.

Overheads are certainly the most difficult costs to deal with due to their lack of identity with the end-product sold to customers. Using suitable location coding numbers we must allocate overheads directly to cost centres wherever possible, and apportion other overheads to cost centres as equitably as possible.

Once all overheads are identified with cost centres we need to absorb them into product costs by using appropriate overhead absorption or recovery rates. The next chapter continues the discussion with a look at the costing of differing end-products found in dissimilar industries.

Further reading

Books
Drury, C. *Management and Cost Accounting,* 2nd edn (VNR).
Lucey, T. *Costing*, 3rd edn (DPP).
Pizzey, A. *Principles of Cost Accountancy*, 5th edn (Cassell).

Articles
Drury, C. Product costing in the 1990s. In *Accountancy* (May 1990).
Drury, C. Activity-based costing. In *Management Accounting* (Sept. 1989).
Jeans, M. & Morrow, M. The practicalities of activity-based costing. In *Management Accounting* (Nov. 1989).
Sheridan, T. Don't count your costs – manage them. In *Management Accounting* (Feb. 1989).
Williamson, D. Incentive payment schemes. In *Management Accounting* (March 1989).

Work-Based Assignment

Where applicable, ascertain the methods used in your organization:

(a) to remunerate direct labour;
(b) to value materials issued from stores;
(c) to charge overheads to product lines.

Questions with answers
(see Appendix 4)

1 Wood & Bark Ltd trade in a single product and maintain a perpetual inventory. The company has valued its stock on the LIFO basis, but is now proposing to change to the FIFO method.

Their records disclose that 2,000 units were in stock at the beginning of the current period, and valued on the basis of a receipt of 5,000 units priced at £2.50, of which 4,000 had been sold before the end of the period, plus 500 from a delivery in 1980 when the cost was £2.00 per unit, plus 500 purchased in 1957 when the cost was £0.50 per unit.

The following transactions took place in the period January 1982 to June 1982:

January	—	Sold	1,500 units at £4.00 each
February	—	Received	10,000 units at £2.50 each
March	—	Sold	8,000 units at £4.00 each
April	—	Received	15,000 units at £2.60 each
May	—	Received	6,500 units at £2.70 each
June	—	Sold	22,000 units at £4.00 each

You are required:
(a) to calculate the stock valuation at 30 June 1982 using
    (i) the LIFO method,
    (ii) the FIFO method;
(b) to calculate the trading profit for the period January to June 1982 using both methods of valuation for opening and closing stocks;
(c) to reply to Mr Wood who suggests, 'In order to be consistent we should value opening stock on the LIFO basis and closing stock on the FIFO basis in the trading account';
(d) to explain the possible reasoning behind the company's decision to change to the FIFO method at the present time;
(e) to summarize the advantages and disadvantages of the FIFO method of stock valuation. (AAT)

2 An industrial concern manufactures three products known as P, Q and R. Each product is started in the machining area and completed in the finishing shop. The direct costs associated with each product forecast for the next trading period are:

	P £	Q £	R £
Materials	18.50	15.00	22.50
Wages:			
Machining area at £5 per hour	10.00	5.00	10.00
Finishing shop at £4 per hour	6.00	4.00	8.00
	£34.50	£24.00	£40.50

There are machines in both departments and machine hours required to complete one of each product are:

Machine area	4	1.5	3
Finishing shop	0.5	0.5	1
Budget output in units	6,000	8,000	2,000
Fixed overheads are:			
Machine area	£100,800		
Finishing shop	£ 94,500		

Required:
(a) An overhead absorption rate for fixed overheads using:
  (i) a labour-hour rate for each department;
  (ii) a machine-hour rate for each department.
(b) The total cost of each product using:
  (i) the labour-hour rate;
  (ii) the machine-hour rate, as calculated in (a) above.
(c) Your comments to the factory manager who has suggested that one overhead rate for both departments would simplify matters.
(d) The fixed cost and the variable rate of overhead cost for the machining area. This has been constant over the previous five periods, and extracted from the following:

Period	Total overhead £	Labour-hours	
1	92,600	21,300	
2	86,200	18,100	
3	95,250	22,625	
4	105,500	27,750	
5	93,200	21,600	(AAT)

3   Geils Supply Company budgets manufacturing overhead at £165,000. Included in this budget is £90,000 of fixed overhead. Overhead is to be charged to products on a machine-hour basis. At normal operating capacity the company should operate for 50,000 machine hours.
(a) What is the overhead rate for costing products?
(b) Assuming that the actual costs are in line with the budget, would you expect the overhead charged to the products to be greater or less than the actual overhead, and by how much, when the company operates at 55,000 machine-hours?
(DMS)

Questions for class use

1   All good wage-incentive schemes should incorporate certain general principles. You are required to list and discuss five such general principles.   (AAT)

2   A company which made one type of product had an actual output this year of 36,000 units compared with a budgeted output of 32,000 units. Sales for the year were 34,000 units at a selling price £34 per unit, while the opening stock for the year was 5,000 units. There was no opening stock in the preceding year. Using an absorption costing system based on budgeted levels of output, unit costs for this year and the preceding year were as follows:

	This year £	Preceding year £
Prime cost	24	22
Production overhead (fixed and var.)	5	4
Selling & admin. overhead (fixed)	1	1
Total cost	30	27
Profit	4	3
Selling price	£34	£30

Fixed production overhead this year was £48,000 and £3 per unit last year.

You are required:

(a) To prepare tabular income statements for this year on the basis:

    (i) that an absorption costing system is in use, based on budgeted levels of output;

    (ii) that fixed production overhead is charged against revenue for the year in which the expense is incurred.

(b) To comment on the reasoning underlying the different results. (AAT)

3 Job and process costing

There are a number of costing methods which are specially designed so that they suit the way in which a particular product or service is made or provided. Basically there are only two types of costing methods – 'job costing' and 'process costing' – which are then adapted to suit the requirements of any industry's output whether it is a product or a service.

These adaptations of job or process costing go under the names of 'batch costing', 'contract costing', 'operation costing' or 'service costing', 'by-product costing' and 'joint product costing'. Whichever of these costing methods is selected as appropriate, the principles of cost allocation and apportionment described in the previous chapters still apply, including the relatively new ideas on activity-based costing. We start with a look at job costing before tackling its many variants.

Job Costing

This system is employed where goods or services are provided on a one-off basis as opposed to being mass produced. Each product or service is distinguishable from others, being designed to the specific requirements of an individual customer. It is therefore the appropriate costing system for engineering firms fabricating to a blueprint, ship repairers, jobbing builders, printing firms and architects.

Job costing is performed for three reasons. It informs managers at any time of the progress of a job in cost terms. It also gives a valuation of work-in-progress on that job, which is needed to prepare final accounts at period ends and so determine profit and balance sheet values. Finally, it identifies the profit or loss on the job at completion which, if fed back to the manager concerned, can provide useful data for future price estimation and control.

In an uncomputerized system a document called a 'job card' will be used to accumulate all costs as the job progresses over its whole life, irrespective of accounting periods. In a computerized accounting system the unique job number allocated as an integral part of the cost code structure will record all costs allocated to each job and overheads absorbed by it. A print-out can be obtained at any moment in time to serve the same effect as the job card, provided the data input is up-to-date.

Any direct costs can be charged straight to the job number through the coding system when applied to timesheets, stores requisitions and invoices. The job will also attract production overheads at the predetermined departmental absorption rates. In this way the costs are built up as the job progresses and at any moment in time represents the value of work-in-progress.

In addition to being charged to individual jobs, production costs on all jobs are also charged to a 'Work-in-Progress Account'. This acts as a check, or control, on the value of all work-in-progress at any time. When a job is completed it is transferred from this 'Work-in-Progress Account' to the 'Cost of Sales Account' if sold immediately, or alternatively it is transferred to the 'Finished Goods Stock Account' at production cost.

Batch Costing

Essentially, batch costing is a variant of job costing where a batch of homogeneous products is treated as an individual job for costing purposes. Costs are recorded against a job number allocated to each batch and the final production cost is divided by the quantity of articles produced to get the production cost per article. It is ideally suited to the cost requirements of mass-production industries such as car components, electrical goods and shoemaking.

Contract Costing

This again is another variant of job costing where costs are accumulated for an individual contract, and has obvious relevance for contruction, civil engineering and shipbuilding. The 'product' is usually individually designed to the client's specification and may take months, if not years, to complete.

With the exception of shipbuilding, in most cases the work is carried out at the client's site rather than at the contractor's own premises. When the work is performed 'on site' some indirect costs can be charged directly to the contract which would not normally be possible with factory work. Examples here include site power, site telephone, use of plant, site administration and site management salaries.

When contracts extend over a long period of time, it is usual for progress payments to be allowed for in the legal document. This avoids the contractor having to provide enormous sums of working capital which it would otherwise be obliged to do. In the case of construction, the value of work completed is usually assessed on a monthly basis by a surveyor or architect.

The monthly certificate of the value of work certified in effect becomes an interim invoice but is normally subject to a deduction of 5% or 10% which is called the 'retention'. These monthly retentions are a safeguard for the client that the contractor will complete the whole job satisfactorily and are not released until some time after contract completion.

The final profit on any contract will not be known with great accuracy until the contract is actually completed and all adjustments agreed with the client. The company needs to report to its shareholders at least twice a year on the profit made in the period. It is usual, therefore, for companies to take some profit on the work as it progresses, without waiting until the end of the contract, which may take years to complete. In this way companies avoid the violent fluctuations in yearly profits which would occur if they were solely dependent on contract completions.

There are two reasons why companies will tend to underestimate the amount of profit made to date. First there is the accounting concept of conservatism which states that profits should not be anticipated before realization. Until a contract is completed, a company cannot be certain that it will not encounter any difficulties with the job and possibly incur unanticipated costs.

Second is the tax angle, which in effect means that because profits are taxable, deferring the declaration also defers the payment of tax on those profits.

This interim profit-taking is a problematical field for construction companies treading a path between the requirements of shareholders, tax authorities and accounting standards. Whatever they agree to do about taking profit on long-term work-in-progress, the policy must be followed consistently from year to year and must not conflict with SSAP No.9.

A typical practice might be to compare the contract sales value of the work certified to date with the cost of the work certified, and so identify the total profit. This is then reduced by the percentage retention and by a further conservative factor, say one-third, to allow for unforeseen events to come.

Example

Suppose a contract for a new bridge was let at a value of £300,000 with monthly progress payments subject to a retention of 10%. The value of work certified to date is £100,000 and the cost of the work including overheads amounts to £90,000. The contractor restricts the profit on work-in-progress to two-thirds. Profit to date is therefore:

	£
Value of the work certified	100,000
Total cost of work certified	90,000
Total profit	£ 10,000

Profit to be taken = (£10,000 − 10%) x ⅔
= £6,000

Process Costing

Unlike job and batch production, where activity ceases when the individual or group of products is completed, process costing applies in industries where production is continuous. In this situation we cannot identify specific costs with individual products. We can say, however, that certain costs were incurred during a particular period of time and relate that to the number of units produced. In this way we arrive at an average unit cost.

In many industries there may be partially completed products at any one time and these need to be converted into 'equivalent whole units' in order to calculate the average unit cost of one complete unit.

Example

A company started a process on 1 February and incurred the following production costs during the month:

	£
Direct materials	30,000
Direct labour	4,000
Production overheads	16,000
Total production cost	£50,000

Output for the month consisted of 2,000 complete products plus 200 partially completed products on which the stage of completion for each cost element was:

Direct materials	70%
Direct labour	40%
Production overheads	40%

We can combine this information in the following statement to calculate the average cost per complete unit as £23.63:

Cost element	Complete units	Equivalent part units	Total equivalent units	Total cost £	Average cost £
D. materials	2,000	200 x 70%	2,140	30,000	14.02
D. labour	2,000	200 x 40%	2,080	4,000	1.92
Prod'n o/heads	2,000	200 x 40%	2,080	16,000	7.69
Total				£50,000	£23.63

Process costing is applicable to industries, not only where production is continuous, but also where production passes through sequential stages, with the output of one process being fed into the next process and so on. If the above example related to the first of a number of sequential processes, then the completed work would be transferred to the second process at £23.63 per unit.

It is also possible that losses normally occur in a process and accounting for these is necessary for control purposes. Such losses increase the cost of the good production.

Example

A firm introduces 1,000 gallons of chemicals into a process at a cost of £10,000, being an average cost of £10 per gallon input. It is normal for a 20% loss to occur through evaporation, so the average cost per gallon of good output is:

$$\text{Cost per gallon} = \frac{£10,000}{(1,000 - 20\%)} = £12.50$$

When a firm uses a 'standard costing system', the abnormal gain or loss compared with the norm level stipulated in the standard cost specification is quantified as a material yield variance. This topic is pursued in Chapter 6.

It is important to distinguish between 'waste' and 'scrap', as their costing treatment is necessarily different. Waste occurs when there are process losses with no recoverable value, the result of which is to enhance the cost of good production as illustrated in the above example.

'Scrap' is a term used to describe losses which have a recoverable value, either by resale to another party or by being fed back into a similar process. In this case any 'recovery value' goes to reduce the cost of the initial process.

A similar treatment is usually given to 'by-products' where the 'net realizable value' goes to reduce the process costs of the main product. A by-product is one which arises in the course of the process to produce the main product(s) and is of relatively insignificant value. The net realizable value is the resale or re-usable value of the by-product after taking account of any handling costs incurred after separation from the main product.

A further situation to examine is where more than one product is produced simultaneously in a process. Each product may have a significant value of its own, either as a final product or as a feed into separate new processes. Such products are called 'joint products' and are primarily distinguished from by-products by their significant value.

When joint products are produced we need to separate their common process costs at the point of separation of the joint products themselves. This can be done in one of two ways:

(1) The common costs can be apportioned to individual products *pro rata* to a 'physical measure' of the quantity of each product produced, *or*

(2) The common costs can be apportioned on the basis of the 'market value' of each joint product at the time of separation.

Example

A particular process is used to manufacture Product A and Product B jointly. The joint process costs for last month amounted to £15,000 and the production, work-in-progress and sales data were as follows.

Product	Production quantity kg	Work-in-progress quantity kg	Sales quantity kg	Sales unit value £
A	6,000	1,000	5,000	2
B	9,000	2,000	7,000	3

We can use this data to apportion the costs between the two joint products, to value the work-in-progress and to calculate the profit per product, comparing the two possible bases.

Physical Quantity Method

This averages the total process cost over the combined quantity of production, namely:

$$\text{Cost per kg} = \frac{£15,000}{6,000 \text{ kg} + 9,000 \text{ kg}} = \frac{£15,000}{15,000 \text{ kg}} = £1.00 \text{ per kg}$$

This unit cost of £1 per kg is now used to value work-in-progress and the cost of sales to arrive at profit.

Product	Work-in-progress kg	£	Cost of sales kg	£
A	1,000	1,000	5,000	5,000
B	2,000	2,000	7,000	7,000
	3,000 kg	£3,000	12,000 kg	£12,000

Product	Sales kg	£	Sales value £	Cost of sales £	Profit £
A	5,000	2.00	10,000	5,000	5,000
B	7,000	3.00	21,000	7,000	14,000
			£31,000	£12,000	£19,000

Market Value Method

This method apportions joint process costs on the basis of the market or sales value of production at the point of separation.

Product	Production quantity kg	Selling price £	Sales value of production £	Apportionment of costs £
A	6,000	2.00	12,000	4,615
B	9,000	3.00	27,000	10,385
			£39,000	£15,000

Now we need to apportion the costs of each product between work-in-progress and the cost of sales.

Product	Costs £	Work-in-progress kg	£	Cost of sales kg	£
A	4,615	1,000	769	5,000	3,846
B	10,385	2,000	2,308	7,000	8,077
	£15,000		£3,077		£11,923

We can now calculate the profit on sales.

Product	Sales kg	£	Sales value £	Cost of sales £	Profit £
A	5,000	2.00	10,000	3,846	6,154
B	7,000	3.00	21,000	8,077	12,923
			£31,000	£11,923	£19,077

Finally we can summarize the two methods and compare them as follows.

Product	Physical quantity method Value of W.I.P. £	Profit £	%	Market value method Value of W.I.P. £	Profit £	%
A	1,000	5,000	50	769	6,154	61
B	2,000	14,000	67	2,308	12,923	61
	£3,000	£19,000		£3,077	£19,077	

With the physical quantity method the relative profitability of the two products differs when profit is expressed as a percentage of the sales value. This is because the joint costs are apportioned on the basis of volume, giving an equal unit cost for both products. Products with higher sales prices therefore have higher profit margins.

Under the market value method, when joint costs are apportioned to products *pro rata* to their sales value, the profit margins must be identical for the products concerned.

A word of caution is appropriate here. Firms will choose whichever of the above two methods seems most relevant to their circumstances. The costing that results will allow them to value stocks and the cost of sales for the purpose of producing final accounts. However, neither method will provide a firm basis for pricing or product mix decisions based on product profitability. The reason for this is the arbitrary way in which joint costs are apportioned as there is no such thing as the 'true' cost of a joint product.

Service Costing

This final method of costing is applicable when a uniform or standard service is provided to clients. Railways, bus companies and transport firms all cost in terms of passenger–miles and tonne–miles. Hospitals relate costs to patient–days and electricity boards to kilowatt–hours.

Example

Suppose a lorry carried a load of 10 tonnes on a journey of 200 miles and the total cost of wages, fuel and operating costs came to £250. The cost per tonne–mile can be ascertained in this way:

$$\text{Cost per tonne–mile} = \frac{\text{Cost incurred for journey}}{\text{No. of tonnes} \times \text{No. of miles}}$$

$$= \frac{£250}{10 \times 200} = 12.5\text{p per tonne–mile}$$

Such information is useful for overall cost control and general pricing policy but care must be exercised in its use on individual pricing decisions. This is because some costs will not vary precisely with the size of the load or length of the journey, a topic pursued in the next chapters.

Summary

This chapter has examined two broad methods of costing called job costing and process costing, and a number of other related methods. It is possible to adapt costing methods to suit any industry's requirements but the principles of cost allocation and apportionment are applied throughout.

Individual job costing, contract costing and batch costing provide few problems in the sense that specific items are being costed. This is not the case with process costing as costs are not specifically related to individual items but to the volume of throughput during a period of time. This requires us to cost for incomplete production, process losses, and joint products produced by the same process.

The next chapter takes costing a stage further, demonstrating one of its uses in cost-based approaches to product pricing.

Further reading	**Books** Drury, C. *Management and Cost Accounting*, 2nd edn (VNR). Lucey, T. *Costing*, 3rd edn (DPP). Pizzey, A. *Principles of Cost Accountancy*, 5th edn (Cassell).

Work-based assignment	Ascertain which costing method(s) your organization uses for the products or services supplied to clients. *Note*: The choice is between job, batch, contract, process or service costing.

Questions with answers (see Appendix 4)	1 You have been given the following details for carrying out a job for a new customer. Direct materials: 6 kg at £15.20 per kg Direct labour:

Dept	Hours	Rate per hour
Assembly	2.0	£6
Testing	0.5	£5
Packing	0.25	£4

Annual budget for overheads (recovered on an hourly basis):

Dept	Hours	Overheads
Assembly	1,000	£20,000
Testing	1,500	£10,000
Packing	500	£ 9,000

Profit and general overheads recovered at 25% on above works costs.
   You are required to calculate the charge that should be made for this job.

(DMS)

2 A specialist manufacturer of purpose-built plant engaged in three separate jobs in May 198X. The following costs were incurred:

	Job A	Job B	Job C
Direct materials purchased	£524	£671	£382
Direct labour:			
Skilled, hours	158	170	16
Semi-skilled, hours	316	190	30
Site expenses	£118	£170	£25
Selling price of job	£3,318	£2,750	£1,950
Completed at 30 April 198X	100%	80%	25%

The following information is available.

Direct materials for the completion of the jobs have been recorded.
Direct labour is paid: skilled £5 per hour; semi-skilled £4 per hour.
Site expenses tend to vary with output.
Administration expenses total £440 per month and are to be allocated to the jobs.
On completion of the work, the practice of the manufacturer is to divide the calculated profit on each job: 20% to the site staff as a bonus; 80% to the company. Calculated losses are absorbed by the company in total.

You are required to:
(a) calculate the profit or loss by the company of Job A;
(b) project the profit or loss by the company of Jobs B and C;
(c) comment on any matters you think relevant to management as a result of your calculations;
(d) advise management whether to accept Job D which must be delivered by 30 June 198X. Job D is identical to Job B, but the customer has agreed to accept a 10% increase in the selling price. As Jobs B and C must also be delivered by 30 June, management is concerned that there may be insufficient labour available as this cannot be increased. No other orders are in prospect.

(AAT)

Questions for class use

1 On 1 January, 10,000 gallons of Devils Drink was in process in a part-finished state, the cost value being £4,750 for direct materials and £4,700 for wages and overheads. During January a further 35,000 gallons was put into process, the direct materials costing £17,250 whilst wages and overheads together came to £18,525. Some 28,000 gallons were completed and sold to breweries whilst 17,000 gallons remained in process at 31 January, being only two-thirds complete so far as wages and overhead were concerned but complete as to material content. Output is valued on a weighted average cost basis.

You are required to calculate:
(i) the value of work-in-progress as at 31 January
(ii) the cost of finished output sold to breweries. (DMS)

2 A Public Works company secures a contract to build a technical college at a fixed contract price of £5 million; completion must be in time to meet the start of the educational session starting two years hence. Work commenced on 1 July and at 31 December the following details had been recorded in the costing records:

	£
Materials purchased	620,000
Wages paid	140,000
Other direct charges	127,000
Plant sent to site (at valuation, 1 July)	180,000
Value of work measured (to 15 December)	860,000
Cash received	774,000

Additionally you ascertain:

	£
Materials on site not used to date	14,000
Work completed, but not measured	74,000

Plant is depreciated at 20% p.a. against valuation.

Required:

(a) A contract account for the period showing the amount of profit/loss you consider should be taken to the profit and loss account.

(b) Explain why the amount taken to profit and loss account may differ from the normal profit.

(AAT)

4 Pricing

Every firm needs to recover all its costs, and make a reasonable profit, to survive in the long run. Some firms live through loss-making periods of a year or two but this partly depends on their liquid resources at the outset. Survival may also depend on their ability and willingness to sell off, or close down, loss-making activities, and on the generation of cash from the sale of surplus assets.

Critical to the health and survival of any firm is the decision of what price to charge its customers for the goods and services it supplies. Obviously the costs a firm incurs are relevant to this decision but there is more than one way to look at these costs, and there are many other non-cost factors to take into account.

Economists lay claim to a model which will help firms determine their optimum selling price. This is based on the premise that firms will set their selling prices at a level which will maximize their profits.

Another assumption made in the model is that, for firms operating under the conditions of imperfect competition (i.e. the vast majority), demand will increase as price is lowered. How responsive demand is to changing price is referred to as the 'price elasticity of demand'.

Demand tends to be more elastic (i.e. responsive) for non-essential items, particularly if close substitutes are available. Demand is more inelastic when the goods or services are more essential in consumers' eyes, and when no close substitutes are available.

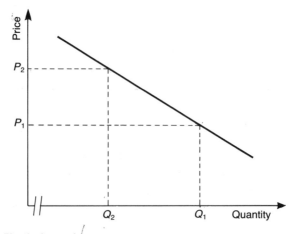

Figure 4a Elastic demand

Figures 4a and 4b show typical demand curves derived from plotting quantity demanded against price in these two situations of elastic and inelastic demand. This illustrates that a change in price from P_1 to P_2 has much more effect on reducing quantity demanded from Q_1 to Q_2 when demand is elastic, as in Figure 4a.

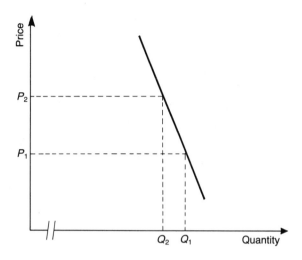

Figure 4b Inelastic demand

Assuming a firm can identify the shape of the demand curve for a product, it then needs to establish which combination of price and quantity is the most profitable. To do this, economists introduce costs into the model. Costs can either be looked at in total or as the cost of one additional unit of output, which is called 'marginal cost'.

Economists now maintain that profits are maximized at a quantity Q_x where the difference between total costs and total revenue is the greatest. This will also equate with the volume Q_x achieved where the marginal cost of one extra sale just equals its marginal revenue. Hence, the optimum selling price is the one that equates marginal revenue with marginal cost. Figures 5a and 5b illustrate these total and marginal situations.

This theoretical approach would be satisfactory in practice, provided firms can readily construct a demand curve for each of their products. However, this is not so easy to do and also ignores the point that demand responds to many factors other than price, for example sales promotion and packaging.

Yet another limiting factor is the premise we started with, that firms seek to maximize profits in the short run. There are many social, legal and environmental reasons why this may not be so plus the fact that managers set goals which may be inconsistent with profit maximization.

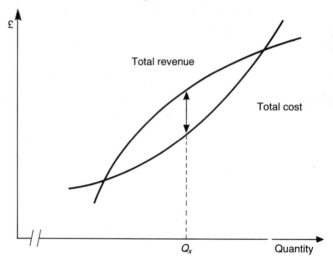

Figure 5a Total cost/revenue

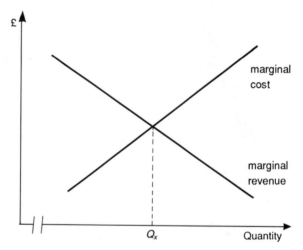

Figure 5b Marginal cost/revenue

These are some of the reasons why firms may not behave as predicted in the economist's model by fixing selling price so that it equates marginal revenue with marginal cost. If firms do not behave this way, how do they fix their prices?

Some firms are of course 'price takers' as opposed to being 'price fixers'. Price takers may be such because there is a dominant supplier in the same market; alternatively, there may be only one or two monopolistic buyers for the product.

For all these reasons we return to costs as one basis for fixing prices. One popular approach to pricing is that known as 'cost plus', where a predetermined profit element is added to the total cost of the product or service being sold. The amount of profit to aim for can be determined from a 'full cost pricing' approach or a 'rate of return pricing' approach; these are now discussed in turn.

Full Cost Pricing

This system of pricing gets its name from the fact that all costs are charged to products. It is also known as 'absorption cost pricing' because products absorb indirect costs in addition to their direct costs. A profit margin is added as a mark-up on the combined total of direct and indirect costs to obtain the selling price. Therefore we can say:

Selling price = Direct costs + Share of indirect costs + Profit margin

---

Example

The following information was taken from the current year's budget of GEM Ltd.

	Machine shop	Assembly shop	Finishing shop
Direct labour hours	20,000	18,000	10,000
Wage rate per hour	£5.25	£4.10	£4.50
Production overheads	£80,000	£36,000	£20,000

An enquiry has been received for a quotation to supply a special piece of equipment and GEM's estimator has collected the following information:

Components to be purchased		£320
Materials from store		£570
Direct labour times:		
Machining	60 hours	
Assembling	20 hours	
Finishing	10 hours	
Delivery cost to customer		£160

GEM recover their administration and selling costs by adding 20% to the cost of manufacture. A further 10% is then added to the total cost for profit. A detailed quotation is required.   (DMS)

From the information supplied it would appear that GEM Ltd use separate hourly recovery rates for the production overheads. These can be calculated as follows:

$$\text{Machine shop: } \frac{\pounds 80,000}{\pounds 20,000 \text{ hours}} = \pounds 4.00 \text{ per hour}$$

$$\text{Assembly shop: } \frac{\pounds 36,000}{18,000 \text{ hours}} = \pounds 2.00 \text{ per hour}$$

$$\text{Finishing shop: } \frac{\pounds 20,000}{10,000 \text{ hours}} = \pounds 2.00 \text{ per hour}$$

Having determined the overhead recovery rates the cost data can now be tabulated into a price quotation:

Direct costs:			£	£
Materials	Purchased components		320	
	Stores issues	570	890	
Labour	Machining	60 h @ £5.25	315	
	Assembling	20 h @ £4.10	82	
	Finishing	10 h @ £4.50	45	442
Total direct costs				1,332
Production overheads:				
Machine shop		70 h @ £4.00	280	
Assembly shop		20 h @ £2.00	40	
Finishing shop		10 h @ £2.00	20	340
Cost of manufacture				1,670
Administration and selling costs (20%)				334
				2,004
Delivery cost				160
Total cost				2,164
Profit (12.5%)				216
Selling price to be quoted				£2,380

One advantage of this approach is its apparent simplicity, enabling senior management to delegate price fixing to a lower level once recovery rates and profit margins have been set. However, a few words of warning are in order.

Both the production and administrative overhead recovery rates are based on budgeted figures for the coming period. By their very nature many of these overheads will be fixed rather than variable. Should the budgeted volume of activity or the budgeted cost of these overheads change in reality, then the overhead recovery rates cease to be appropriate because the fixed cost per hour will have changed.

Margins and Mark-Ups

A further question to address is the size of the profit mark-up to be used. The above example begs the question by quoting the mark-up to be applied to total costs for this purpose. It is perhaps appropriate that we digress for a moment to examine the difference between a profit margin based on selling price and a profit mark-up based on total cost. A simple illustration should suffice.

Example

	£	
Total cost	80	
		25% profit mark-up on cost
Profit	20	
		20% profit margin on selling price
Selling price	100	

Although the money value of profit is the same £20 in both cases, the percentage profit varies because it is calculated on different bases. We now need to consider how this profit is assessed.

Many industries have a normal mark-up peculiar to that particular trade. In retail trade, mark-ups are normally applied to the buying-in cost of the goods being resold which, in effect, is at the gross profit level. In the engineering industry, mark-ups may be applied to total costs, which relate more to the net profit level.

Whichever way profit is expressed, we cannot assume that firms can charge either the profit mark-up they want, or what is the norm for their industry. If one firm's costs are high, it may have to trim its mark-up to remain competitive. If general market conditions are poor, then all participating firms in that industry may have to trim their prices and profit margins.

In conditions of low demand a firm needs to have a flexible pricing policy and not to stick to a rigid profit mark-up on total costs. It is better to make sales at a lower-than-normal profit, or sometimes even at a small loss, than not to make any sales at all. This approach is explained later in this chapter under 'Marginal Cost Pricing' and we return to it again in Chapter 10.

The size of the target profit margin is really determined by the required rate of return on capital. Capital comes from the two main sources of shareholders' funds and borrowed capital. Each of these sources has its own cost which can be amalgamated into a weighted average cost of capital. This encapsulates the return required by owners and the interest needed to service any loans.

The required return on capital is therefore the weighted average cost of capital, which varies from firm to firm and industry to industry. Factors influencing the required rate of return are the track record of the company, the perceived risk of its industry, and its future prospects.

Even when two firms have the same required rate of return, this does not mean that it will be achieved in an identical way. Some industries are capital-intensive and others not. Some industries have a rapid stock turnover rate whilst others have a very long operating cycle from the start of work to eventual payment by the customer.

Contrast in your mind a food supermarket turning over its stocks every two weeks and receiving immediate cash settlement, with a heavy engineering firm taking months to assemble products and then waiting a further two months for settlement. These factors all find expression in a trio of key performance ratios which are more fully discussed in Chapter 8. Meanwhile we can say:

Rate of return on capital p.a. = Profit margin $\times$ Rate of turnover of capital p.a.

For example, $$20\% = 10\% \times 2$$

We can now turn this relationship round to identify the required profit margin:

$$\text{Profit margin} = \frac{\text{Rate of return on capital required}}{\text{Rate of turnover of capital p.a.}}$$

Using the illustrative figures above:

$$\text{Profit margin} = \frac{20\%}{2} = 10\%$$

This 10% profit margin can therefore be achieved by a mark-up of just over 11% on total costs. On average, should all work be done for its budgeted cost, then an 11% addition to total costs will broadly achieve a 10% profit margin on selling prices.

Rate of Return Pricing

Essentially, rate of return pricing is just another variation on full cost pricing with the emphasis being transferred from the profit margin to the return on capital. As mentioned earlier, the target return on capital is determined primarily by the weighted average cost of capital, which incorporates the cost of loan interest and the return expected by shareholders on all their funds. This target return on capital can be used for long-term price fixing in the following way.

Example

Haphi Ltd have a target rate of return on capital of 20%. Their total costs are £5m and capital employed amounts to £2.5m. The percentage mark-up needed to earn a 20% return on capital can be found from the following formula:

$$\text{Target mark-up on total costs} = \text{Target return on capital} \times \frac{\text{Capital employed}}{\text{Total annual costs}}$$

$$= 20\% \times \frac{£2.5m}{£5.0m}$$

$$= 10\%$$

This can be verified, for a 10% mark-up on £5m total costs yields a profit of £0.5m which represents a 20% return on the £2.5m capital employed. A 10% mark-up on total cost is consistent with a 9% profit margin on the £5.5m sales value as follows:

$$\text{Return on capital} = \text{Profit margin} \times \text{Turnover of capital}$$

$$= \frac{£0.5m \times 100\%}{£5.5m} \times \frac{£5.5m}{£2.5m}$$

$$20\% = 9\% \times 2.2$$

When using the rate of return pricing approach, two points should be borne in mind. In a multi-product firm it will be necessary to apportion the capital employed to individual product lines; inevitably this apportionment may be arbitrary at times.

It should also be remembered that the capital employed, and not just total costs, relates to a specific level of output. The amount of working capital included in capital employed will vary roughly *pro rata* with the volume of production and sales. The capital employed on fixed assets, however, may not vary very much whatever the level of output, provided it is within present capacity limits.

With both full cost pricing and rate of return pricing, some further points should be remembered. It will be necessary to apportion fixed costs to individual products, regardless of the general nature of some overheads and the somewhat arbitrary way this may be done.

Both pricing methods represent a static rather than a dynamic picture as they relate to long-term objectives. Prices may have to be discounted to cope with short-term demand conditions. Also, it is not easy to see the effects of changing volumes on prices or profit, hence the marginal costing approach is more useful for firms facing rapidly changing demand conditions.

Marginal Cost Pricing

'Marginal costing' is the term applied to the separation of total costs into their fixed and variable categories, as described in detail in the following chapter. In marginal costing, fixed costs are not apportioned to individual products but are left as a total sum for the firm. This overcomes the arbitrariness of overhead apportionment inherent in full cost pricing. When the variable costs of one product are deducted from its sales revenue we get what is termed its 'contribution':

$$\text{Sales revenue} - \text{Variable costs} = \text{Contribution}$$

The contributions of all products go to pay for total fixed costs and provide the profit. The aim of marginal cost pricing is to maximize the contribution towards fixed costs and profit. This approach allows firms to charge different prices in different markets or in changing market conditions. An example of marginal cost pricing is found on the railways when the same journey can have varying prices depending on the time of day, or the season of the year, or the competition from other forms of transport.

It is very easy to say that firms should maximize their contribution, but salespersons will find it reassuring to have some target contribution in mind. We can supply the answer by reference to the budgeted plans that firms make to achieve their objectives. Consider the following case.

Example

A firm sets its sales budget at £10m for the coming year, composed of a number of different products. Its fixed costs in various departments come to £2m in total for the year and a satisfactory return on the capital employed would be £1m. The total contribution required by this firm is therefore £3m, which represents 30% of the total sales value. This 30% figure is often referred to as the 'contribution ratio' or 'profit/volume ratio'. Provided that the sales force are well informed of the contribution earned by each individual product, they can attempt to maximize contribution in the prices they obtain whilst bearing in mind the overall contribution ratio required.

Should the budgeted sales value be subject to some uncertainty, then the contribution ratio could be calculated for varying levels of sales in this way:

Sales	£8m	£9m	£10m	£11m
Contribution target	£3m	£3m	£3m	£3m
Contribution ratio	37.5%	33.3%	30.0%	27.3%

These falling contribution ratio requirements do not mean that the firm should necessarily reduce its prices at higher overall sales levels. Profit-maximizing firms would certainly not do so and it should be borne in mind that a higher profit element is required at higher levels of sales to provide a return on the extra working capital. In reality, therefore, the £3m contribution target will not remain static. The fixed cost element in contribution will, however, remain constant.

Examples of marginal costing applied to pricing in special situations are contained in Chapter 10 which deals with short-term decision making.

Summary

In this chapter we started with the economists' approach to pricing, contrasting that with the two broad cost-based approaches. Full cost pricing says that all costs are charged to individual product lines, direct costs directly so but indirect costs being apportioned in as relevant a manner as possible. To this total of direct and indirect costs is then added a profit element to arrive at the selling price. This profit element is related to the long-term return on capital objective. In the short term, such prices may not necessarily be obtainable due to demand conditions, and few firms stick rigidly to full cost prices.

In a study conducted in 1986 Mills found that full/absorption costing was the primary cost-related pricing method used by 71% of manufacturing and 65% of service companies responding (the article by Mills is listed below, under 'Further reading').

The other broad cost-based approach is based on marginal costing principles. This takes the view that fixed costs for the firm should be left as a total sum and not apportioned to individual product lines at all. In this way the somewhat arbitrary nature of overhead apportionment inherent in full cost pricing is avoided.

Each product line is said to make a contribution towards the firm's total fixed costs and profit target, as only variable costs are charged against sales. A firm's objective should be to maximize contributions from its sales and not to adhere to rigid full cost selling prices. Sales personnel are therefore given more flexibility to respond to short-term demand conditions but they may be given an overall contribution ratio at which to aim.

It cannot be emphasized too strongly that marginal cost pricing must be undertaken with great care. In the long term, any firm's survival depends on it covering all its costs and making a reasonable rate of return on the capital employed. If a firm takes orders on a contribution basis, that do not fully pay for fixed overheads, then that firm's growth and survival are at risk. Nevertheless, marginal cost pricing can be a very useful tool if properly understood and applied.

Further reading

Books
Arnold, J. & Hope, T. *Accounting for Management Decisions* (PHI).
Drury, C. *Management and Cost Accounting*, 2nd edn (VNR).

Article
Mills, R.W. Pricing decisions in UK manufacturing and service companies. In *Management Accounting* (Nov. 1988).

Work-based assignment

Find out whether your organization fixes prices on a full cost basis, a marginal cost basis, or some other basis. If your organization is a price taker, check whether product profitability is calculated on a full cost or marginal cost basis.

Questions with answers
(see Appendix 4)

1 Your company makes a single product, the Betascope.
   (a) You have been asked to calculate the unit selling price by the company, from the information provided below, based on a monthly output of 1,000 units:

   17 units of raw material at £7.50 per unit
   125 hours of direct labour at £2.50 per hour
   Variable overheads at 40% of direct labour cost
   Fixed overhead is to be recovered at the rate of 10% of total variable cost
   Mark-up is 50% of total cost

   (b) The company's monthly potential productive capacity is 1,000 units. For the coming month it is forecast that the factory will only produce at 80% of its potential. Also, you are informed that raw materials, wages and variable overheads are expected to rise by 15%, 10% and 5% respectively. Fixed costs of £56,500 will not alter.

   Using a marginal cost approach, calculate the new unit selling price on the basis that the financial director requires the factory output to yield a constant amount of monthly profit.   (IOM)

2 You have been given the following details for carrying out a job for a new customer:

Direct materials: 4 kg at £10.50 per kg
Direct expenses: £36.50
Direct labour:

Dept	Hours	Rate per hour
Machine shop	2	£5
Assembly dept	1	£4
Packing shop	0.2	£3

Annual budget for overheads:

Dept	Hours	Variable overheads	Fixed overheads
Machine shop	1,000	£20,000	£30,000
Assembly dept	1,500	£15,000	£ 7,500
Packing shop	800	£10,000	£16,000

Profit and administrative overheads recovery rate: 25% of all above costs.

You are required to:
   (a) Calculate the charge that should be made for the job

(b) If the customer rejected your price and offered £200, what would be the advantages and disadvantages of accepting the order? State any premise on which your decision is based. (DMS)

Question for class use

1 The Flexible Tool Company manufactures and sells three industrial power drills. The company's policy is to apportion fixed overheads month by month on the basis of monthly direct labour hours. Wages are paid at a rate of £2.50 per hour. The forecast fixed overheads for November, 198X are £14,000.

The variable unit costs relating to components and assembly for each type of drill are:

	Drill type		
Costs:	D123	D456	D789
Parts	£15.00	£25.50	£30.00
Direct labour	£5.00	£7.50	£10.00
Variable overhead	£1.50	£3.00	£2.00

The company calculates its selling price by doubling the total cost (i.e. variable costs plus apportioned fixed overheads). The sales forecast for November, 198X is as follows:

	D123	D456	D789
Units	400	500	300

You are required to calculate the unit selling price of each drill, showing your workings in a clear manner. (IOM)

Part II
Planning and control

Overview

One description of management views it as a cycle of three key activities, namely:

- Planning   Deciding what to do, who is to do it and when to do it
- Implementing   Putting the plan into operation
- Controlling   Monitoring whether the plan is working and taking corrective action when necessary

This definition of management has obvious relevance to management accounting, and to the second part of this book in particular. The following chapters go on to explain the planning and control techniques of profit/volume planning, standard costing and budgetary control.

Once plans are made, however, they need constant monitoring to highlight any problem areas at an early stage and so allow corrective action to be taken in good time. Much of this book is concerned with financial performance measurements that are used to compare actual results with planned activities.

Some of these measurements may be absolute, as with budgets or standards, when we calculate the variance – the difference between actual and planned values – in money terms. Other financial measurements are relative measures using ratios such as the return on capital employed or the more sophisticated idea of residual income recommended for decentralized organizations.

First, we turn to profit/volume planning to examine more closely the link between costs and levels of activity, and so to determine how profit varies with fluctuations in the level of output.

5 Profit/volume planning

The basic separation of costs into only two categories – 'fixed' or 'variable' – was briefly mentioned in two previous chapters. This classification of costs by their behaviour, relative to changes in the output level, is at the heart of an accounting technique called 'marginal costing'. This has many applications in helping management to carry out their roles of planning, control and decision making.

We have, of course, already met one application of the technique in the previous chapter dealing with marginal cost pricing (Chapter 4). Examples of its use will also be found in later chapters dealing with standard marginal costing (Chapter 6), flexible budgeting (Chapter 7), short-term decision making (Chapter 10) and long-term investment decisions (Chapter 11). In this particular chapter we will examine the role of marginal costing in profit/volume planning.

The simplistic view of cost behaviour is that fixed costs remain a constant total sum over a range of output levels and that total variable costs increase in linear fashion with output. Both these costs can be combined to show total costs. These start at the level of fixed costs and increase from that point as more and more variable costs are required for the increased output. This situation is shown in Figure 6.

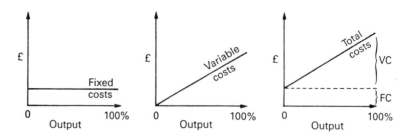

Figure 6 Cost behaviour (simplistic view)

It is clearly not realistic to assume that costs will behave in this fashion over a wide range of output levels. Some fixed costs, such as rent and rates, will be constant from zero output through to maximum capacity. Other fixed costs, e.g. administrative salaries, may increase in a series of stepped rises as staff become unable to cope without further hired help.

The assumption of linear variable costs is also suspect. Firms expect greater discounts for bulk purchase of goods or materials; this would reduce the slope of the variable cost curve as output increases. Other economies of scale may result from the division of labour but eventually diseconomies of scale may set in near maximum capacity with, for example, the use of overtime working.

These two more realistic pictures of fixed and variable costs are shown in Figure 7.

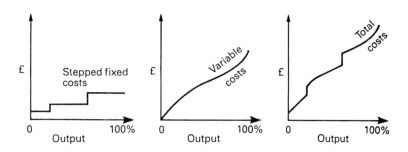

Figure 7 Cost behaviour (realistic view)

Having looked at the non-linearity of costs in real life it may seem surprising that the assumption of linearity still exists, and even more surprising that we are about to make the same assumption! The reason for this is that although cost linearity, as shown in Figure 8a below, is patently untrue at both low or high levels of output, it could be realistic for the range of output levels normally concerning a particular firm.

The range of output levels of practical significance to a firm is referred to as the 'relevant range'. The total cost is shown in Figure 8b to be linear within that range.

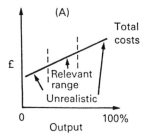

Figure 8a Linear costs

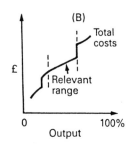

Figure 8b Non-linear costs

A similar assumption of linearity is also made for sales revenue. It would be quite feasible to draw the sales revenue curve with a decreasing slope at higher output depicting the possible need to reduce unit price to achieve greater volume sales. Within the relevant range of output for a firm it could be that the unit sales price is constant and hence the total revenue curve is assumed to be linear throughout. This is illustrated in Figure 9.

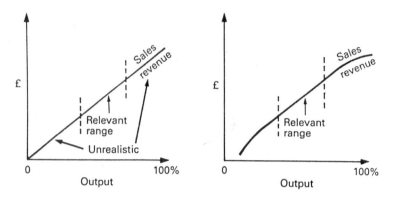

Figure 9 Sales revenue curves

Break-Even Analysis

The study of the relationship of costs and sales revenue to various levels of sales volume is often referred to as 'cost/volume/profit analysis' (CVP) or 'break-even analysis'. With the proviso that it is looking at a short-term situation where fixed costs and unit variable cost are unlikely to change within the relevant range, break-even analysis can be a useful planning technique for managers. Some of its uses are:

- Finding the level of activity where total sales revenue equals total costs (i.e. the break-even point) or where a certain level of profit will be achieved
- Determining the margin of safety between the existing sales level and the break-even point
- Visualizing the effect of a change in any variable on the break-even point and profit
- Determining contribution ratios as indicators of product profitability
- Calculating the level of operating gearing as an indicator of the effect on profit of a given change in sales

All of these uses are now examined in turn.

Break-Even Chart We start our look at break-even analysis with a single-product break-even chart. This will allow us to see at a glance how profit or loss varies with the change in volume. It is also useful in depicting the approximate effects of a change in the cost structure, say a switch from manual labour to automatic machinery which reduces variable costs but increases fixed costs.

Example

A firm makes only one product which sells for £10. The variable cost per unit is £5 and fixed costs total £75,000 per annum. Maximum capacity would be about 25,000 units per annum but the firm normally operates around the 80% capacity level. Figure 10 shows the break-even chart drawn from this information.

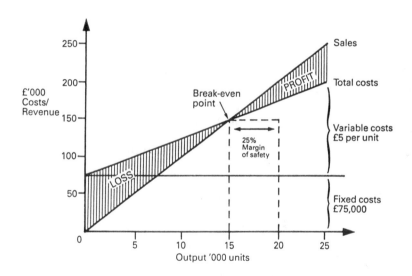

Figure 10 Break-even chart

Break-even is reached at 15,000 units when sales revenue exactly equals the total costs of £150,000. Output of less than this amount results in a loss, whilst greater output makes a profit.

The size of the profit or loss at any output can be read off the graph at a glance. To do this we use the scale on the vertical axis to evaluate the gap between the total cost line and the sales line.

Margin of Safety

Also represented on the break-even chart is the 'margin of safety', which represents the amount by which output can fall from its present level back to the break-even point. This cushion, or safety margin, is usually expressed as a percentage and gives management an idea of how far away they are from a loss-making situation.

In the example illustrated the present level of output of 20,000 units can fall by 25% (5,000 units) before a loss would result.

Calculation of Break-Even Point

If our firm happened to be operating below the break-even level at the present time, then we could use the graph to calculate the percentage increase in sales needed to return to a profit-making situation. If sales were, say, only 10,000 units at present, then an increase of 5,000 units, equivalent to a 50% increase, would be needed to get back to the break-even point. Alternatively we can calculate the break-even point.

If we assume that selling prices and variable costs are linear, then we can also assume that total sales revenue and total variable costs will move *pro rata* with sales volume. This means that every sale will yield a constant surplus of revenue over its variable cost. The special name we give to this surplus is 'contribution', and it is of fundamental importance in marginal costing.

$$\text{Contribution} = \text{Sales} - \text{Variable costs}$$

The notion of contribution applies both to an individual unit sale and also to total sales. In the above break-even example, a selling price of £10 was assumed, together with a unit variable cost of £5 and fixed costs of £75,000 per annum. If we sell a product for £10 that has a variable cost of only £5, then we are gaining a contribution of £5 from each unit sale. The number of sales we need to pay for our fixed costs equals the number of £5 contributions needed to make up £75,000, i.e. 15,000 units. We can therefore say:

$$\text{Break-even point} = \frac{\text{Fixed costs}}{\text{Contribution per unit}}$$

$$= \frac{£75,000}{£5}$$

$$= 15,000 \text{ units}$$

Calculation of Target Volume

If we need to know what volume of sales will yield a certain target profit then we extend the above break-even analysis by adding profit to the fixed costs and so find the total contribution required.

Using the same example but now also assuming that the firm wants to make a profit of £30,000 per annum, the total contribution required will equal £105,000. As each unit sale contributes £5, then 21,000 unit sales will be needed to achieve the target profit of £30,000 as follows:

$$\text{Target volume} = \frac{\text{Fixed costs} + \text{Required profit}}{\text{Contribution per unit}}$$

$$= \frac{£75,000 + £30,000}{£5}$$

$$= 21,000 \text{ units}$$

Contribution Ratio

Instead of expressing the break-even point or target volume in numbers of units, it is equally possible to express them in sales revenue terms. This uses the concept of 'contribution ratio' which measures the proportion of contribution to sales as either a percentage or a decimal.

Taking the same example of a £5 contribution on a £10 selling price this gives a contribution ratio of 50% (or 0.5 when expressed in decimal terms) as follows:

$$\text{Contribution ratio} = \frac{\text{Contribution}}{\text{Sales price}} \times 100\%$$

$$= \frac{£5}{£10} \times 100\%$$

$$= 50\%$$

Target Sales Value

The sales value necessary to earn any required contribution is found by dividing that contribution by the contribution ratio when expressed as a decimal. Continuing with the same example, when a target profit of £30,000 is required in addition to recovering the £75,000 fixed costs, we find:

$$\text{Target sales value} = \frac{\text{Total contribution required}}{\text{Contribution ratio}}$$

$$= \frac{£105,000}{0.5}$$

$$= £210,000$$

Operating Gearing The angle at which the total cost line crosses the sales line on a break-even chart is called the 'angle of incidence'. Large fixed costs relative to sales value will result in a wide angle, whilst a low level of fixed costs to sales value will result in a narrow angle.

The significance of this angle is that it indicates the speed with which losses or profits accumulate when output changes. A large angle of incidence depletes profit more rapidly than a small angle when sales volume falls. Conversely, profits are made more quickly with a large angle when sales volume rises.

These relationships are also expressed in what is termed 'operating gearing' which quantifies how much effect a given change in sales will have on profit. To find the operating gearing we divide the contribution by the net profit.

Example

Assume that a firm makes a contribution of £80,000 and a net profit of £20,000. What is the operating gearing ratio?

$$\text{Operating gearing} = \frac{\text{Contribution}}{\text{Profit}}$$

$$= \frac{£80,000}{£20,000}$$

$$= 4$$

The application of this gearing figure is a fourfold change in profit for any given change in sales. If, for instance, sales were to fall by 10% then there would be a 40% (10% x 4 gearing ratio) drop in profit as a consequence.

We can now look at an example which applies many of the above techniques.

Example

The following cost statement relates to a product which sells for £10.00 per unit.

	(£ per unit)	
Direct materials	3.00	
Direct wages	2.00	
Variable overhead	1.00	
	6.00	
Fixed overhead	2.00	(Based on normal output level of 30,000 products)
Total cost	8.00	

You are required to calculate:

(i)   the break-even point;
(ii) the contribution ratio;
(iii) the margin of safety;
(iv) the percentage increase in profit if sales volume is increased by 20%;
(v)   the number of sales needed to maintain the existing profit level if the selling price is reduced by 10%.   (DMS)

(i)   Unit contribution = Selling price – Variable cost

$$= £10 - £6$$

$$= £4 \text{ per unit}$$

$$\text{Break-even point} = \frac{\text{Fixed costs}}{\text{Contribution per unit}}$$

$$= \frac{£60,000}{£4} = 15,000 \text{ products}$$

(ii) Contribution to sales ratio $= \dfrac{\text{Contribution per unit}}{\text{Selling price per unit}} \times 100\%$

$$= \frac{£4}{£10} \times 100\% = 40\%$$

(iii) Margin of safety $= \dfrac{\text{Present output} - \text{Break-even point}}{\text{Present output}} \times 100\%$

$$= \frac{(30,0000 - 15,000)}{30,000} \times 100\% = 50\%$$

(iv) % Profit increase = % Increase in sales × Operating gearing ratio

$$= 20\% \times \frac{\text{Contribution}}{\text{Profit}}$$

$$= 20\% \times \frac{£4}{£2} = 40\%$$

(v)   Existing profit level = £2 × 30,000 products = £60,000

$$\text{Target sales} = \frac{\text{Total contribution required}}{\text{New contribution per unit}}$$

$$= \frac{£60,000 + £60,000}{£3} = 40,000 \text{ products}$$

Planning for Change

One of the uses of break-even charts is to examine the possible effects of a change in any of the data, be it a different selling price or a change in cost structure. Take, for example, the original situation of a selling price of £10 with a unit variable cost of £5 and fixed costs of £75,000 per annum. This information is now amended to show the effects of an increase in selling price to £12 per unit (Figure 11).

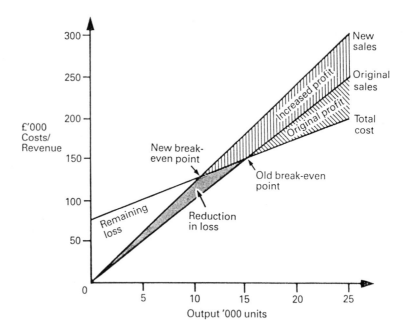

Figure 11 Effect of changed selling price

The shaded area between the original sales line and the new sales line shows the reduced loss/increased profit that would result from such a move. It also shows the reduction in the break-even point brought about by the higher unit sales price. What it does not predict of course, is the number of sales that would be achieved at a higher price. To answer that question would require some market research and an estimate of the so-called 'price elasticity of demand'. The concept of price elasticity examines the relationship of sales volume to different selling prices and thus helps marketing people decide on pricing policy.

Break-even charts can also show the effects on profits of any change in the cost structure. The example mentioned earlier of a switch from manual labour (variable cost) to automated production (fixed cost) is a case in point. This situation would show as an increase in fixed costs coupled with a reduction in variable costs so that the total cost line would start at a higher point but rise at a less steep slope than before.

The before and after situations are shown in Figure 12. It gives an indication of whether such a change will be worthwhile and what sales volume is needed for savings in variable costs to cover the increase in fixed costs. In this case sales volume needs to exceed 12,000 units before it would be worthwhile.

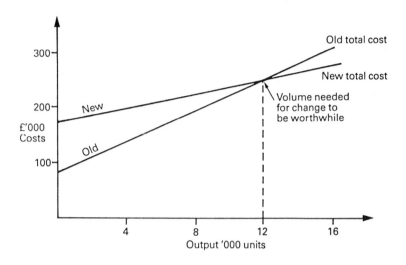

Figure 12 Changed cost structure

Multi-Product Chart

Previous examples and discussions of break-even charts have been limited to single-product situations, which in practice are hard to find. Very few firms supply only one product and although a break-even chart can be drawn for one product in a multi-product firm, the problem of fixed cost apportionment inherent in the system of absorption costing remains.

It is perfectly feasible to draw a break-even chart for the whole product range. The only difference in the layout of the chart is that the horizontal axis needs to be scaled in terms of total sales revenue, rather than units of products. This is because the products may be very dissimilar, and adding them together in unit terms may be likened to mixing chalk and cheese.

Example

Let us take the case of a two-product firm where the following information applies:

		Product A	Product B	Total
	Sales quantity	10,000	2,000	
	Sales price	£10	£50	
	Variable cost per unit	£5	£35	
	Sales revenue	£100,000	£100,000	£200,000
Less:	Variable costs	£50,000	£70,000	£120,000
	Contribution	£50,000	£30,000	£80,000
Less:	Fixed costs			£60,000
	Profit			£20,000

This information is laid out in the break-even chart in Figure 13 showing that break-even is achieved when sales revenue equals £150,000 for the two products combined.

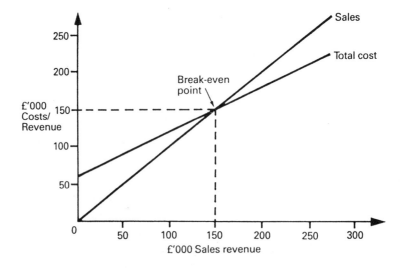

Figure 13 Multi-product break-even chart

The weakness of this presentation is that the chart shows the profit or loss at various levels of sales but it assumes the same proportionate mix throughout. Should those proportions change then a new break-even chart is required.

Summary

When relating costs or profit to volume we need to identify which costs are fixed and which are variable with output. We can then express this information on charts to show readily the profit or loss at any particular output level, in addition to the break-even point.

The classification of costs into these fixed and variable categories also allows us to identify the contribution a product makes towards fixed costs and profit. Contribution is a key concept in accounting and comprises the sales value less variable costs only.

The break-even point and the volume required to make a target profit can both be calculated by dividing the total contribution required by the contribution per unit.

When contribution is expressed as a percentage of sales value we get the 'contribution ratio' or 'profit/volume ratio' as it is sometimes called. This is used as a measure of product profitability in other chapters, but here it is used to calculate target sales value and the operating gearing ratio.

We return to this analysis of costs by behaviour and the concept of contribution many times in later chapters. Standard marginal costing, flexible budgeting and short-term decision making are all based on these ideas, as we shall see.

Further reading

Books
Arnold, T. & Hope, T. *Accounting for Management Decisions* (PHI).
Drury, C. *Management and Cost Accounting*, 2nd edn (VNR).
Lucey, T. *Costing*, 3rd edn (DPP).
Pizzey, A. *Principles of Cost Accountancy*, 5th edn (Cassell).

Work-based assignment

Give examples of fixed costs and variable costs in your own organization

(a) from your own department;
(b) from other departments.

Questions with answers
(see Appendix 4)

1   Snow White Ltd make plastic sledges of a standard size. Each sledge contains 2 kg of raw material which is moulded by machine after which the finished article is packed. The following information is available.
(a) Raw material is bought in 20-kg bags costing £22 each. Packing materials cost £0.25 per sledge.
(b) The variable cost of machine time, including operator's wages, amounts to £12 per hour.
(c) Two persons are employed on packing at an hourly rate of £4 each and together take 3 minutes to pack one sledge, just keeping pace with production.
(d) The total fixed overheads for the sledge moulding and packing amounts to £300 for a 38-hour week.
(e) The selling price is £6.50.

You are required to calculate:

(i) the cost of each sledge on a marginal costing basis;

(ii) the number of sledges per week that must be sold to break even (*Note:* a break-even chart is not required);

(iii) the new break-even point should the raw material price rise by 50%. (DMS)

2 The board of directors of your company is about to make a decision as to the installation of equipment which will result in the redundancy of a number of operating staff. The overall effect will be a reduction of variable cost but an increase in fixed costs, and a potential increase in production.

You have been requested to prepare notes of the points they need to consider, with special reference to the effects of operating gearing. (Certified Diploma)

3 An electrical component manufacturer budgets to sell 36,000 units although the factory has the capacity to produce 40,000 units in normal circumstances.

Variable costs per unit are:

Wages	£2.00
Materials	£8.00
Overheads	£4.00

Fixed costs for the period are expected to be £201,600.

The selling price is £20 per unit.

You are required:

(a) To calculate how many units must be made and sold in order to break even during the period. Express the information on a break-even chart for presentation to the management.

(b) To ascertain the budgeted profit for the period, assuming opening and closing stocks are the same.

(c) To state the number of units to be manufactured when the amount of capital invested in this production is £330,000 and the directors require a 15% return on this.

(d) To advise the management on the results calculated in item (c) above, stating any reservations you may have. (AAT)

Questions for class use 1 Precision Ltd manufacture a metal fastener for the motor trade and its management want your advice. The following information is available:

(a) The amount of capital employed in the business is £1m.

(b) The product takes 12 minutes to make and assemble at an average rate of pay of £4 per hour.

(c) Raw materials cost 25p per product.

(d) Variable overheads cost £5 per hour.

(e) Fixed overheads amount to £90,000 p.a.

(f) The proposed selling price is £2.50 per product.

You are required:

(i) To calculate the number of units that Precision Ltd will have to sell to break even (ignoring the cost of capital).

(ii) To calculate the number of units needed to be sold to earn a 20% return on capital.

(iii) To draw a break-even chart, clearly labelling the break-even point.   (DMS)

2   Solo Ltd manufacture one product only and their budget for the coming year shows the following:

		£000
Sales of 30,000 units at £20		600
Variable costs	280	
Fixed costs	200	480
Profit for the year		120

You are required:

(a) To draw a break-even chart, identifying the break-even point and the margin of safety.

(b) To indicate the effect on profit on separate break-even charts for each of the following situations:
   (i)   a decrease in fixed costs;
   (ii) an increase in variable costs;
   (iii) a decrease in selling price;
   (iv) an increase in sales volume.   (DMS)

6 Standard Costing

'Standard costing' is the name given to a detailed accounting technique, the aim of which is to plan and control both costs and revenue, and hence profit. It is centred on the products of mass production industries where a repetitive manufacturing or processing activity is carried out. The list of industries where it can be applied is endless but includes brewing, food, paper, textiles, electrical goods, furniture, clothing, chemicals, pharmaceuticals, car components and building materials – to name but a few.

The standard cost of a product is the total cost of direct labour and materials plus a share of overheads that may be incurred in the production process. Standard costing is the continuous comparison of the standard costs with the actual costs of the products. This comparison may take place daily, weekly or even monthly. Inevitably differences will occur between the standard and actual results, so these are examined for their causes in order to improve future performance.

There are a number of advantages claimed for standard costing:

- Setting up standards requires a thorough review of materials used and methods of operation.
- Continuous monitoring engenders cost consciousness and increases motivation if standards are realistic.
- It frees senior management from day-to-day routine when 'management by exception' is practised.
- It provides a firm basis for price fixing and stock valuation.

The Control Cycle

Control is one of a small number of key management functions and is often described as a cycle of five sequential stages. Standard costing is an excellent example of one such control cycle and we go on to examine its five stages. These can be expressed diagrammatically as shown in Figure 14.

The conclusions we draw from these five stages are that:

(1) Setting standards of performance means the preparation of a standard cost specification for each and every product to be included in the standard costing system.

(2) Defining performance measurements is the identification of the detailed variances to be used for this purpose.

(3) Measuring actual performance is the recording of actual costs and revenue for each product.

(4) Comparing actual with standards identifies any significant variances to draw to management's attention.

(5) Taking corrective action if and when necessary completes the control cycle.

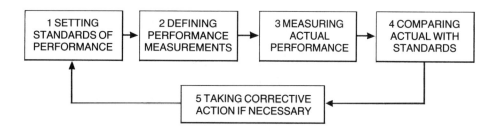

Figure 14 Standard costing control cycle

Standard Cost Specification

The setting of direct labour and material standards involves determining the best layout, methods of operation and most suitable materials for the job. This is where management science plays a role in the person of an industrial engineer bringing techniques like method study, work measurement and value analysis into play.

When first applying standard costing to any product the starting point is to specify quantities and grades of the labour and material elements, and include an apportionment of budgeted overheads to arrive at the total standard cost. This standard cost specification will be set out on a standard cost card or sheet, and these days it is stored in a computer system.

The setting-up process may yield economies over existing costs due to the painstaking investigation of all aspects of operations. Such economies may also occur when standards are revised occasionally in the light of changed working conditions.

When setting standards it is important that they are realistic. There is no point in setting 'ideal' standards that are only capable of achievement under perfect conditions, without waste, breakdowns, disputes or other disruptions. The more realistic standards are called 'expected standards', as they reflect what can reasonably be expected to be achieved within the timescale of the budget year.

Example

The following standard cost data refer to one unit of Product GR 49:

Direct material:
    Material M77   9.0 kg at £2.67 per kg
              M210   12 units at £6.90 per unit
    Material reclamation allowed   1.8 kg at £0.90 per kg

Direct labour:
    Machining   10.5 hours at £4 per hour
    Assembly   3.6 hours at £3.50 per hour

Variable overhead:
    Machining   £1.40 per direct labour hour
    Assembly   70% of direct labour cost

Fixed overhead:
    Machining normal capacity   40,000 labour hours per year
    Annual budget   £100,000
    Assembly normal capacity   200,000 labour hours per year
    Annual budget   £60,000

The standard cost sheet is required for Product GR49 to show the total standard cost of one unit and the profit when the unit selling price is £200.

(Certified Diploma)

It is helpful to set out the standard cost sheet in a similar order, quoting quantities, unit cost and value for each element of cost. Fixed overhead absorption rates need to be calculated from the annual budget information of the two departments if the standard cost is based on absorption costing. An alternative marginal costing approach will be discussed later. If the unit sales price is also included, the profit or loss is simply the difference between the total standard cost and the standard selling price.

Standard Cost Sheet for Product GR49 (one unit)

	Quantity	Rate	Value	Total
Direct material:				
Material M77	9.0 kg	£2.67	£24.03	
M210	12 units	£6.90	£82.80	
Material reclamation	1.8 kg	£0.90	(£1.62)	
				£105.21
Direct labour:				
Machining	10.5 hrs	£4.00	£42.00	
Assembly	3.6 hrs	£3.50	£12.60	
				£54.60
Variable overhead:				
Machining	10.5 hrs	£1.40	£14.70	
Assembly	70% × 3.6 hrs	£3.50	£8.82	
				£23.52

Fixed overhead:			
Machining	10.5 hrs	£2.50	£26.25
Assembly	3.6 hrs	£0.30	£1.08
			£27.33
Total standard cost			£210.66
Loss per unit			(£10.66)
Standard selling price			£200.00

The total standard cost is seen to be £210.66, which is more than the selling price of £200 per unit. The resulting loss is therefore £10.66 per unit, which demands immediate management action.

Variances

Periodically, the actual costs of labour, materials and overheads are compared with the predetermined standards laid down in the specification. Differences are almost bound to occur: the accounting term for these is 'variances', which are given the symbol letter (F) when favourable or (A) when adverse.

Favourable variances are so called because they increase the expected profits whilst adverse variances reduce profits. It is also possible to express variances as either positive or negative figures. The accuracy of this approach depends on the formulae (see later) being used the correct way round.

Variances arise because the quantity and/or the cost of the resources used differs from what should have been consumed for that amount of production. Management have to decide which variances are relevant to their situation; those selected become performance measurements for that firm.

Basically there are only two main types of variance – those relating to the unit price of labour, material and overhead resources, and those relating to the quantity or volume of resources consumed. We examine both these types by reference to material M77 in the standard cost specification above.

Example

Suppose the firm made 100 products last week using 920 kg of material M77, which it purchased at £2.50 per kg. We want to compare this actual cost of material with the standard cost specified to identify any variance, as follows.

Standard cost of M77	= 900 (i.e. 100 × 9) kg × £2.67 =	£2,403
Actual cost of M77 =	920 kg × £2.50 =	£2,300
Total material M77 cost variance	=	£103 (F)

This variance of £103 results from two causes and not just one. On one hand, extra costs are incurred by using 20 kg of material more than was specified for that level of production. When these 20 kg are priced at the standard price, the excess cost amounts to £53.40 (A) which is called the material usage variance. On the other hand, the firm bought the material more cheaply than it expected and saved 17p on each of the 920 kg used. This resulted in what is called a material price variance of £156.40 (F).

In summary, therefore, we can say that the firm saved £156.40 on the buying-in price of material M77 but that it used £53.40 too much in quantity. These two separate variances net off against each other, as one is favourable and the other adverse, to comprise the total material cost variance as follows.

Material price variance   = £156.40 (F)
Material usage variance   = £ 53.40 (A)
Total material cost variance   = £103.00 (F)

Variances for other costs and for sales can be similarly divided into two main types relating to price and volume although they are given different names. A full list of these basic variances is given in the table below, based on an absorption costing approach.

Types of basic variances

Element	Price variance	Volume variance
Direct materials	Material price	Material usage
Direct labour	Labour rate	Labour efficiency
Variable overheads	Variable O/H expenditure	Variable O/H efficiency
Fixed overheads	Fixed O/H expenditure	Fixed O/H volume
Sales	Sales price	Sales margin volume

Before we look at a more comprehensive example we need to define each variance carefully and explain the reasons why they occur in more general terms. Various symbols are used in the formulae and these are based on the following key:

A = Actual   S = Standard   P = Price   Q = Quantity
C = Cost   B = Budgeted   SAR = Standard absorption rate
O/H = Overhead   ( ) = Difference between values

Materials

The 'material price variance' represents the difference between the actual and the standard purchase prices of material for the total quantity purchased. Unlike other cost variances which are calculated at the time production takes place, this variance is normally calculated at the time of purchase.

Material price variance = (SP–AP) AQ

Example

When the 920 kg of material M77 were actually bought in at £2.50 as opposed to the standard price of £2.67 the calculation is:

$$\text{Material price variance} = (SP - AP) \times AQ$$
$$= (£2.67 - £2.50) \times 920$$
$$= £156.40 \text{ (F)}$$

The material price variance is the responsibility of the buyer or purchasing officer. Reasons why the variance occurred could include a switch to a new supplier, a fall in market price, extra discount received or a lower quality of material purchased.

If the material price variance is calculated at the time of purchase, it is because the materials are put into stock at their standard cost. When they are subsequently issued to production there will be no price variance at that point in time.

The 'material usage variance' represents the difference in the cost of material used that is caused by its more, or less, efficient use compared with that specified. It is important to note that the principle of flexible budgeting is applied to materials and all other variable costs in standard costing. This means that whatever the level of actual production turns out to be, we compare the actual cost of any variable cost with its flexed budgeted cost.

The material usage variance is calculated from the difference between the actual quantity of material used and the standard quantity specified for that level of production. This quantity difference is evaluated at the standard price because any difference in the actual price is subsumed in the material price variance.

$$\text{Material usage variance} = (SQ - AQ)\,SP$$

Example

The above firm used 920 kg of material M77 instead of the 900 kg specified for the 100 products made. The calculation is:

$$\text{Material usage variance} = (SQ - AQ) \times SP$$
$$= (900 - 920) \times £2.67$$
$$= £53.40 \text{ (A)}$$

This material usage variance could be the responsibility of the buyer if sub-standard material were to blame, but normally the responsibility lies with the production supervisor or manager. Other possible reasons for the variance include machine faults, unskilled labour, poor supervision and mishandling.

Where a number of materials are combined in a mix, as say with chemicals, then it would be useful to analyse the material usage variance into two further parts called mix and yield variances.

Labour

The 'labour rate variance' represents the difference in direct labour cost caused by any variations from the standard rates of pay and is akin to the material price variance, using the same formula. It is calculated from the difference between the standard and actual rates per hour multiplied by the actual number of hours paid. Where more than one grade of labour is employed then a labour rate variance will be calculated for each one.

$$\text{Labour rate variance} = (SP - AP)\,AQ$$

Example

The standard machining time allowed for one unit of Product GR49 is 10.5 hours at a standard rate of pay of £4 per hour. When 100 units were made last week they took 1,120 hours to complete and were paid at £3.60 per hour. The calculation is:

$$
\begin{aligned}
\text{Labour rate variance} \quad &= (SP - AP) \times AQ \\
&= (£4.00 - £3.60) \times 1120 \\
&= £448.00 \ (F)
\end{aligned}
$$

Responsibility for this variance would lie with the production supervisors if they had switched to a lower grade of labour. It is unlikely that the reduced rate is the result of collective bargaining but in any new permanent situation the standard cost specification should be revised.

The 'labour efficiency variance' represents the difference in labour cost caused by the degree of efficiency in the use of labour compared with the standard specified. Again it is akin to the material usage variance and is calculated in the same way.

$$\text{Labour efficiency variance} = (SQ - AQ)\,SP$$

Example

The firm should have used 1,050 hours to produce the 100 units taking 10.5 hours for each one. It actually took 1,120 hours to complete production. The calculations are:

$$
\begin{aligned}
\text{Labour efficiency variance} &= (SQ - AQ) \times SP \\
&= (1,050 - 1,120) \times £4.00 \\
&= £280.00 \ (A)
\end{aligned}
$$

In summary therefore, the firm has saved £168 on the cost of labour overall. The £448 saved by paying a lower-than-normal rate per hour has been partially offset by paying £280 for the excess hours worked. The total labour cost variance can be summarized as follows.

Labour rate variance	£448 (F)
Labour efficiency variance	£280 (A)
Total labour cost variance	£168 (F)

Variable Overheads These are overheads whose total cost should vary *pro rata* with the level of production, as opposed to fixed overheads whose total cost remains constant irrespective of fluctuations in production levels.

The 'variable overhead expenditure variance' represents the difference between the actual cost of the variable overheads and the total amount recovered on the actual level of production at the standard absorption rate. It is calculated from the difference between the quantity of output multiplied by the standard absorption rate per unit and the actual variable overheads:

$$\text{Variable overhead expenditure variance} = (AQ \times SAR) - AC$$

Example

Assuming for the moment that variable overheads are recovered at the rate of £14.70 per unit of product then the total recovery amounts to £1,470 for the 100 products. If the actual variable overheads cost £1,555 then we get the following calculation:

$$
\begin{aligned}
\text{Variable overhead expenditure variance} &= (AQ \times SAR) - AC \\
&= (100 \times £14.70) - £1,555 \\
&= £85 \text{ (A)}
\end{aligned}
$$

Because variable overheads are supposed to vary with the level of production, this variance represents the difference in spending between actual cost and the standard cost allowed for that level of production. However, where variable overheads are absorbed on a direct labour hour basis, there are two possible reasons for the variation in variable overhead costs: the above reason, namely that the actual overheads cost more or less than expected; or the other reason, that the direct labour carried out their work with a greater or lesser degree of efficiency than allowed in the standard cost specification. This results in a 'variable overhead efficiency variance'.

Example

We will again assume that the actual variable overheads cost £1,555 in total but this time the variable overhead standard absorption rate was set at £1.40 per labour-hour for machining. Each product was allowed 10.5 hours for completion. The variable overhead expenditure variance now becomes:

(Actual hours × Standard absorption rate) − Actual cost

(1,120 × £1.40) − £1,555 = £13.00 (F)

The variable overhead efficiency variance represents:

(Standard labour hours − Actual labour hours) × SAR

(1,050 − 1,120) × £1.40 = £98.00 (A)

The total variable overhead variance is now seen to be composed of two elements:

Variable overhead expenditure variance	£13	(F)
Variable overhead efficiency variance	£98	(A)
Total variable overhead variance	£85	(A)

The £13 favourable variance represents a saving in the actual cost of the overheads incurred, whilst the adverse efficiency variance of £98 represents the extra cost of spending too long on the work and mirrors the direct labour efficiency variance.

Fixed Overheads

There are also two reasons why fixed overheads can vary from the standard cost allowed. On the one hand the actual cost of the fixed overheads can turn out to be more than that budgeted, e.g., when a higher rate bill than expected is received from the local authority. On the other hand fixed overheads are recovered on the basis of a standard absorption rate of £x per product or per hour.

When the level of production exceeds that budgeted then more overheads will be recovered than are actually incurred. This leads to a favourable fixed overhead volume variance. The converse is also possible when a shortfall in production leads to an under-recovery of overheads because the standard absorption rate anticipated overheads being spread over more units of production. The 'fixed overhead expenditure variance' represents the difference between the actual cost and the budgeted cost:

Fixed overhead expenditure variance = (BC − AC)

Example

Suppose the actual fixed overheads for the machining department were £2,800 whilst the budgeted cost was £2,887 then the fixed overhead expenditure variance is £87 (F).

The 'fixed overhead volume variance' represents the under- or over-recovery of fixed overheads caused by the actual volume of production varying from the budgeted volume used to set the standard absorption rate. When this standard absorption rate is based on a unit of production (as opposed to an hourly rate) the volume variance is calculated from the difference between actual and budgeted volume multiplied by the standard absorption rate per unit.

$$\text{Fixed overhead volume variance} = (AQ - BQ)\,SAR$$

Example

Assume the standard absorption rate for machining fixed overheads was £26.25 per unit of product irrespective of hours taken to produce it. The budgeted level of production last month was 110 products but only 100 were actually produced. The fixed overhead volume variance is therefore:

$$(AQ - BQ) \times SAR$$
$$(100 - 110) \times £26.25 = £262.50\ (A)$$

When fixed overheads are absorbed on the basis of an hourly rate, then the above volume variance is composed of two separate elements which can be separately evaluated. On the one hand the under- or over-recovery is affected by the actual level of production compared with that budgeted. This is known as the 'capacity variance'. On the other hand the overhead recovery is also affected by the actual number of hours taken to produce the goods compared with the standard hours allowed. This part is known as the 'efficiency variance'. Together the capacity and efficiency variances make up the volume variance.

Sales

Variances occur when sales are made at non-standard prices and/or when the actual volume of sales differs from the budgeted level. In this latter case it is the profit margin which is gained/lost on the extra/lost sales. The 'sales price variance' represents the profit lost or gained by selling at non-standard prices. It is calculated from the difference between the actual and standard selling price multiplied by the actual sales quantity:

$$\text{Sales price variance} = (AP - SP) \, AQ$$

Example

The standard selling price of Product GR49 is £200 but £205 was achieved because smaller-than-normal discounts were allowed. During the month 100 products were sold. The sales price variance is:

$$(AP - SP) \times AQ$$
$$(£205 - £200) \times 100 = £500 \text{ (F)}$$

The 'sales volume variance' represents the profit margins gained or lost on the variation in sales from the budgeted level. It is calculated from the standard profit margin multiplied by the difference between actual sales volume and budgeted sales volume:

$$\text{Sales volume variance} = (AQ - BQ) \times \text{Standard profit margin}$$

Example

The sales volume was budgeted at 110 but turned out to be only 100 last month. The standard profit margin is £13.26. The sales volume variance is:

$$(AQ - BQ) \times \text{Standard profit margin}$$
$$(100 - 110) \times £13.26 = £132.60 \text{ (A)}$$

The total of these two sales variances does not measure the difference in sales value between budgeted sales and actual sales. It does measure the difference in the profit earned that is brought about through sales effort, either by selling at a non-standard price, or by selling a different quantity from that budgeted.

So far we have seen how standard costing sets yardsticks, or standards of performance, in money terms. Actual results are compared with these predetermined yardsticks and variances are identified which, if significant, lead to managerial action. In this way the control cycle is completed.

Management does not always have time to sift through large quantities of detailed cost variances and wants information in a global or summarized form. One way to satisfy this need is to calculate standard costing ratios which measure aspects of overall efficiency and activity. Another way is to produce a management control statement on profit and loss account lines. We now look at these ideas in turn.

Standard Costing Ratios

Chapter 8 examines the use of accounting ratios to measure aspects of company performance and liquidity. At this point we are restricting our discussion to measures of company performance associated with the standard costing technique, additional to the variances already discussed.

Central to these other measures is the concept of the 'standard hour' which represents the amount of work which can be done in one hour under standard conditions. This standard hour is a useful commom denominator with which to aggregate different operations and different products.

With this definition of a standard hour, we can measure the operating efficiency of a firm by relating the 'standard hours equivalent of the work produced' to the actual hours taken:

$$\text{Efficiency ratio} = \frac{\text{Standard hours produced}}{\text{Actual hours worked}} \times 100\%$$

Example

Suppose last week a firm took 500 actual hours to produce goods equivalent to 450 standard hours. The efficiency ratio is:

$$\frac{450}{500} \times 100\% = 90\%$$

It is theoretically possible for the efficiency ratio to reach 100% or even to exceed it. Much will depend on the realism of the standards and the motivation (including payment incentives) of the labour force. Like many other ratios it is a comparison with previous performance that may inform most.

Another ratio is used to measure the 'level of activity' as opposed to the level of efficiency with which that activity was carried out. The 'activity ratio' relates the actual work produced to the budgeted work for that period, both being expressed in standard hours.

$$\text{Activity ratio} = \frac{\text{Standard hours produced}}{\text{Budgeted standard hours}} \times 100\%$$

Example

Taking the same example where the actual standard hours produced were 450, let us now assume that there were 475 budgeted standard hours. The calculation is:

$$\frac{450}{475} \times 100\% = 94.7\%$$

The activity ratio of 94.7% measures the shortfall from the budgeted level of activity of 100%

A third ratio measures 'capacity usage' by relating the actual hours worked to the budgeted standard hours.

$$\text{Capacity ratio} = \frac{\text{Actual hours worked}}{\text{Budgeted standard hours}} \times 100\%$$

Example

Using the same figures from the previous illustrations, when 500 actual hours were worked but the firm had budgeted for 475 standard hours, the calculation is:

$$\frac{500}{475} \times 100\% = 105.3\%$$

This capacity ratio indicates that more hours were worked than planned, whereas the activity ratio states that less production was achieved than planned. This apparent anomaly is explained by the efficiency ratio, which states that more time was taken on production than should have been taken.

We now turn our attention to another way of measuring overall performance which combines budgeted profit, variances and actual profit in one explanatory statement to management.

Management Control Statement

The variances we examined in the previous chapter all rely on the preparation of budgets and standards which detail costs, income and output. This means that a firm operating budgetary control and standard costing systems should be able to predict the future profit from its trading operations.

If the sales and cost variances are negligible, then the actual profit made will more or less equate with the budgeted profit. Any significant variances will radically affect the profit actually achieved but the nature of a particular variance will give a good insight into its possible cause. Adverse variances reduce the actual profit from the budgeted level whilst favourable variances enhance it.

A common practice is to incorporate standard costing variances into a management control statement. This takes the form of a standard costing profit and loss account reconciling the budgeted profit with the actual profit achieved. The reasons why the actual profit varies from the budgeted level are contained in the cost and sales variances which replace the absolute values of costs and sales found in a conventional profit and loss account. A comprehensive example based on a 'standard absorption costing system' now illustrates this approach.

Example

Carr Chemicals Ltd are a one-product firm. The company uses a standard absorption costing system and prepared the following budget for last month which was expected to result in a profit of £7,000.

Budget for last month

	£	Units	£
Sales at £6 per unit		10,000	60,000
Direct materials			
10,000 kg at £1 per kg	10,000		
Direct labour			
5,000 h at £4.80 per h	24,000		
Variable overheads			
10,000 units at 50p each unit	5,000		
Fixed overheads			
£7,000 per week (70p per unit)	7,000		
Total cost of sales		10,000	46,000
Budgeted profit at standard profit margin of £1.40			£14,000

Unfortunately, Carr Chemicals did not produce and sell as many products as they had planned, yet they made a greater profit. The actual results were:

Actual results for last month

	£	Units	£
Sales at £6.20 per unit		9,000	55,800
Direct materials			
9,500 kg at 90p per kg	8,550		
Direct labour			
4,500 h at £4.90 per h	22,050		
Variable overheads	4,000		
Fixed overheads	6,500		
Total cost of sales		9,000	41,100
Actual profit			£14,700

We can now draw up a statement reconciling the actual profit of £14,700 with the £14,000 budgeted profit by detailing the adverse or favourable variances for the month. These variances explain how the extra profit was achieved. Management examining this statement are not asked to look at absolute cost and sales values, but are pinpointed to the deviations from planned activities. If they consider any variance to be significant it can be discussed and/or further examined to see if anything can be learned to improve future performance.

Standard costing profit and loss account

	(F)	(A)	£
Budgeted profit for the month			14,000
Variances:	(F)	(A)	
Sales price variance (£6.00–£6.20) 9,000	1,800		
Sales margin volume var. (9,000–10,000) £1.40		1,400	
Material price variance (£1.00–£0.90) 9,500	950		
Material usage variance (9,500–9,000) £1.00		500	
Labour rate variance (£4.90–£4.80) 4,500		450	
Labour efficiency var. (4,500–4,500) £4.80	—	—	
Variable o/head exp.var. £4,000–(9,000×50p)	500		
Fixed o/head exp. variance (£6,500–£7,000)	500		
Fixed o/head volume var. (9,000–10,000)70p		700	
	3,750	3,050	700 (F)
Actual profit for the month			£14,700

(Note that the standard quantity of material and labour used in the material usage and labour efficiency variances, respectively, are based on the quantities that should have been used for the actual level of production i.e. 9,000 products. In other words a flexed budget approach is used to quantify the standards for labour, materials and also variable overheads.)

Standard Marginal Costing

The above example, and the variances discussed so far, were based on absorption costing principles, as opposed to marginal costing principles. It is equally possible to base standards on this latter approach.

Referring back to the original budget for Carr Chemicals we find that the standard profit amounted to £1.40 per product and the fixed overheads were budgeted at 70p per product. The actual output turned out to be 1,000 products less than the quantity expected and therefore the firm would lose £2.10 on each of the 1,000 sales shortfall, making £2,100 in total.

Standard absorption costing separates the effects of this sales shortfall into two variances, which quantify the lost profit and the under-recovery of overheads as:

	£	
Sales margin volume variance	1,400	(A)
Fixed overhead volume variance	700	(A)
Total	£2,100	(A)

These two separate variances were included in the standard costing profit and loss account illustrated above, but it would have been equally valid to combine them in a marginal costing approach.

Marginal costing, you may recall, does not apportion fixed overheads to products but takes the view that products make a contribution towards fixed costs and profit. In brief we can say:

$$\text{Sales} - \text{Variable costs} = \text{Contribution}$$

and

$$\text{Contribution} = \text{Fixed costs} + \text{Profit}$$

Standard marginal costing combines the lost profit and under-recovery of overheads on the 1,000 units in the one contribution volume variance. Using the same example from Carr Chemicals above, we find:

$$
\begin{aligned}
\text{Contribution volume variance} \quad &= (AQ - BQ) \times \text{Unit contribution} \\
&= (9,000 - 10,000) \times £2.10 \\
&= £2,100 \text{ (A)}
\end{aligned}
$$

The final effect is the same for both standard marginal and standard absorption costing, because each shows that the 1,000 lost sales resulted in a reduction in profit of £2,100.

A third and final approach to standard costing systems is to restrict the calculation of standards to direct costs only. Variances would therefore be limited to those pertaining to direct materials, direct labour and direct expenses. This would leave overheads to be controlled by a system of fixed departmental budgets with the option of flexible budgets should the situation demand it.

Summary

This chapter introduces the idea of yardsticks being set against which future performance can be measured. Standard costing can therefore be seen as a control cycle, an idea which applies in other spheres of management. A study by Lyall, Okoh & Puxty (cited under 'Further reading') points to the continued use of standard costing in industry.

Standard specifications can be set for unit prices and volumes, for each cost element and for sales. When actual results are compared with these standards, we get both price and volume variances.

Favourable variances explain how extra profit was gained whilst adverse variances show how profit was lost. Both can be combined in a management control statement to show why actual profit turned out different from that budgeted.

The variances we have encountered so far provide a good grounding for most standard costing systems. However, it should not be assumed that all standard costing systems will use exactly the same basis.

As mentioned earlier, the variable overhead variances depend on the way that overheads are absorbed by products. Fixed overhead volume variances are capable of sub-division into capacity and efficiency variances. In certain industries the material volume variance is capable of further analysis into mix and yield variances. The labour efficiency variance is also capable of further breakdown into root causes although, with increasingly automatic processes, direct labour is more dependent on machine pacing rather than on human effort in many industries.

There is danger in all this, however, that too much detailed analysis of variances by accountants may hinder rather than help the managers being informed. Firms should use the system best suited to their industry, to their costing methods and, in particular, to their management requirements. As Dugdale suggests in his article (listed under 'Further reading' below), textbook techniques should never be a substitute for hard thinking about the specific problem to be solved.

Standard costing provides information which can be used by management as a monitoring and control device. This can be done in a global way by using ratios based on the concept of the standard hour and also by the preparation of standard costing profit and loss accounts.

Standard costs can be based on absorption, marginal or direct cost principles. Obviously, there are differences in the types of variances that can be extracted from these different systems, but their basic purpose – to plan and control costs and selling prices, and thereby performance – remains the same. We now go on to discuss budgetary control, a complementary planning and control system based on functional departments.

Further reading

Books
Drury, C. *Management and Cost Accounting*, 2nd edn (VNR).
Lucey, T. *Costing,* 3rd edn (DPP).

Articles
Dugdale, D. Standard costing – where theory and practice diverge. In *Management Accounting* (Oct. 1988).
Lyall, D., Okoh, K. & Puxty, A. Cost control into the 1990s. In *Management Accounting* (Feb. 1990).
Walker, J. The analysis of production overhead variances. In *Management Accounting* (Jun. 1989).

Work-based assignment

Ascertain whether or not your organization uses a system of standard costing. If so, is it based on direct costs only, or on variable costs only, or on all costs? Obtain a sample of the management control statement used to inform management of the effect of standard costing variances on profit. Ascertain possible causes for each individual variance.

Questions with answers
(see Appendix 4)

1 It has been decided that the performance of the assembly department of your company is to be measured using ratios based upon standard hours.

During two succeeding periods the following information was obtained:

	Period 1	Period 2
Budget production in standard hours	2,000	2,250
Actual hours worked	1,800	2,400
Actual production in standard hours	1,750	2,250

(a) You are required to produce the following for each of the above periods:
  (i) the efficiency ratio,
  (ii) the activity ratio,
  (iii) the capacity ratio.

(b) You are also required to comment on the figures you have produced in (a).

(Certified Diploma)

2 (a) Calculate the material and labour variances from the following data:

Standard cost of component XY:

Material cost	£0.60 per kg
Material weight to produce one component	1.5 kg
Wage rate, per hour	£3.80
Time required to make one component	36 minutes
Standard selling price, per component	£3.50

The following was recorded in the month of May 198X:

Components manufactured and sold	3,510
Sales income	£12,285
Materials purchased and issued	(i) 2,740 kg at £0.58
	(ii) 2,315 kg at £0.62
Wages paid for the production	(i) 880 hours at £3.90
	(ii) 1,300 hours at £3.65

(b) Present the answers to the above information in a statement to management disclosing the reasons for the differences between standard and actual gross profit.

(c) A consultant recently stated that 'Past performance is the best guide to ascertaining standard costs'.

Analyse this statement in detail and indicate whether or not you agree with it.

(AAT)

Questions for class use

1 You are given the following information in relation to the month just finished:

Budget production	3,200 units	Actual production	3,050 units
Actual hours worked	25,250	Actual labour cost	£60,600
Standard labour rate per hour	£2.60	Standard hours per unit	8

You are required:

(a) to calculate   (i)   the efficiency ratio,

                     (ii)   the capacity ratio,

                     (iii)   the activity ratio;

(b) to calculate   (i)   the labour efficiency variance,

                     (ii)   the labour rate variance,

                     (iii)   the labour cost variance;

(c) to comment on the results.   (AAT)

2 The standard material cost of fabric specified for a particular garment is £4.50, comprising 3 metres at £1.50 per metre. The standard time allowed for making up the garment is 15 minutes paid at the rate of £3 per hour. Last week 1,000 garments were made using 3,200 metres of fabric which was purchased at £1.40 per metre. The total time taken to make up these garments was 230 hours which were paid at the standard rate.

You are required to:

(a) Calculate the   (i)   material cost variance,

                     (ii)   material usage variance,

                     (iii)   material price variance.

(b) Calculate the   (i)   labour cost variance,

                     (ii)   labour efficiency variance,

                     (iii)   labour rate variance.

(c) Suggest any possible reasons why these variances may have occurred.   (DMS)

3 The sales budget for the last quarter for a division of a large company which markets two similar products was as follows:

Sales budget	Units	Value
		£
Model:		
'Prestige'	5,000	10,000
'Superior'	5,000	7,500
	10,000	17,500

The standard variable cost per unit was 'Prestige' £1.30 and 'Superior' 70p. Although the two products are not completely interchangeable it is thought that one type is purchased in lieu of the other, despite being sold through different outlets.

The results for the last quarter were as follows:

Actual sales	Units	Value
		£
Model:		
'Prestige'	7,500	14,250
'Superior'	2,800	4,480
	10,300	18,730

The costs charged were as standard.

The management have expressed their disappointment at the results and have asked you to prepare:

(a) a standard variance analysis;

(b) suggestions as to how this state of affairs can be prevented or anticipated in the future.   (Certified Diploma)

7 Budgetary control

There are many similarities between a system of budgetary control and the standard costing technique described in the preceding chapter. Much detailed preparatory work is common, as both are concerned with detailed costs and revenues. Also, both techniques are concerned with the planning and control of operations by the continuous monitoring of actual results against those budgeted. Significant variances arising from this comparison are then subject to further investigation and management action as appropriate.

Where the two systems differ is in the unit of application. Standard costing is product-based: the standard costs, particularly for overheads, are not confined to one single department but straddle a number of departments. Budgets, on the other hand, are prepared for differing functions, each of which is likely to mirror the departmentally based structure of the firm.

Corporate strategy and strategic planning are concerned with the broad objectives of the firm over a future timescale of a few years. Budgetary control, however, is often described as the expression of detailed financial plans to meet corporate objectives. These plans are essentially short-term for the coming months up to one year ahead. They are based on short-term objectives such as a target return on capital, a sales value, or a certain percentage share of the market. These short-term plans must, of course, be compatible with the longer-term corporate objectives.

Why Budget?	By the use of budgeting systems, senior management can carry out their roles of planning, delegating, co-ordinating, controlling and motivating. The preparation of detailed plans leads to the identification of the resources – people, materials, equipment and money – needed to bring those plans to fruition.

Responsibility is delegated to departmental managers who can see how their function fits into the global plan and how their separate departmental activities are co-ordinated to a common goal.

Motivation to achieve targets is a key feature of budgetary control, provided budgets have not been imposed without consultation. Imposed budgets are likely to lead to adverse behavioural consequences. Managers may seek to charge costs to incorrect locations or blame colleagues for adverse variances.

Using budgeting systems, senior management can communicate company objectives, delegate responsibility and concentrate solely on any deviations from plans without getting bogged down in day-to-day activities. They thereby practise the principle of 'management by exception'.

Organizing for Budgetary Control

It is the responsibility of top management, personified in the board of directors in a private sector company, to specify the broad objectives for the coming year. These are communicated to a budget committee comprising representatives of both the board and key functional managers. This committee then interprets these objectives into outline plans for each departmental head, who in turn submits his/her detailed proposals.

This process may have to be repeated a number of times to get the necessary integration and co-ordination of the individual budget proposals into a viable state. The detailed procedures to be followed, coding numbers, inflation policy and similar matters should all find expression in a budget manual which is issued to each manager involved.

Some firms approach budget preparation on an incremental basis. This approach takes the previous year's figures to date and adjusts them for anticipated changes in the level of activity and for changes in price levels. Such an approach assumes that there is no slack in the system. An alternative approach is to build budgets up from a 'zero base' and so justify all resources requested in a budget.

Vigilance must be exercised that managers do not pad their budgets and so ensure that variances will be favourable. Similarly, the budgets must be realistic targets at which to aim, being neither too optimistic to please the boss nor too tight to be attainable.

When finally accepted by the budget committee, the functional budgets are aggregated into a master budget consisting of monthly profit and loss accounts, a balance sheet at the year end and a statement of sources and applications of funds for the year. If approved by the board this becomes the policy to be pursued for the coming year.

In many firms the procedure outlined in Figure 15 is assisted by an accountant or budget officer, who provides information and advice to all concerned. Regrettably, in some firms, the complete system of budgetary control is run by accountants for accountants, and imposed on other managers without proper consultation. Consequently the technique loses much of its motivating appeal as it is very important for it to be seen and implemented as a management tool.

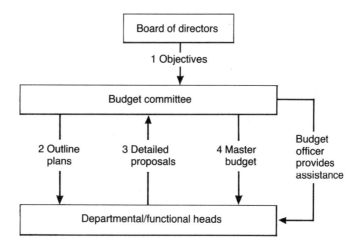

Figure 15 Budget preparation

Identification of the Key Factor

The starting point with budgeting is to identify the key or limiting factor which restricts the firm's growth at this moment in time. In most firms this key factor will be sales volume but it could equally be a shortage of space, skilled labour, raw materials, machinery or even working capital. Assuming sales is the key or limiting factor for a firm, this places the major responsibility for budgeting on the shoulders of the sales manager or director, as all other functions will be geared to this level of activity.

The sequential budgeting process is summarized in Figure 16.

We now examine each of these budget statements in turn to see the principles on which they are prepared and the most suitable layout with which to express them.

Sales Budget

This budget is not just one total sales figure for the coming year, but must be broken down and classified by:

- individual product lines
- differing distribution channels e.g. wholesale, retail
- sales areas or regions
- months in which sales will occur

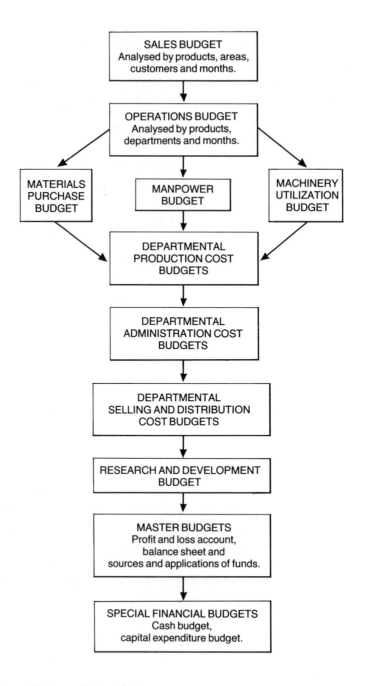

Figure 16 Sequential budgeting process

An extract from such a budget, with random figures, could be set out in the following matrix manner which is a layout applicable to many other budgets:

Sales Budget for 198*X*

Product			Jan	Feb	Mar	Apr	May	Jun	(etc.)	Total
P1	Units	'000	10	10	10	11	12	11		132
	Value	£000	20	20	20	22	24	22		264
	Wholesale	£000	12	13	13	12	14	12		150
	Retail	£000	8	7	7	10	10	10		114
										264
	Area 1	£000	6	5	6	7	8	7		84
	Area 2	£000	9	9	8	10	9	8		114
	Area 3	£000	5	6	6	5	7	7		66
										264
P2 (*Repeat as above*)										

Information to compile a sales budget for an existing business will be drawn from many sources, including:

- current sales level
- past seasonal trends
- sales representatives' reports
- market research, economic trends
- price/demand relationships

Production Budget

On the assumption that sales is the key or limiting factor, then the production/operations level is determined by the sales budget quantities. When production capacity is insufficient, resort may be made to subcontracting. Assuming capacity is sufficient, then the production levels are determined by the length of the production/operations cycle, target stock levels and the month in which the sale is budgeted to occur.

Example

Using the sales volumes for product P1 in the sales budget above let us assume that the product takes one month to complete and the firm carries sufficient finished goods stock at any month end to satisfy all the budgeted sales in the following month. Assuming stock on 1 January was 8,000 units, the production budget can now be set out in the following way:

Production Budget for 198X ('000 units)

	Jan	Feb	Mar	Apr	May	(etc.)	Total
Closing stock	10	10	11	12	11		
Sales during month	10	10	10	11	12		—
	20	20	21	23	23		
Less: Opening stock	8	10	10	11	12		—
Completed prodn reqd	12	10	11	12	11		

Once the production/operations budget is determined the resources of materials, manpower and machinery needed to carry out such production can be determined.

Materials Purchase Budget

There are two main purposes of this particular budget. Advance warning of global requirements for the coming year enables the buying department to arrange supplies on the best possible terms to ensure delivery, quality and the most competitive price. It also provides essential information to feed into the cash budget at a later stage.

A purchase budget follows a very similar pattern to a production budget when both opening and closing stocks, in addition to the materials consumed in the production process, are taken into account. Requirements may be based on past consumption but a more recent trend is to plan materials requirements on the basis of orders received and/or expected.

Example

The formula for making a fertilizer consists of two ingredients mixed in the following proportions:

2 parts Chemical X costing £250 per tonne
1 part Chemical Y costing £200 per tonne

The ingredients required for production in a particular month are bought in the preceding month and the month's output is sold in the following month. The sales forecast is as follows:

Month	Tonnes
February	65
March	70
April	80
May	65
June	60

The separate quantities and cost values of ingredients X and Y are required for purchases in each of the three months January, February and March.

The material content of the sales quantities can be derived as follows:

Sales forecast	Product tonnes	$\frac{2}{3}$ X tonnes	$\frac{1}{3}$ Y tonnes
February	66	44	22
March	72	48	24
April	84	56	28
May	63	42	21
June	60	40	20

Taking into account that materials are purchased two months before the sale of the finished product takes place, then the material purchase quantities and values are:

Material Purchase Budget

	X		Y	
	tonnes	£	tonnes	£
January	48	12,000	24	4,800
February	56	14,000	28	5,600
March	42	10,500	21	4,200

Manpower Budget

This aims to tell the personnel department the manpower requirements for the coming year so that adequate recruitment, training or retraining can take place. It also feeds information into the production cost and cash budgets.

Example

The budget committee of an engineering division of a plc are working on the preparation of budgets for the coming year. The assistant personnel manager is preparing that section of the manpower budget relating to direct operatives, based on the production budget which has already been approved by the committee. The following details are available.

Machining Department

Component	Quantity units	Standard labour-hours per unit
T1	53,000	2
T2	52,500	2
V1	39,000	2
V2	39,500	4

Assembly Department

Product	Quantity units	Standard labour-hours per unit
T	52,000	3
V	39,000	4

Sales and production levels are evenly spread throughout the year and there are no seasonal variations. A 40-hour week will be worked throughout the 52 weeks of the year and no overtime is envisaged. Each employee is entitled to 12 days' holiday plus 8 statutory days and is expected to average 5 days' absence through sickness.

A calculation of the number of direct operatives to be employed next year (to the nearest whole number) is required for each of the two departments.

In this example, the annual number of effective working hours per person is 47 weeks × 40 hours = 1,880 hours per annum (excluding the odd extra day in each year). The assistant personnel manager can therefore multiply the units produced by the hours taken per unit to get the total hours required. These total hours are divided by the effective working hours per annum for one person. The computations are as follows.

Machining Department

Component	Quantity units		Hours per unit		Total hours
T1	53,000	×	2	=	106,000
T2	52,500	×	2	=	105,000
V1	39,000	×	2	=	78,000
V2	39,500	×	4	=	158,000
					447,000

$$\text{Manpower required} = \frac{447,000}{1,880} = 238 \text{ persons}$$

Assembly Department

Product	Quantity units	Hours per unit	Total hours
T	52,000	3	156,000
V	39,000	4	156,000
			312,000

$$\text{Manpower required} = \frac{312,000}{1,880} = 166 \text{ persons}$$

Machinery Utilization Budget

The procedure for calculating machine time requirements follows an identical pattern to that of the above manpower budget. The resultant information is used to determine if any new asset purchases are required after allowance has been made for downtime due to routine maintenance and breakdowns. This mirrors the allowances built into the manpower budget for sickness and holidays.

Production Cost Budget

This summarizes the cost of resources consumed by each separate production department and includes direct costs and indirect costs. The complete budget feeds into both the budgeted profit and loss account (after allowing for stock changes) and the cash budget. A suitable layout for a departmental production cost budget is:

Departmental production cost budget

	Jan	Feb	Mar	Apr	May	Jun	(etc.)	Total

Direct costs:
  Labour
  Materials
  Expenses								

Total direct costs								

Indirect costs:
  Labour
  Salaries
  Materials
  Expenses
  Depreciation								

Total indirect costs								
Total departmental costs								

Administration, Selling and Distribution Cost Budgets

These all comprise indirect costs for the firm and can be displayed in the same manner as the indirect costs in the production cost budgets above. The level of each budget should not just be an inflated figure from the previous year but a genuine attempt to measure the resources needed to give the level of service demanded from the department.

In the case of administrative costs this may be achieved by a 'zero-based budgeting' approach. This literally starts from scratch with no prior assumptions about previous spending levels and lists the resources required to perform various functional tasks. These tasks can then be prioritized and the budget prepared on the basis of what is deemed essential, or how far the money allocated will stretch. This 'priority-based budget' approach may also prove particularly helpful in public sector service departments.

The selling and distribution departments' budgets are directly linked to the level of activity contained in the sales budget. Some selling and distribution costs may be fixed in nature irrespective of the exact level of activity, whilst other costs may vary directly with the level of sales. The following example illustrates this approach and includes some sample figures.

Selling and Distribution Cost Budget

	Jan	Feb	Mar	Apr	May	etc.
Sales quantity, '000 units	20	20	25	30	30	
Variable costs:	£000					
Sales commission at 10%	2.0	2.0	2.5	3.0	3.0	
Vehicle fuel and servicing	0.4	0.4	0.5	0.6	0.6	
Fixed costs:						
Basic salesmen's salaries	9.0	9.0	9.0	9.0	9.0	
Advertising	6.0	6.0	6.0	6.0	6.0	
Office salaries	8.0	8.0	8.0	8.0	8.0	
Drivers' wages	9.0	9.0	9.0	9.0	9.0	
Vehicle standing charges	5.0	5.0	5.0	5.0	5.0	
Total budget	39.4	39.4	40.0	40.6	40.6	

Budget Reports

The accounting year is the natural choice for the budgeting process, although it is broken down into months for regular comparison with budgeted figures. These months may be of the calendar or lunar variety, or some other constant working period. This avoids distorted comparisons due to the incidence of works and statutory holidays. Some firms also work on a rolling year, adding a new month's budget as each month passes.

The comparison of actual results with budget takes place on two different time planes. Each departmental manager is fed information about the costs (and income) under his/her control on a regular basis, normally every month. This monthly report compares actual costs/income with budgeted costs/income for the month under review and for the cumulative months of the accounting year so far elapsed. Figure 17 illustrates this approach.

Dept:		Monthly Budget Report						Month:
Cost code	Description	Current month			Cumulative			
		Budget £	Actual £	Variance £	Budget £	Actual £	Variance £	
612	Salaries	5,200	5,400	+200	15,600	16,100	+500	

Figure 17 Typical monthly budget report

Controllable Costs

A problem often arises in budgeting, somewhat similar to the one examined in Chapter 9 on responsibility accounting for decentralized organisations. Reduced to its basics, the problem amounts to how far to go in recharging costs to cost centres for budgeting and monitoring purposes.

When costs actually incurred by a departmental manager are charged against that same department, there is a strong motivating element at work. However, if the cost centre is charged with apportionments of establishment charges over which the departmental manager has little control, if any, then the practice may have a demotivating effect. On the other hand, if all costs are not charged or apportioned to departments, then the cost of functional activities are understated and a manager may be unaware of the true cost of the function's existence.

A compromise might seem to be to report back at two levels. The first stage of the budget monitoring report should include controllable fixed and variable costs which are agreed to be the direct responsibility of the departmental manager. The second stage of the report can include apportioned general overheads which are not seen as the direct responsibility of the departmental manager. In this way both purposes are served. The departmental manager can concentrate on the controllable costs which are his prime responsibility while also being aware of the remaining costs incurred on behalf of his/her department.

Research and Development Budget

Normal accountancy policy, as expressed in SSAP No.13, is that revenue expenditure on research and development activities is charged to the profit and loss account as and when incurred. This would include depreciation on fixed assets which themselves are shown in the balance sheet statement.

Many firms think of research and development as just another overhead and allocate a small percentage of income to cater for its costs. It is perfectly feasible to think of research and development as just another department and to budget for it in the same way as administrative, selling and distribution expenses and to subject it to the same kind of monthly report back.

Such practice will provide useful global feedback on the elements of costs, but misses the distinguishing feature of this kind of expense. From a control and report-back point of view, research and development have much in common with capital expenditure. In both cases money is committed to individual projects which may take years, rather than weeks, to complete.

What is useful in both cases is additional information on the nature of expenditure on each individual project together with an estimate, where possible, of the further expenditure required until completion. The former provides valuable information to each project manager and department head on the state of each project whilst the latter allows top management to exercise judgement on the continued viability of particular projects. At this point the reader may wish to look at the section on capital expenditure budgets later in this chapter.

Up to this point we have seen how budgets are set for individual departments or functions, all integrated towards common objectives set by top management. Such functional budgets are used to monitor progress and feed formation back to the manager concerned by a regular comparison with actual results.

We now want to look at the way top management and accountants draw all the detailed budgets together to obtain an overall view of both viability and performance.

Master Budgets

These are so called because they summarize the detailed transactions contained in the various functional budgets and look at them from different points of view. The budgeted profit and loss account summarizes the planned income and expenditure month by month to arrive at the budgeted profit for the year. A typical example would look like the table below.

A number of tests for viability can now be carried out on the budgeted profit figures to see if the projected trading results are acceptable. These would include an examination of the absolute monthly and yearly profit figures with the same period in the previous year.

Comparisons can also be made with profit objectives laid down by top management. Use is also likely to be made of ratio analysis to quantify profit margins, return on capital, and rate of turnover of capital. These ideas are explored in the following chapter.

Just as departmental budgets are subject to constant monitoring as the budgeted year progresses, so will the budgeted profit and loss account be

Budgeted Profit and Loss Account

	Jan	Feb	Mar	Apr	May	Jun	(etc.)	Total
Sales, £000	100	100	100	110	115	110		
Less:								
Direct labour	12	12	12	13	13	13		
Direct materials	20	20	20	22	23	22		
Direct expenses	2	2	2	2	2	2		
Production overheads	15	15	15	15	16	15		
Administration costs	10	10	10	10	10	10		
Selling costs	12	12	12	13	14	13		
Distribution costs	15	15	15	17	19	17		
Total costs	86	86	86	92	97	92		
Profit/(Loss)	14	14	14	18	18	18		

compared with the actual result for the same month and with the cumulative total to date. Where a manufacturing or processing firm uses standard costing then a different type of profit and loss account can be prepared showing the reasons why the actual profit differs from that budgeted. This was explained in Chapter 6.

A budgeted balance sheet will also be projected for the end of the budget year, showing the assets owned and the sources of finance with which they were acquired. This statement is required to calculate the projected profitability of operations and also to do various tests on the liquidity and capital structure resulting from a further year's trading. A typical balance sheet in vertical Companies Act 1985 format looks like the one shown below.

Budgeted Balance Sheet

	£000	£000
Fixed assets		2,000
Current assets:		
Stocks and work-in-progress	3,000	
Debtors	1,500	
Bank balance and cash	500	
	5,000	
Less: Creditors due within one year	2,000	
Net current assets (working capital)		3,000
Total net assets (capital employed)		5,000
Less: Creditors due after one year		1,000
Share capital and reserves		4,000

The final statement making up the trio of master budgets is the budgeted statement of sources and applications of funds. This could be projected monthly but even the yearly statement will provide valuable information for management. In essence this is a statement about cash flow, summarizing the different ways cash has been received during the period and the ways in which it has been used.

The balancing figure between total inflows and outflows of cash represents the change in the liquidity position. The main causes of liquidity problems and the size of the potential problem are both identifiable from this statement. It is therefore of great use to management in pinpointing candidates for remedial treatment.

The format of the statement as laid down in SSAP No.10 is as follows.

Statement of Sources and Application of Funds

			£000
Sources of funds:			
Profit before tax			105
Add back: Depreciation			15
Total cash generated from trading operations			120
Other sources:			
Issue of new shares			45
New loan			15
Total sources of funds			180
Less: Applications of funds:			
Payment of tax		40	
Payment of dividend		35	
Purchase of fixed assets		50	
			125
			55
Increase in working capital:			
Increase in stocks		47	
Increase in debtors		30	
Increase in creditors		(27)	50
Movement in net liquid funds			5

Special Financial Budgets

These comprise the cash budget and the capital expenditure budget and are primarily working tools for the accountant although summarized information from both will be fed to top management.

Taking the cash budget first, this is a very detailed statement showing all the planned receipts and payments of cash for the coming year broken down into monthly intervals. It therefore quantifies any potential surpluses or deficits of cash, and their expected duration, in time for any necessary action to be implemented.

Unlike the statement of sources and applications of funds it does not summarize the reasons for the monthly surplus or deficit. For example, purchases are shown as a cash payment in the month when actually paid, without distinguishing between materials consumed and those remaining in stock. The sources and application of funds statement separates this one transaction and charges materials consumed against profit whilst showing any change in stocks as a movement of working capital.

A cash budget includes all revenue and capital transactions with one exception. Purchases of fixed assets are included in the cash budget whereas depreciation on them is not. To do otherwise would be to doublecount the same transaction but, even more importantly, it would ignore the fact that depreciation is not a cash expense but a notional expense designed to spread the initial cost over a number of years' profit and loss accounts.

The two important things to remember when compiling a cash budget are to ignore depreciation and to allow the necessary time lags on credit transactions. The following example will illustrate this.

Example

You have been presented with the following information relating to Midas Ltd.

Forecast Trading and Profit and Loss Account

	Jul	Aug	Sept	Oct	Nov	Dec	Total
	£	£	£	£	£	£	£
Sales	30,000	25,000	26,000	28,000	30,000	40,000	179,000
Less:							
Purchases	15,000	12,500	13,000	14,000	15,000	20,000	89,500
Gross profit	15,000	12,500	13,000	14,000	15,000	20,000	89,500
Wages	9,000	9,200	8,500	9,500	9,600	12,000	57,800
Expenses	3,000	3,600	7,000	4,000	3,000	3,100	23,700
Depreciation	1,500	1,500	1,500	1,500	1,500	1,500	9,000
	13,500	14,300	17,000	15,000	14,100	16,600	90,500
Net profit or (loss)	1,500	(1,800)	(4,000)	(1,000)	900	3,400	(1,000)

No account has been taken of cash discounts allowable or receivable in the above figures.

As the company's future is uncertain you have been asked by the Sales Director to prepare a cash forecast for the six months to 31 December 198X, given the following additional information:

(i)	Sales	50% of sales are made for cash; 30% are settled in the month following the month of sale and are subject to a 2% prompt settlement discount; the remaining 20% are received the following month.
(ii)	Purchases	The company's policy is to pay suppliers in the month of delivery, claiming a 5% discount.
(iii)	Wages and expenses	Paid in the month to which they relate.

(iv) It is anticipated that, during the six months, the following receipts and payments will occur:

August	Sale proceeds from the disposal of freehold property £40,000.
September	Proceeds from disposal of investments £6,100 Rent on leaseback of premises sold in August now payable at £6,000 per annum, payable half-yearly in advance.
November	Purchase of machinery £7,500.

(v) The company's bank balance at 1 July is £7,500 overdrawn.

(vi) Sales for May and June amount to £18,000 and £21,000 respectively.

(IOM)

The cash forecast/budget can be laid out in a matrix format similar to the profit and loss account. However, the individual items are not the same. Each month the cumulative cash position can be determined and the continued viability, or otherwise, of the company ascertained.

Our interpretation of the cumulative cash balance is that the initial bank overdraft of £7,500 ceases to be a problem in August when the once-and-for-all sale and leaseback is expected to take place. Thereafter the cash balance remains strongly positive despite the increasing working capital requirement brought on by rising sales. In the event of the property sale not taking place, however, this would have serious consequences for the level of overdraft required.

The trading and profit and loss account paints a gloomier picture. There is a net loss in three months out of six and a marginal loss of £1,000 in total for the period. Although Midas Ltd can survive this scale of loss for a number of years it would find it difficult to attract new capital and hence its long-term survival is open to question.

Cash Forecast/Budget

	Jul £	Aug £	Sept £	Oct £	Nov £	Dec £
Cash in:						
Cash sales	15,000	12,500	13,000	14,000	15,000	20,000
Credit sales						
net of discount	6,174	8,820	7,350	7,644	8,232	8,820
	3,600	4,200	6,000	5,000	5,200	5,600
Asset sales		40,000	6,100			
Total cash in	24,774	65,520	32,450	26,644	28,432	34,420
Cash out:						
Purchases (net)	14,250	11,875	12,350	13,300	14,250	19,000
Wages	9,000	9,200	8,500	9,500	9,600	12,000
Expenses	3,000	3,600	7,000	4,000	3,000	3,100
Rent			3,000			
Machinery					7,500	
Total cash out	26,250	24,675	30,850	26,800	34,350	34,100
Monthly +/(−)	(1,476)	40,845	1,600	(156)	(5,918)	320
Cumulative balance	(8,976)	31,869	33,469	33,313	27,395	27,715

Capital Expenditure Budget

As mentioned earlier in the chapter, this budget has a close affinity with the budgeting of research and development activities. The total spend requires monitoring, and individual project spending projected to completion also needs watching carefully to avoid any serious overspends.

The techniques of individual project appraisal are discussed in Chapter 11 dealing with investment appraisal. There it is explained how the profitability of investments is assessed using discounted cash flow techniques which also assist us in choosing between competing projects.

Before any selection can take place, however, top management have to decide how much capital to make available for the coming year. Because of the long-term nature of many investments they will also have to give serious thought to more than one year ahead so that projects, once started, are not starved of funds before completion in a subsequent year.

Sources of funds for capital expenditure include:

- depreciation provision for the year on existing fixed assets
- sales of scrap and surplus/redundant assets
- grants
- new capital in the form of loans or share issues

To some extent a chicken-and-egg situation can exist, with top management not being able to decide how much capital to put into the pool without knowing the investment requirements of line management. This is partly answered by their own corporate strategy. If, say, they wanted to pursue growth by expansion or acquisition, then they must allocate sufficient funds for that purpose.

When compiling the total capital budget for the coming year a useful way forward is to categorize various types of investment and allocate funds to programme areas before selecting the individual projects that can proceed, as shown in the table below.

Investment category	Amount requested	Amount allocated	
	£	£	%
Legal/safety requirements	20,000	20,000	100.0
Replacement vehicles	100,000	80,000	80.0
Cost saving/efficiency	250,000	170,000	68.0
New products	500,000	500,000	100.0
Total	870,000	770,000	88.5%

The implication of this budget is that top management agree that the company must meet its legal and safety obligations in full. They are also fully committed to implementing the new products which are probably part of their corporate strategy. This means that the other two categories must be cut back as the total amount requested exceeds by £100,000 the £770,000 capital that is available for investment.

Notwithstanding that regular replacement of vehicles is company policy, they are prepared to trim this category back in the light of other demands for capital this year. The same observation applies to cost saving investments where there is insufficient capital being made available to allow all viable projects to proceed. Selection will be based on those which offer the maximum benefit for each pound invested, which forms the basis of the 'profitability index' calculation mentioned in Chapter 8.

Once projects have been authorized, their progress needs careful monitoring and each project manager should receive monthly reports on the costs incurred to date, analysed by element of cost and by stages of the project. A suitably designed job number, as an integral part of the cost code structure mentioned in Chapter 1, will facilitate this process.

Top management also need updating on the state of the capital budget as a whole. They need to know how the total spend compares with the total budgeted for the year and, more particularly, how each individual project spend relates to the amount allocated. A suitable form of presentation for this purpose is shown below.

Capital Budget Report

Project number	Title	Actual/projected costs				
		Last year £	*This year* £	*Total to date* £	*Projected to complete* £	*Authorized amount* £

We have now completed our examination of functional budgets but there remains the discussion of two somewhat opposing types of budgeting systems.

Flexible Budgeting

The system of budgeting described throughout this chapter is based on 'fixed' budgets, which remain unchanged irrespective of the actual level of activity achieved. If this actual level is significantly different from the budgeted level there will be significant 'volume' variances.

When standard costing systems are used, the difference in profit attributable to the variation in activity level from that budgeted is quantified in specific volume variances. In the absence of a standard costing system the solution to the problem of variable levels of activity lies in the use of a 'flexible budget'.

This is defined by the Chartered Institute of Management Accountants as a 'budget which is designed to change in accordance with the level of activity attained'. Essentially, the flexible budget consists of not one budget but a series of budgets, each being based on a different level of activity within the expected range.

For example, if a firm never expects activity to fall below 70%, it can prepare four budgets of income and expenditure at 70%, 80%, 90% and 100% levels of the maximum capacity. Should the actual level turn out to be, say, 85%, then the budget for that level can be derived by interpolating the 80% and 90% budgets. Comparison of actual results can then be made with the budget for the same level of activity. Any resulting variances are of a controllable nature as the change in volume has been eliminated.

Flexible budgeting obviously entails the separation of costs into fixed and variable categories to forecast expenditure at different levels of activity. This is not the same analysis as into indirect and direct costs because some indirects, for example power, vary with the level of activity and some directs, possibly wages in certain circumstances, are fixed.

We can compare the variances arising under a fixed budget system with those obtaining under a flexible budget system in the following example.

Example – Comparison of Fixed and Flexible Budget Systems

Illustration of a fixed budget report:

	Fixed budget for month	Actual results for month	Variances
Activity level	100%	85%	15% (A)
	£	£	£
Direct labour	33,000	31,000	2,000 (F)
Direct materials	27,000	23,700	3,300 (F)
Overheads	36,000	34,100	1,900 (F)
Total	£96,000	£88,800	£7,200 (F)

Flexible budget for the same month:

	Flexible budget at:			
Activity level	70%	80%	90%	100%
	£	£	£	£
Direct labour	27,000	29,000	31,000	33,000
Direct materials	18,900	21,600	24,300	27,000
Variable overheads	10,500	12,000	13,500	15,000
Fixed overheads	21,000	21,000	21,000	21,000
Total	£77,400	£83,600	£89,800	£96,000

Flexible budget report for the same month:

	Flexed budget	Actual results	Variances
Activity level	85%	85%	0%
	£	£	£
Direct labour	30,000	31,000	1,000 (A)
Direct materials	22,950	23,700	750 (A)
Variable overheads	12,750	12,600	150 (F)
Fixed overheads	21,000	21,500	500 (A)
Total	£86,700	£88,800	£2,100 (A)

Firms may use a mixture of fixed and flexible budgets for different departments, for example fixed budgets in administrative and sales administration departments, and flexible budgets in production, operations and distribution departments. Alternatively, a system of fixed budgets only may be used, coupled with a standard costing system to disclose relevant volume variances. In environments where standard costing is inapplicable, then flexible budgeting is most appropriate where the level of activity is very uncertain.

Summary

Just as we in our private lives need to budget and monitor our finances to achieve objectives, say to buy a new car, so firms need to plan and control their activities to achieve corporate objectives.

The planning and control mechanism used by firms is known as budgetary control and consists of monthly plans for all functions covering all departments within the firm. All plans are interlinked because no one function acts independently and the level of activity in each function must be linked to the key or limiting factor at that point in time.

Plans need to be consistent with the corporate objectives laid down by top management and their viability will be tested in this light, perhaps by a return on capital criterion. Once those plans have been accepted for the coming year, then regular monitoring on a monthly basis will ensure that management's attention is directed to any significant deviations.

The way in which budgeting systems are implemented is very important from the behavioural point of view. Systems should not be imposed by accountants but implemented by a management committee seeking the co-operation of all managers. If responsibility for plans is to be vested in managers, and their success or otherwise judged by such performance, then they should be involved in the detailed planning process.

Further reading

Books
Drury, C. *Management and Cost Accounting*, 2nd edn (VNR).
Lucey, T. *Management Accounting*, 2nd edn (DPP).
Pizzey, A. *Principles of Cost Accountancy*, 5th edn (Cassell).

Article
Wise, D. Better budgeting for better results: the role of zero base budgets. In *Management Accounting* (May 1988).

Work-based assignment

(a) Identify the key or limiting factor in your organization.
(b) Obtain a sample of the budget monitoring statement that relates to your department. Ascertain to what degree of significance a variance must be, to attract management action.
(c) If such a statement does not exist, draw up a suitable format, inserting the names of the costs involved and the variances you wish to disclose.

1 In the preparation of budgets it is important to separate controllable costs from non-controllable costs.

    (a) Distinguish between:

        (i)   controllable costs, and

        (ii) non-controllable costs.

    (b) Sketch a budget statement, which is to be presented on a monthly basis, for a small workshop, showing four controllable costs and four non-controllable costs.

    (c) Outline the duties of a budget committee.   (AAT)

2 (a) Why would a firm prepare a Manpower Budget as part of an annual budgeting system?

    (b) The Personnel Department of CJM Ltd are working on the Manpower Budget for the coming year starting 1 July 198X. You are helping in the preparation of that section of the budget which deals with direct operatives, based on the following Production Budget which has already been approved:

Production budget

Machining centre:

Component	Quantity p.a. (components)	Standard labour-hours per component
xa	53,000	2
xb	52,500	4
ya	39,000	1
yb	39,500	3

Assembly centre:

Product	Quantity p.a. (products)	Standard labour-hours per product
X	52,000	3
Y	39,000	4

A 40-hour week (8 hours × 5 days) is worked throughout the 52 weeks of the year. Each employee gets 20 days' holiday (including statutory days) and sickness averages 5 lost days per employee per annum.

You are required to:

    (i) Calculate the number of employees needed to complete the machining and assembly work in the coming year.

    (ii) State how many employees you would employ for the above work on the assumption that machining staff can produce any components and assembly staff can assemble either product but that machining and assembly staff are not interchangeable. Assume also that any overtime hours are 30% more expensive than regular time.   (DMS)

3   (a) (i) Explain the purpose of a cash budget.
        (ii) From what principal source is the cash budget prepared?

    (b) On 31 December, the summary balance sheet of Kingsley & Dickens Ltd, booksellers, was as follows:

	£		£
Capital	10,000	Shop equipment	3,750
Creditors	5,000	Stock of books	6,000
Proposed dividends	750	Debtors	3,750
		Cash in bank	2,250
	£15,750		£15,750

The following transactions are anticipated for the next three months:

	Credit sales	Cash sales	Credit purchases	Cash purchases
January	£3,750	£3,500	£6,000	£500
February	£4,500	£1,250	£5,750	£250
March	£5,000	£3,000	£6,750	£250

Additionally, you are informed:

Wages paid will be £250 per month.
Postage and packing is to be 20% of credit sales, and paid in the month of sale.
Debtors normally pay one month after books are sold to them.
Creditors are paid one month after receipt of books.
Shop equipment will be replaced on 1 January. The new equipment will cost £6,000 and payment will be made in equal instalments in February, March and April. The old equipment will realize £2,000 in February.
Depreciation of the new equipment will be 10% p.a. and charged to accounts monthly.
Half the dividends proposed will be paid in March, half in July next.
The company expects a gross profit of ⅓ on selling price.

Required:
(i)   A cash budget for the three separate months ending 31 March.
(ii) A forecast trading and profit and loss account for the same three months in total only.
(iii) A forecast balance sheet as at 31 March.

    (c) Miss Kingsley cannot understand why the cash balance does not equate with the profit and loss account surplus. How would you respond?
        (AAT)

Questions for class use

1   Two products are produced by a company. The sales forecast for the first seven months of the coming year is:

	Product A units	Product B units
January	500	1,400
February	600	1,400
March	800	1,200
April	1,000	1,000
May	1,200	800
June	1,200	800
July	1,000	900

Finished goods equal to one-half of the sales of the next month are to be in stock at the end of each month. This requirement was met on 31 December last. No work-in-progress stock is held at the end of a month.

Direct material and direct labour costs are:

	Product A £	Product B £
Direct material per unit	28	12
Direct labour per unit	8	7

Prepare a production budget for each product line for the first six months of the year and convert it into a material and labour cost budget. (DMS)

2 (a) Explain the term 'limiting factor'.
   (b) Give an example of how it may be recognized, and explain how the cost accountant may assist management in overcoming the problem.
        (AAT)

3 You are contemplating leaving your full-time employment and starting a consultancy business specializing in marketing research.

   You have looked into the possibility and discovered the following facts:
   (i)   Your available capital is £5,000. This you would pay into your business bank account at the beginning of June 198X.
   (ii) You estimate there are 200 working days in the year. In the first six months you anticipate charging clients for the following days:

June	5	September	10
July	8	October	12
August	10	November	12

   Your daily charge rate is £150.
   (iii) Your clients will take one month's credit.
   (iv) Expenses, which will be recovered from clients with the fee charges, will amount to 15% of the fees charged. These costs will be paid by you in the month in which the consultancy is undertaken.
   (v)   Office equipment, having an estimated life of 5 years, will be purchased in June on the following terms:

Cost	£5,500
Deposit	£500

   12 monthly instalments from July of £500 each (including interest of £83 per instalment)

(vi)   Secretarial and administration costs are likely to be £300 per month. These will be paid monthly as incurred.

(vii) Premises can be rented on the following terms:

Premium for a five-year lease	£500
Annual rental payable in advance on 1 June	£1,200

You are required to prepare:

(a)   the cash forecast for your consultancy for the six months to 30 November;

(b)   the profit forecast for the six months ending 30 November. Work to the nearest £.   (IOM)

8 Ratio analysis

We saw in Chapter 7 that detailed financial plans are summarized in a master budget consisting of a budgeted profit and loss account and a budgeted balance sheet. Control can be exercised by a comparison of actual figures with the budgeted figures, but extensive use is likely to be made of accounting ratios. These can be used in the setting of targets or budgets and also in the subsequent control process to ensure company objectives are being achieved.

A 'ratio' is the relationship between a pair of figures, taken from the profit and loss account and/or the balance sheet, which is used to measure some aspect of financial performance. A typical example is the 'return on capital', which relates the profit earned in a year to the amount of capital employed by the business to earn it. In this case one figure is taken from each of the two statements, but some ratios use both figures from the same statement.

The quotient of two figures brought together in this way is called a ratio, even though it may be expressed as a percentage, or one figure as a multiple of the other. The absolute sizes of ratios rarely have any meaning as they are usually used in the context of comparisons with target ratios, or with previously achieved ratios, or with other firms' ratios.

Ratios can be used to measure and/or control the following:

- Profitability
- Cost efficiency
- Use of fixed assets
- Working capital requirements
- Liquidity
- Gearing
- Debt level
- Investment performance

Throughout this chapter, examples of ratios will be drawn from the following typical profit and loss account and balance sheet drawn up in the recommended style.

Profit and Loss Account

		£000
Sales		10,000
Less: Cost of goods sold	6,000	
Administrative expenses	1,500	

		£000
Selling and distribution expenses	1,000	
Research and development	500	9,000
Operating profit		1,000
Interest payable		140
Profit before tax		860
Corporation tax		260
Profit after tax (earnings)		600
Dividends paid and proposed		200
Retained profit		400
Earnings per share		10p

Balance Sheet

		£000
Fixed assets		2,000
Current Assets:		
Stocks	3,000	
Debtors	1,500	
Bank balance	500	
	5,000	
Less: Creditors due within one year	2,000	
Net current assets (working capital)		3,000
Total net assets (capital employed)		5,000
Less: Creditors due after one year		1,000
Ordinary share capital and reserves		4,000

Profitability

We have already met the key ratio for any profit-seeking organization, which is its return on capital. This expresses the annual profit as a percentage of the capital employed in the business. This is influenced by two further ratios, namely, the 'profit margin' (net profit as a percentage of sales) and the 'rate of turnover of capital' (sales divided by capital).

Example

Assuming profit is £1m, sales are £10m and capital is £5m, then:

Return on capital = Profit margin × Turnover of capital rate

20%   10%   2

which are calculated in the following way:

$$\frac{\text{Profit £1m} \times 100}{\text{Capital employed £5m}} \% = \frac{\text{Profit £1m} \times 100}{\text{Sales £10m}} \% \times \frac{\text{Sales £10m}}{\text{Capital employed £5m}}$$

The return on capital varies from firm to firm, industry to industry, and from year to year. However, many industries produce a return on capital within the range of 15–25% before charging interest and tax, but wider variations may be found in their profit margins and rates of capital turnover. The table below shows how a 20% return on capital could be achieved in different industries.

Industry	Return on capital		Profit margin		Rate of capital turnover
Heavy engineering (capital-intensive)	20%	=	10%	×	2
Food retailing (material-intensive)	20%	=	2%	×	10
Construction (labour- + material-intensive)	20%	=	4%	×	5

Profit margins in food retailing may be only of the order of 2% but this is offset by a very high rate of turnover of capital. In more capital-intensive industries with a long production cycle, the low rate of capital turnover is compensated by a relatively high profit margin.

These three key ratios are only the starting point from which a number of subsidiary ratios can be calculated relating operating costs or assets to sales. Figure 18 illustrates this approach; then precise definitions and an example are given for each ratio.

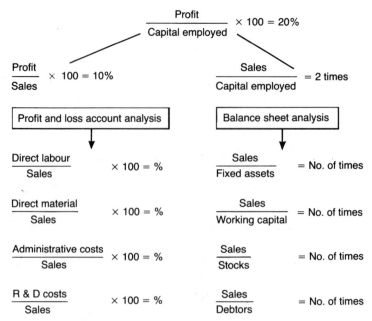

Figure 18 Performance ratios

Return on Capital   This ratio is always expressed as a percentage in the way we might personally think about our financial investments in, say, a building society. When applied to firms we need to consider which profit and whose capital is used in the ratio, as the choice depends on the use to which the ratio is put.

Looked at from the owners' viewpoint, the concern is with the profit earned for them relative to the amount of funds they have invested in the business. The relevant profit here is after interest, tax and any preference dividends have been deducted. This leaves the profit solely attributable to the ordinary shareholders and is often referred to as the 'earnings'. The capital to which earnings relate is the share capital plus accumulated reserves which make up the total shareholders' funds invested in the business. Therefore:

$$\text{Return on shareholders' funds or equity} = \frac{\text{Profit after interest, tax and preference dividends}}{\text{Ordinary shareholders' funds}} \times 100\%$$

$$= \frac{\pounds 0.6\text{m}}{\pounds 4\text{m}} \times 100\% = 15\%$$

This ratio will be influenced not only by the trading performance of the company but also by tax allowances on investment and the mix of owners' capital relative to borrowed capital.

A wider view of company performance that ignores these latter influences and concentrates just on company performance, is the ratio normally referred to as the return on capital or return on investment. Often this ratio is abbreviated to the initial letters ROC or ROI. It is calculated by taking the profit before interest, tax and any dividends and expressing it as a percentage of the total capital employed, irrespective of whether it is owners' capital or borrowed capital. Therefore:

$$\text{Return on capital} = \frac{\text{Profit before interest, tax and dividends}}{\text{Total capital employed}} \times 100\%$$

$$= \frac{\pounds 1\text{m}}{\pounds 5\text{m}} \times 100\% = 20\%$$

When calculating either the return on equity or the return on capital employed, it may be necessary to take account of the change in the capital figure during the year. This recognizes the fact that retained profit has not been available in full for a whole year and to take the year-end capital, as is normally done, ignores this fact. If a new loan was introduced partway through a year, then the year-end figure is again not representative. The average of year-start capital with year-end capital can be used to overcome this problem but if this is still not accurate enough then one can resort to a monthly average figure for capital employed.

Profit Margin

There are two levels at which profit margins can be calculated. The gross profit is obtained by deducting the cost of sales from the sales value before all the general expenses are taken into account. The 'gross profit margin' is this gross profit expressed as a percentage of sales in the same time period:

$$\text{Gross profit margin} = \frac{\text{Gross profit}}{\text{Sales}} \times 100\%$$

$$= \frac{\text{£4m}}{\text{£10m}} \times 100\% = 40\%$$

In retail trade the gross profit represents the profit on sales when only the buying-in cost of the goods sold is taken into account. In the construction industry, the gross profit is after site costs have been deducted from sales turnover. In manufacturing, the gross profit is struck after only the manufacturing costs of goods sold are deducted from sales.

The second and more important ratio relates the final net profit to the sales value, again as a percentage. It is usual to take the net profit before interest, tax and dividends have been allowed. This is because all three of these factors can vary over time for reasons which have nothing to do with the actual trading performance being monitored by the ratio. What we are really saying is that profit margins are determined by operating costs and selling prices rather than the capital mix or effective tax rate at any point in time.

$$\text{Net profit margin} = \frac{\text{Net profit before interest, tax and dividends}}{\text{Sales}} \times 100\%$$

$$= \frac{\text{£1m}}{\text{£10m}} \times 100\% = 10\%$$

Turnover of Capital

This ratio is usually expressed as the number of times £1 of capital generates £1 of sales in the year. For example, if capital is £5m when sales are £10m, we say capital employed was turned over twice during the year, which is the same as saying that each £1 of capital generated £2 worth of sales. Therefore:

$$\text{Turnover of capital} = \frac{\text{Sales}}{\text{Capital employed}}$$

$$= \frac{\text{£10m}}{\text{£5m}} = 2 \text{ times}$$

Cost Efficiency

An extension of the profit margin is to express every profit and loss account expense separately as a percentage of sales. Here is an example from the same profit and loss account used earlier:

Profit and Loss Account Analysis

Cost of goods sold/Sales	£6.0m/£10m	=	60%
Administration/Sales	£1.5m/£10m	=	15%
Selling and distribution/Sales	£1.0m/£10m	=	10%
R & D/Sales	£0.5m/£10m	=	5%
Net profit/Sales	£1.0m/£10m	=	10%
			100%

In a manufacturing context it would be advisable to break down the cost of goods sold into direct labour cost, direct material cost and production overheads, all expressed as percentages of sales value.

Again it must be stressed that the absolute size of the above ratios have little value. Each one should be compared with what it was in previous time periods, with a budgeted or target figure, or with other firms' ratios in the same industrial segment.

Use of Fixed Assets

The intensity of use of any asset, fixed or current, is measured by its relationship to sales value. Fixed assets may be examined in this way as a total group or in suitable sub-categories of buildings, plant and equipment, vehicles, fixtures and fittings.

Example

When sales are £10m and fixed assets are £2m, then:

$$\text{Fixed asset turnover} = \frac{\text{Sales}}{\text{Fixed assets}} = \frac{£10m}{£2m} = 5 \text{ times}$$

If, for example, the 'fixed asset turnover' ratio had been averaging about 7 times in recent years, then the above performance is a marked deterioration, warranting further investigation. An alternative explanation could be that a relatively large replacement programme has just been completed.

When comparing this ratio with previous time periods, we need to ensure that the fixed assets are at up-to-date values and not at outdated historic costs. Sales are less of a problem as they will always be relatively up-to-date since they refer to the last 12 months.

Working Capital Level

A somewhat similar calculation can be performed on working capital to identify the velocity of circulation of the same money being used over and over again in the same year. To illustrate this let us take sales of £10m and working capital of £3m:

$$\text{Rate of turnover of working capital} = \frac{\text{Sales}}{\text{Working Capital}}$$

$$= \frac{£10m}{£3m} = 3.33 \text{ times}$$

In effect, £1 of working capital generated £3.33 of sales within a one-year period. The faster this velocity, then the smaller will be the working capital required. As a result the company will be more profitable as less interest will be payable on the reduced amount of capital.

Working capital is primarily composed of stocks, debtors and creditors, so each of these three items can be related to some appropriate measure of the level of activity. The resulting ratio finds expression as a number of times per annum or as a period of time. These approaches are now explored.

Stocks and work-in-progress are always valued at their purchase cost or manufactured cost for their present state. It would be invalid to relate such stocks to sales, as this compares a cost price with a selling price. A more valid approach is to relate stocks to the cost of goods sold during the year.

Example

Assume stocks were valued at £3m at the year end whilst the cost of goods sold was £6 for the year with little seasonal variation in sales.

$$\text{Stock turnover rate} = \frac{\text{Cost of goods sold}}{\text{Stocks}}$$

$$= \frac{£6m}{£3m} = 2 \text{ times per annum}$$

Ratios based on asset values in a balance sheet are snapshots at a moment in time. If there are seasonal fluctuations in sales then stock levels may also fluctuate in anticipation of demand, or to smooth out production in the case of manufacturing companies. Care must be taken to compare like with like when using such ratios to compare with other time periods or with other companies' ratios.

An alternative way of looking at the stock turnover rate is to express the stockholding as being equivalent to the cost of goods sold for a period of time. In the above example a stock turnover rate of 2 times per annum equates to a stock level sufficient for 26 weeks' sales. This is calculated from:

$$\text{Stockholding period} = \frac{\text{Stocks}}{\text{Cost of goods sold}} \times 52 \text{ weeks}$$

$$= \frac{£3m}{£6m} \times 52 \text{ weeks}$$

$$= 26 \text{ weeks}$$

Debtors can be looked at in a similar way to the stockholding period. We are familiar with credit customers taking such and such a number of weeks to pay their invoice in line with the credit period allowed in the normal course of business. Some customers take longer and very few pay early unless motivated by a cash discount. The average time taken to pay, again assuming no marked seasonal bias in yearly sales, can be found by relating the debtors at a moment in time with the sales for the previous 12 months. When sales are £10m for the year and debtors £1.5m we get:

$$\text{Credit period taken} = \frac{\text{Debtors}}{\text{Sales}} \times 52 \text{ weeks}$$

$$= \frac{£1.5m}{£10m} \times 52 \text{ weeks}$$

$$= 7.8 \text{ weeks}$$

The credit control department can be assessed for its efficiency by a comparison of this 7.8 weeks with the time previously taken by customers, or by an interfirm comparison, or with the average time allowed.

When examining other companies' annual accounts we may be interested in how long they take to pay their suppliers. If we are able to identify both trade creditors at the year end and total purchases for the year, then the calculation is on the same lines as those above for debtors.

Liquidity

Previous ratios have examined the performance of a company from a viewpoint of profitability, encompassing the control of operating costs and the capital tied up in assets. In order to survive, companies must also watch their liquidity position, by which is meant keeping enough short-term assets to pay short-term debts. Companies fail when they cannot pay monies due to employees, bankers, suppliers or the taxman. There are two main ratios used to examine the liquidity position of a company, namely the liquidity ratio and the current ratio.

The 'liquidity ratio' is sometimes referred to as the 'quick ratio' or the 'acid test ratio' because this is the one that really matters. It examines the ratio of liquid assets to current liabilities. A 1:1 ratio means a company has sufficient cash or near-cash to pay its immediate debts.

Liquid assets are defined here as all the current assets excluding stocks and work-in-progress on the basis that these latter items cannot normally be converted quickly into cash. In effect, liquid assets are debtors, cash, bank balances and any other short-term investments.

Example

Using the balance sheet information at the start of this chapter we find that:

	£000
Current assets:	
Stocks and work-in-progress	3,000
Debtors	1,500
Bank balance	500
	5,000
Current liabilities:	
Creditors due within a year	2,000

$$\text{Liquidity ratio} = \frac{\text{Liquid assets}}{\text{Current liabilities}} = \frac{£2.0m}{£2.0m} = 1:1$$

The above ratio is obviously satisfactory but it will rarely hit this precise figure for most firms. When it is slightly in excess of 1:1 this is also acceptable but if it significantly exceeds parity then thought should be given to alternative uses of any cash balances.

Where a bank overdraft is included in current liabilities a liquidity ratio of less than 1:1 may be quite satisfactory but only on the premise that the borrowing facility will not be withdrawn. In some industries work-in-progress is turned into cash as quickly as trade creditors are due for payment. A case in point here is the construction and civil engineering industry where liquidity ratios of, say, 0.7:1 can be found in published company accounts.

The other test of a company's liquidity includes stocks and work-in-progress on the grounds that stocks eventually turn into debtors and later into cash itself. This 'current ratio' is calculated by relating all current assets to current liabilities; a norm of 2:1 is regarded as satisfactory in most industries. This value is somewhat arbitrary and a better guide may be to look for the norm for a particular industry, as published by a trade association or magazine, or by one of the commercial firms collating such statistics. Using the above balance sheet data we get:

$$\text{Current ratio} = \frac{\text{Current assets}}{\text{Current liabilities}} = \frac{£5m}{£2m} = 2.5\text{:}1$$

Although above the quoted norm, this current ratio of 2.5:1 may be acceptable for its particular industry. Even if the ratio is less than 2:1 it also may be quite satisfactory, as in the case of the construction industry for the same reasons quoted for the liquidity ratio.

Gearing

The distinguishing features of borrowed capital, as opposed to owners' capital, are that borrowings must be serviced by interest payments and the capital sum repaid at the agreed time(s). There is no such legal obligation to pay dividends to owners nor is the share capital normally repayable before the liquidation of the company.

From a liquidity point of view, too much borrowing is risky, as the higher the proportion of capital raised by loans (or permanent overdrafts), the higher will be the proportion of profit going as interest. A measure of this proportion can be gained by expressing the annual interest payment as a percentage of the annual profit before interest, tax and dividend payments.

This ratio is known as 'income gearing'. The smaller the percentage, then the less vulnerable the company will be to any setback in profits or rise in interest rates on variable-rate loans. The larger the percentage, then the more risk that level of borrowing represents to the company. The risk is that of liquidation should a company be unable to meet its interest or repayment obligations.

Example

If we take the figures from the earlier profit and loss account we find that interest is £140,000 and the operating profit is £1m, so that:

$$\text{Income gearing} = \frac{\text{Annual interest charge}}{\text{Annual operating profit}}$$

$$= \frac{£0.14m}{£1m} \times 100\% = 14\%$$

At this level the company does not appear very vulnerable to anything but a total collapse in profits. If, however, income gearing exceeds (say) 50%, then this leaves the company very vulnerable to any profits setback. Bank managers and other lenders certainly keep an eye on this ratio.

An alternative way to calculate income gearing is to divide the operating profit by the annual interest charge to find the interest cover:

$$\text{Interest cover} = \frac{\text{Annual operating profit}}{\text{Annual interest charge}}$$

$$= \frac{£1m}{£0.14m} = 7.1 \text{ times}$$

The other aspect of borrowed capital is the ratio of the amount of capital put in by the owners to that provided by financial institutions as loans. This relationship is known as 'gearing' because the profit earned for shareholders can be levered up by getting surplus profit on borrowed capital after the interest has been paid. Normally, bank managers and other lenders will not let this ratio get too high, but circumstances can arise which were not originally envisaged.

Example

Using the balance sheet information previously provided, when shareholders' funds were £4m and long-term loans were £1m, then:

$$\text{Gearing ratio} = \frac{\text{Borrowed capital}}{\text{Shareholders' funds}} \times 100\%$$

$$= \frac{£1m}{£4m} \times 100 = 25\%$$

Another common way to express the gearing ratio is to find the proportion which borrowed capital bears to the total capital employed. Using the same figures as above this total capital must equal £5m, being the combination of owners' capital (£4m) and borrowed capital (£1m).

$$\text{Gearing level} = \frac{\text{Borrowed capital}}{\text{Total capital employed}} \times 100\%$$

$$= \frac{£1m}{£5m} \times 100\% = 20\%$$

Care must be exercised when considering gearing ratios to know precisely which definition is being discussed. The suggestion is sometimes made that not only have accountants invented a language of their own to confuse other managers, but they have more than one term to mean the same thing!

There is no one level of gearing one can point to for all companies. Whether a company has borrowed too much or too little capital depends very much on its past record and future prospects. It should also be borne in mind that some industries are more cyclical than others and subject to a higher degree of commercial risk. This should not be compounded by exposing the company to too high a degree of financial risk by being overgeared.

A wider view of money owed to any party, as opposed to just lenders, is contained in the 'debt ratio'. This looks at the total amount of debt and relates it to the total assets of the company to identify what proportion of total assets are financed by money owed to third parties. Total debt includes loans and overdrafts but also includes future tax payments and all current liabilities. Total assets comprise all fixed and current assets. From our previous balance sheet we can identify total assets as £7m and total debt as £3m so that:

$$\text{Debt ratio} = \frac{\text{Total debt}}{\text{Total assets}} \times 100\% = \frac{£3m}{£7m} \times 100\% = 43\%$$

Predicting Failure

The ratios discussed so far have examined a company's finances from profitability, efficiency and liquidity points of view. In essence, these ratios are control and monitoring devices used by a company on itself, or its divisions, and are essentially backward-looking.

It is possible to use such ratios in a forward-looking context to assess the financial state of health of a company, as to whether it is likely to be financially stable or subject to financial difficulties in the future.

Altman identified a group of five ratios which are combined by individual weightings to produce a single 'Z score'. The size of this Z score for any one company is measured against datum levels to predict likely success or failure. The five ratios selected by Altman and their weightings were:

1. Net current assets/Total assets (1.2)
2. Retained earnings/Total assets (1.4)
3. Profit (pre-interest and tax)/Total assets (3.3)
4. Market value of equity/Book value of total debt (0.6)
5. Sales/Total assets (1.0)

Using assumed figures for the above five ratios the Z score calculation becomes:

$$
\begin{aligned}
Z &= 1.2(0.4) &+ 1.4(0.05) &+ 3.3(0.2) &+ 0.6(1.5) &+ 1.0(1.5) \\
&= 0.48 &+ 0.07 &+ 0.66 &+ 0.90 &+ 1.5 \\
&= 3.61
\end{aligned}
$$

Companies with Z scores of above 3.0 were found to be unlikely to fail, whilst scores below 1.8 gave cause for concern about failure in the next year or two. The Altman model correctly classified 95% of the total sample of 66 American manufacturing firms used. There is something of a grey area in between these datum scores.

There are some practical difficulties in using this prediction model. Deciding what market value to place on equity, when it may vary daily, is a case in point. Another drawback is the use of past financial accounts to obtain the data for the ratios. These do not disclose 'off-balance sheet' finance nor do they take account of any current loss of market, for example, when an interest rate hike hits housebuilding and related consumer goods.

Companies in different sectors have different methods of financing to reflect their operating cycles and relationships with suppliers and customers. Construction, retail and service sectors, for example, may need different ratios/weightings compared to manufacturing companies on which the above model was based. There is some evidence that the predictability of failure also varies with the size of the company. (See article by Briggs and MacLennan listed under 'Further reading'.)

Investment Performance

An avid reader of the City pages of our serious newspapers may already be familiar with some of the financial ratios used to evaluate shares. Typical of such ratios are the 'gross dividend yield', the 'dividend cover' and the 'price/earnings ratio'.

The term 'earnings' is often found in the published profit and loss account of companies. It is a short way of describing the profit attributable to the ordinary shareholders after interest, tax and any preference dividends have been deducted. This does not mean that ordinary shareholders will receive all this profit by way of dividends as some is usually retained in the company to provide further capital.

If we divide the earnings for the year by the number of shares in existence we get what is known as the 'earnings per share'. If we then divide the current market price of one share by the earnings per share we find the 'price/earnings ratio'.

Example

Suppose a company had earnings of £600,000 for the last year and had three million shares in issue currently trading at £2.40 each.

$$\text{Earnings per share} = \frac{\text{Earnings}}{\text{Number of issued shares}}$$

$$= \frac{£0.6m}{3m} = 20p$$

$$\text{Price/earnings ratio} = \frac{\text{Market price per share}}{\text{Earnings per share}}$$

$$= \frac{£2.40}{20p} = 12$$

The earnings per share is used to compare performance from one year to the next when both the profit and the number of shares in issue may have changed. The price/earnings ratio, however, is used to compare the market rating of one company against that of similar companies in the same industry. If, say, one brewery had a price/earnings ratio of 10 whilst other brewers were rated at about 13 then the performance expected of this company is below average.

As a generalization, high price/earnings ratios denote good management in growth industries whilst low price/earnings ratios could signify poor management, risk or cyclical activities. An exceptional profit or loss in the previous year or a rumoured takeover bid may lead to unusual price/earnings ratios but by and large the ratio can be used as an independent assessment of a company's performance.

As previously mentioned, all profit is not distributed as dividends in most companies. The proportion of profit so distributed can be found from the 'dividend cover'. If half the profit is distributed then the dividend is covered twice. If all the profit is paid out, then the cover is a bare once and the dividend would be in danger should profits fall.

The dividend yield measures the money income per annum that a shareholder receives on his/her investment. Although dividends are paid net of income tax at the standard rate, the dividend yield is expressed gross of income tax so that it can be compared with the yield from alternative investments.

Example

Assume that the earnings per share are 20p and that the net dividend paid is 7.5p. The standard rate of income tax is 25% and the present market price is £2.40 per share.

$$\text{Dividend cover} = \frac{\text{Earnings per share}}{\text{Dividend per share}}$$

$$= \frac{20p}{7.5p} = 2.7 \text{ times}$$

$$\text{Dividend yield} = \frac{\text{Gross dividend per share}}{\text{Market price per share}}$$

$$= \frac{10p}{£2.40} \times 100\% = 4.2\%$$

Inter-firm Comparisons

Mention was made earlier that ratios can be used to compare aspects of one company's performance with its competitors. It is quite possible to conduct such an exercise oneself in a rather crude fashion. Published annual accounts for selected competitors can be requested from the company secretary.

Information can also be found more discretely by reference to a database such as Extel located in large public or college libraries. Alternatively, reference can be made to Companies House in Cardiff for photocopies of relevant information. A number of agencies offer to perform this kind of service. Finally, many companies subscribe to credit agencies like Dun and Bradstreet who can provide business information on many companies.

Sometimes a particular trade association conducts a survey of firms in its industry. Alternatively an organization called the 'Centre for Interfirm Comparisons' invites companies in a specified industry to participate in such a study from time to time. A participating firm submits its detailed profit and loss account and balance sheet in confidence as the published results never disclose the names of the firms involved. The data are then adjusted to a common basis for all firms so that ratio comparisons are as valid as possible.

Uniform Cost Comparisons

You will be relieved to hear that uniform costing is not yet another system of costing! The term only means that a number of different organizations use the same costing systems so that cost comparisons may be made between them. Imagine central government trying to collate information from all the local authorities if they had differing descriptions and code numbers for all their income and expenditure.

Here are some typical organizations where uniform costing can be applied and two sample cost comparisons that can be made:

Local authority	— Refuse collection cost per house
	— Social service cost per thousand people
General hospital	— Cost per bed/day
	— Cost per hernia operation/recovery
Electricity board	— Generation cost per kw
	— Cost per meter reading
Polytechnic	— Cost per annum per degree student
	— Income per lecturer hour
Pig farm	— Cost per lb carcass of meat
	— Income per lb carcass of meat
Food supermarket	— Staffing cost per £ sales
	— Establishment cost per £ sales

Uniform costing can be based on either absorption or marginal costing principles, provided all member units use the same coding and classification system. Accounting policies regarding stock valuation, depreciation, fixed asset valuation, length of accounting periods and the like, must also be uniform.

Cost comparisons by themselves are insufficient to justify the rigidities imposed on members by operating their costing system in a uniform way. The publication of cost comparisons will, it is hoped, lead to the adoption of best practice and the elimination of waste.

Summary

Ratios are pairs of figures related to each other, either as a percentage or as a proportion. Most ratios use information from the profit and loss account and/or balance sheet but yardsticks can also be constructed by relating a selected cost to some unit of output. They are mainly used as a tool to measure a company's profitability, efficiency, liquidity and gearing.

The absolute size of a ratio often has little meaning and they are mainly used in a relative way by making comparisons with the previous period, with budgeted ratios or with competitors' ratios. We can liken ratios to clues in detective work. They do not tell us the answers directly but are useful in pointing management to areas that require further investigation.

We must be aware of some limitations of using ratios drawn from annual accounts, particularly when these have been prepared on an historic cost basis. For example, the book value of fixed assets, and hence also of capital employed, may bear no resemblance to their up-to-date values. Also, when comparing different companies' ratios, rented or leased assets in one company will distort some ratios in comparison with another company which wholly owns all its assets.

A modern development of the application of ratios is contained in Z-score analysis which is used to assess the overall financial viability of a company and its trend.

Further reading

Books
Altman, E.I. *Corporate Bankruptcy in America* (Heath-Lexington).
Lucey,T. *Management Accounting*, 2nd edn (DPP).
Slatter, S. *Corporate Recovery* (Penguin).
Westwick, C.A. *How to Use Management Ratios* (Gower).

Article
Briggs & MacLennan, The Prediction of Private Company Collapse, in *European Management Journal*, Vol. 12, 1983.

Work-based assignment

(a) Obtain a copy of your organization's most recent annual report and calculate any relevant ratios for the two years shown. Decide whether each ratio has moved favourably or adversely in the later year and if there is any overall trend or not.

(b) Conduct your own interfirm comparison by obtaining a copy of a competitor's annual report or using a financial database (e.g. Extel) held by some large public or academic libraries.

Questions with answers
(see Appendix 4)

1   From the following annual accounts of New Horizon Limited you are required to calculate the following ratios and comment on the results, indicating what other information you require.

(i)	Gross profit percentage	(vi)	Stock:turnover
(ii)	Net profit percentage	(vii)	Fixed assets:turnover
(iii)	Return on total assets	(viii)	Return on shareholders' funds
(iv)	Quick assets ratio	(ix)	Current ratio
(v)	Debtors collection period	(x)	Debt ratio

Balance Sheet at 30 April 198X

	£000
Share capital	450
Retained profits	240
	690
12% Debentures	700
Trade creditors	620
Proposed dividend	45
	£2,055
Fixed assets net of depreciation	875
Stocks	310
Debtors	770
Bank balance	100
	£2,055

Extracts from year's Profit and Loss Account

	£
Sales for the year	3,100,000
Gross profit	1,725,000
Expenses	805,000
Depreciation	250,000

(IOM)

2   The management of your firm are worried about their poor financial performance and have obtained some financial information on a competitor firm X as follows:

Profit and Loss Accounts

	Your firm		Firm X	
	£000	£000	£000	£000
Sales		100		200
Less: Direct materials	40		70	
Direct labour	20		30	
Administration	20		38	
Selling and distribution	15	95	36	174
Net profit before tax and interest		5		26
Interest		1		4
Taxation		2		10
Profit earned for shareholders		2		12

Balance Sheets

	Your firm		Firm X	
	£000	£000	£000	£000
Plant and machinery (net)	20		60	
Motor vehicles (net)	10	30	20	80
Stocks and work-in-progress	25		30	
Debtors	20		40	
Cash	5	50	–	70
		80		150
Shareholders' funds		65		70
Loan (repayable in 5 years)		10		40
		75		110
Creditors	3		20	
Tax due within 1 year	2		10	
Bank overdraft	–	5	10	40
		80		150

You are required to suggest how your firm may improve its performance where it is significantly worse than Firm X with reference to any appropriate ratios. (DMS)

Questions for class use

1 Compare and contrast the 'return on capital' ratio with the 'return on shareholders' funds' ratio. In what circumstances would each be used? (DMS)

2 You have been asked to check the credit-worthiness of a potential customer and have been given a copy of their latest annual accounts.
    Explain how you would use such information for this purpose. (DMS)

3 The following ratios have been calculated for TTT Ltd to enable them to be compared with the average ratios of a number of firms in the same industry. Adjustments have been made to put both sets of ratios onto a comparable basis.
    Write a commentary on these ratios to advise TTT Ltd what areas they should investigate to improve their performance and suggest possible remedial action.

Ratios	TTT Ltd	Average, all firms
Key ratios:		
1 Operating profit/Capital employed	10.0%	17.9%
2 Operating profit/Sales	9.5%	14.9%
3 Sales/Capital employed	1.05 times	1.20 times
Departmental costs:		
4 Production costs/Sales	80.9%	77.2%
5 Distribution and marketing costs/Sales	3.3%	3.7%
6 Administration costs/Sales	6.3%	4.2%
Production costs:		
7 Materials cost/Sales value of prodn	39.1%	38.1%
8 Works labour cost/ Sales value of prodn	29.2%	24.8%
9 Production overheads/Sales value of prodn	12.6%	14.3%
Asset turnover rates p.a.:		
10 Total assets	1.05	1.20
11 Current assets	1.60	1.72
12 Fixed assets (net)	3.11	4.05
Current asset turnover rates p.a.:		
13 Material stocks	9.49	13.74
14 Work-in-progress	14.11	11.11
15 Finished stocks	4.83	5.17
16 Debtors	4.14	4.42

(DMS)

9 Responsibility accounting

As firms grow in size, either organically or by amalgamation, top management find it impossible to control everyday events and make all the decisions. They get swamped by the minutiae and lose sight of the longer-term objectives and strategy. This leads them to delegate responsibility for day-to-day decision making and operational control to lower levels of management. Such a process is described as decentralization but the degree to which it is exercised can vary widely.

The main purposes of decentralization are therefore to allow central management to concentrate on corporate strategy and allow local management to make local operational decisions that they alone should have the knowledge to do best. Motivation of local management should also be enhanced and communication problems with head office removed by this increase in local autonomy.

However, it should not be assumed that decentralization can be carried out without giving rise to any problems. Much thought may need to be given to the degree of autonomy to allow to local management, which finds expression in the types of responsibility centre used. Care must be taken to avoid situations which allow sub-optimal decisions to be taken by one centre which increases its benefits at the expense of another centre within the group, or to the detriment of the group overall.

Thought must also be given to which services, if any, are to be provided centrally, to avoid possible wasteful duplication within each decentralized unit. A particularly thorny problem occurs where one unit sells goods or services to another within the same ownership. The performance of each of these two units will be influenced by the price at which these transfers are effected. We return to a fuller discussion of so called 'transfer pricing' later.

It is appropriate at this point that we now examine the various types of responsibility centre and see the context in which they may be used. Reference has already been made in earlier chapters to one type of financial responsibility centre, namely the cost centre. This was defined as any section or department of a business over which one person has the responsibility and authority for expenditure. Later again this theme was referred to as being part of the rationale behind systems of budgetary control.

In addition to cost centres, there are also a number of other types of financial responsibility centres which may be appropriate to autonomous or semi-autonomous parts of large organizations that are decentralized or divisionalized. We start by examining the typical features of the main types of responsibility centres and suggest examples where each can be applied in a decentralized organization:

- Managed cost centre – where the manager is responsible for giving the best level of service whilst keeping within his/her budget. This type of centre is appropriate to administrative departments, but both inputs and outputs can be hard to measure. Other management techniques such as work measurement, zero-based budgeting and management by objectives could play a useful role in either the budget setting or monitoring processes.
- Standard cost centre – this is relevant for production and operations departments where the manager is responsible for achieving the standard costs set for products. Standards will normally incorporate controllable costs to include direct labour, direct materials and variable overheads. Performance will be measured by reference to the size of favourable or adverse cost variances.
- Revenue centre – where the manager has the responsibility for maximizing sales revenue whilst keeping within his/her agreed cost budget. Normally such managers have no discretion to incur extra costs on additional resources nor to vary selling prices in a bid to maximize sales revenue in this type of responsibility centre. A typical application of revenue centres might be found in the retail trade of small branch outlets of a large chain. As the size of the branch increases it is likely that the manager's discretion increases and we move into the next category.
- Profit centre – this removes the limitations of a revenue centre by allowing a manager complete discretion over both costs and revenues. A new car showroom or a leisure centre are appropriate examples. The prime objective here is the maximization of profit, with local managers being free to make their own decisions regarding the costs they incur and the prices they charge and any trade-offs between them. No charge for interest on capital employed is included in costs which distinguishes this type of responsibility centre from the next one.
- Investment centre – this takes the profit centre on a stage further by relating the profit objective to the capital employed in making it. The financial objective is likely to be expressed either as a percentage return on capital or as a profit target after deducting a charge for the amount of capital employed. This latter kind of profit target is usually referred to as 'residual income' or 'residual profit'. Investment centres are often seen as the most appropriate form of responsibility centre for relatively autonomous divisions of a large organization. A holding company with a number of separate trading divisions can regard each as an investment centre, responsible for costs, revenue and the amount of capital employed. This does not necessarily mean that each division has control over new capital expenditure but that it will be charged with the cost of servicing the divisional capital employed in the business.

Divisional Reporting When one small homogeneous firm wishes to decentralize, a judicious mixture of managed cost centres, standard cost centres and revenue centres may suffice. Large organizations and conglomerates with disparate activities are almost certain to divisionalize their organization structure and so create a number of near-autonomous units. Performance of these divisions is most likely to be judged by reference to the profit they achieve, but there are a number of ways in which profit can be used for this purpose.

Profit targets can be expressed either as an absolute sum of money, say £5m, or as a percentage return on capital invested in the division, say 20%. Before we look at the pros and cons of these two basic approaches we need to define what we mean by profit in the context of divisionalization. The following example lists sequentially the possible items that can be included in a divisionalized profit and loss account. It puts labels on the different kinds of profit and gives some idea of the factors that need to be considered.

A Divisional Profit and Loss Account

Sales Revenue
Less: Direct costs
Divisional overheads incurred locally

= Controllable profit
Less: Depreciation on divisional fixed assets
Charges for central services
Apportionment of central administration costs

= Divisional profit
Less: Interest charges on divisional capital employed

= Residual profit/income

There are three levels of profit described in this statement, any one of which could be used as an absolute profit target for a division. The 'controllable profit' is the least contentious as only the local costs under the control of the divisional management are taken into account. Where the division also controls its own investment in new fixed assets, then depreciation should also be included as a controllable cost.

The 'divisional profit' takes the controllable profit one stage further by including costs incurred on behalf of the division but not under its direct control. Depreciation comes into this category if fixed asset investment is controlled by central management. Also deducted are charges for any services provided by central units to the division for which it would otherwise have to pay an outside supplier. Included in the central apportionment is a charge for general administration and top management salaries.

To the extent that divisions see these charges as reasonably fair and equitable, then a divisional profit is a good yardstick by which to judge performance, as it incorporates all the costs controlled by or incurred on behalf of the division. When central apportionments for depreciation, services or administration are seen as unfair, the use of divisional profit may have adverse behavioural consequences. In this case the exclusion of the contentious item, or reversion to controllable profit, may be preferable.

The last level of profit which can be used to measure performance is the 'residual profit' (or income), so called because it is the profit remaining after interest has been charged on the capital invested in the division. This interest is calculated at the firm's cost of capital, the calculation of which is included later, in Chapter 11.

It should be appreciated that other definitions of profit are possible. Interest and depreciation charges can be deducted from controllable profit to get a 'residual controllable profit'. Tax may or may not be imputed as a charge against a division's profit. Because many of the factors leading up to the ascertainment of a pre-tax profit are somewhat arbitrary, (e.g. central administration, capital allowances, interest), then a tax charge may be inappropriate.

At this stage we should attempt to line up the differing types of absolute profit targets with appropriate profit-orientated responsibility centres.

Profit centre	*Investment centre*
Controllable profit	Controllable residual profit
or	or
Divisional profit	Residual profit

There remains one important performance measure to discuss, namely the divisional 'return on capital'. In the preceding chapter on ratios this was described as the key performance ratio for any profit-seeking organization. If this relative measure is used to assess overall performance for a group then it appears on the face of it to be equally reasonable to apply the measure to any component part, such as a division.

This brings us back to a problem faced in the discussion on depreciation – whether or not it should be deducted before calculating controllable profit. If divisional management do not control their own investment, then they may react against a performance measure like return on capital when one of the factors in the ratio is outside their control.

Even when investment is totally within divisional control, a decision has to be made as to the value of fixed assets to be used. A choice lies between historic cost, which can be either gross or net of depreciation, or current replacement cost, which similarly can be either gross or net. The historic cost convention overstates profit by allowing insufficient depreciation and it also understates capital employed by retaining fixed assets in the balance sheet at their original cost.

The combination of these two factors overstates the return on capital earned in real terms. A valuation of fixed assets and therefore capital employed in current (real) terms has more attraction, particularly if the group assesses its own performance this way. Unfortunately, at the time of writing, interest in inflation accounting adjustments appears to be on the wane and therefore historic cost asset values are likely to be the norm.

The choice betwen gross and net for either historic or current cost assets is easier to understand. As each year's depreciation is cumulatively deducted in the balance sheet, then the capital employed is reduced, so increasing the return on capital. The use of gross asset values is therefore recommended, regardless of whether they are historic or current-cost based.

The profit figure to be used in a return on capital calculation for a division could be either the controllable profit or the divisional profit, or some slight variant of them. It will never be appropriate to use a residual profit figure as interest would then be counted twice, once in the residual profit and again in the target return on capital. For the reasons outlined earlier, a pre-tax profit is preferred to a post-tax profit. We now turn our attention to a comparison of these two alternative profit measures.

Return on Capital (ROC) v Residual Profit

Without doubt, these two performance measurements are the most appropriate ways of appraising divisions as fully fledged investment centres. However, they are not identical in approach, and the residual income is generally maintained to be the superior of the two. One reason for this is that the ROC measure can persuade divisional management to forego new investments that earn less than their current ROC. Their reasoning is that the new project will reduce their overall ROC in the future and will be counted against them. Even when the new project is expected to earn more than the group's cost of capital it will be rejected. This may be a valid decision from the division's viewpoint, but for the overall group it is definitely a sub-optimal one.

Example

Division X currently earns an ROC of 30% and is considering whether to invest in a new project which is expected to earn an ROC of about 25%. After the new project is implemented the average ROC for Division X would be 28%. The cost of capital for the group is 20% and capital is freely available for projects earning in excess of this rate.

Group management would be happy for this investment to go ahead as it is expected to yield in excess of its cost of capital. The division is likely to reject this project, however, as the ROC yardstick on which they are to be judged will show a worse performance of 28% against their current 30%.

A solution would be for the group to set a divisional target in residual profit terms. If this were done in the above example, then the division would happily go ahead with the project as it would earn an additional profit of 8% on the capital invested after the cost of capital had been allowed for in the residual profit target. We now look at a more comprehensive example showing this residual profit approach.

Example

The following information applies to the budgeted operations of the Goodman division of the Telling Company:

	£
Sales (50,000 units at £8)	400,000
Variable costs at £6 per unit	300,000
Contribution (margin)	100,000
Fixed costs	75,000
Divisional profit	25,000
Divisional investment	150,000

The minimum desired return on investment is the cost of capital of 20%.
Required:
- (a) (i) Calculate the divisional expected ROI (Return on Investment)
  - (ii) Calculate the division's expected RI (Residual Income)
  - (iii) Comment on the results of (i) and (ii)

- (b) The Manager has the opportunity to sell 10,000 units at £7.50. Variable cost per unit would be the same as budgeted, but fixed costs would increase by £5,000. Additional investment of £20,000 would also be required. If the Manager accepted the special order, by how much and in what direction would his Residual Income change?

- (c) Goodman expects to sell 10,000 units of its budgeted volume of 50,000 units to Sharp, another division of the Telling Company. An outside firm has promised to supply the 10,000 units to Sharp at £7.20. If Goodman does not meet the £7.20 price, Sharp will buy from the outside firm. Goodman will not save any fixed costs if the work goes outside, but variable costs will be avoided.
  - (i) Calculate the effect on the total profit of the Telling Company if Goodman meets the £7.20 price.
  - (ii) Calculate the effect on the total profit of the Telling Company if Goodman does *not* meet the price and the work goes outside.

(Certified Diploma)

The expected divisional ROC/ROI is the divisional profit expressed as a percentage of the divisional investment, namely:

$$\text{Return on investment} = \frac{£25,000}{£150,000} \times 100\% = 16.7\%$$

The expected residual income (profit) is the divisional profit less the minimum desired return on the divisional investment, which in this instance results in a negative balance as follows:

Divisional profit	£25,000
Minimum desired return (£150,000 × 20%)	£30,000
Residual income	(£5,000)

Although the minimum desired return on investment is given as 20%, the Goodman division is only expecting to achieve an ROI of 16.7%. This also shows up in the calculation of the target residual income as the expected profit of £25,000 is less than the £30,000 minimum return required, resulting in the negative £5,000 residual income.

When the new opportunity to sell a further 10,000 units is taken into account we can show the change in the original budget and the target residual income as follows:

	Original budget £	Additional budget £	Combined budget £
Sales	400,000	75,000	475,000
Variable costs	300,000	60,000	360,000
Contribution	100,000	15,000	115,000
Fixed costs	75,000	5,000	80,000
Divisional profit	25,000	10,000	35,000
20% Cost of capital	30,000	4,000	34,000
Residual income target	(5,000)	6,000	1,000

The target residual income changes from a negative balance of £5,000 to a positive one of £1,000 as a result of the new opportunity. This occurs because the £10,000 expected profit from the additional order is offset by a further £4,000 cost of capital, thereby increasing residual income by £6,000.

Any transfer price for the sale of 10,000 units by Goodman division to Sharp division will have no effect on the total profit for the Telling Company. It will however affect the profit performance of each separate division as discussed in the next section. Were the order to be placed with another company the total profit of Telling Company would suffer as follows:

		£
Goodman loses contribution of 10,000 x £2 per unit	=	20,000
Sharp gains 10,000 x 80p per unit on buying-in	=	8,000
Overall effect on Telling Company is a loss of		£12,000

Transfer Pricing

Transfer pricing as a problem area only arises when there are internal transfers of goods or services and the performances of the individual centres are monitored. The practice of transfer pricing will be most prevalent in vertically integrated companies when, say, raw materials are passed to a related company to process further or manufacture.

From the global company point of view, overall profitability is not affected one iota by transfer prices between constituent centres. If these centres are treated as revenue, profit or investment centres, however, then the value of the transfer price will have a direct bearing on their individual performances.

For example, if a transfer price is set too low then the selling centre's profitability is reduced and the buying centre's profitability is overstated. This may lead to the misallocation of new resources and will certainly demotivate the management of the selling centre. Should the transfer price have been set too high, then an autonomous buying centre may shop elsewhere to the detriment of the combined group.

When setting transfer prices a number of criteria should be borne in mind. The whole purpose of decentralization is to allow local autonomy and to measure the overall results achieved on a profit centre or investment centre basis. Transfer prices should distort neither the decisions made by local management nor the performance appraisals carried out by central management. Above all, transfer prices should allow goal congruence to take place, which in effect means that the objectives of divisional managers are compatible with the objectives of the parent company.

In practice it may be hard to fix transfer prices that satisfy all these criteria. There are three broad bases possible for fixing transfer prices, but numerous options are available within each one:

(1) Cost-based – variable cost; actual or standard full cost; full cost plus profit; opportunity cost.
(2) Market-based – open market price; market price less cost savings on inter-group sale; variable cost plus proportion of contribution earned on final sale.
(3) Negotiation-based – between the divisional managers concerned or with the assistance of a group manager who may impose a settlement in the absence of agreement.

Wherever possible, reference should be made to the value of identical products or services in a competitive market environment. This values the transaction at arm's length as though it were conducted with a third party.

In many instances, particularly with intermediate products, market-based transfer pricing may not be feasible, so reference must be made to the costs of provision. Only a full cost transfer with a profit mark-up is likely to satisfy the selling division but this may have built-in inefficiences and may lead to too high prices when fixed costs are apportioned to a low level of activity. In this case it would be preferable to set the transfer price on a full standard cost basis.

The final approach is to allow the two divisions to negotiate the price between them. If the divisions are of equal bargaining power this may be possible without the unwanted intervention of central management. In many cases it is likely that either buyer or seller, or both, are in a monopoly situation where they are forced to deal with each other because of the absence of alternative sources of supply. In the event of non-agreement, a transfer price will have to be imposed by group management, bearing in mind the criteria originally mentioned.

Transfer pricing between countries can be distorted for reasons that are irrelevant to domestic transfers. Multinational companies may consider the tax rates levied on profits earned in different countries with a view to reducing the worldwide tax bill. This can be influenced by using suitable transfer prices for components, goods and services transferred between group companies in different countries, so that profit arises in lowly taxed as opposed to highly taxed countries.

Apart from these tax implications, there are other implications for transfer pricing between countries. The hardness of the currencies concerned and the ability, or otherwise, to remit dividends abroad, will also influence a multi-national as to where it wishes to take the profit on inter-group transfers.

Summary

When firms decentralize, they need to appraise the performance of the separate units which then become financial responsibility centres. These range from simple cost centres through revenue centres to fully fledged profit or investment centres. The choice of appropriate responsibility centres largely depends on the degree of autonomy allowed by central management.

The performance of divisions is measured in profit terms but there are a number of definitions possible. The profit measure can be an absolute or a relative one. Relative measures such as return on capital can lead to sub-optimal decision making, and an absolute measure like residual profit is preferred.

Although attractive in concept, there is little evidence of widespread use by companies of residual profit as a measure of performance of their investment centres. A survey (listed under 'Further reading') by Reece & Cool of 459 American companies showed that two-thirds used ROI only, whilst one-quarter used a combination of ROI and residual profit. Only 2% used residual profit on its own.

A particular problem arises when there are inter-company sales and purchases of goods and services. These demand the fixing of a transfer price which, if set at the wrong level, distorts the performance measurement of the divisions concerned.

Further reading

Books
Drury, C. *Management and Cost Accounting*, 2nd edn (VNR).
Lucey, T. *Management Accounting*, 2nd edn (DPP).
Pizzey, A. *Principles of Cost Accountancy*, 5th edn (Cassell).

Article
Reece, J. S. & Cool, W.R. Measuring investment centre performance. In *Harvard Business Review*, (May/Jun 1978).

Work-based assignment

(a) Identify the type of financial responsibility centre that relates to the division, department or section where you work.
(b) If your department recharges another part of the same organization for any work done, ascertain the basis of the transfer charge and judge whether it is equally fair to both parties or not.

Questions with answers
(see Appendix 4)

1 (a) What are the principal types of financial responsibility centre? Describe the financial objectives of the manager of each centre.
  (b) What are the main considerations which will affect the choice of the definition and measurement of these responsibility centres?
  (c) What criteria should be used for deciding which measure of financial responsibility to use for each organizational unit?   (Certified Diploma)

2 Select and justify the type of financial responsibility centre you think is most appropriate to each of the following:
  (a) an autonomous division of a large conglomerate plc;
  (b) the social services department of a local authority;
  (c) a branch of a chain of high street shops, supported by national advertising organized by headquarters.   (DMS)

Questions for class use

1 You have recently been appointed as a consultant to a small engineering company with a sales turnover of £80m. The directors have been considering a decentralization scheme which will involve the creation of five divisions with profit responsibilities. The finance director has been quoted: 'This change will create a climate in which the divisional managers will be judged by their own performance'.

You are required to prepare a briefing for the managing director which:

(a) identifies the advantages and disadvantages of making an interest charge based on divisional capital employed;

(b) outlines any problems in defining and measuring the capital employed on which to base an interest charge. (Certified Diploma)

2 A recent American study has shown that despite the alleged conceptual weaknesses in measuring the performance of divisions, the majority of divisionalized companies use a percentage figure of Return on Investment (ROI) and not a figure, expressed in dollars, of the Residual Income (RI) remaining after making a charge for the use of the capital invested in the division.

Required: A description, with examples, of the alleged conceptual weaknesses and an explanation why, nonetheless, ROI is used. (Certified Diploma)

Part III
Decision making

Overview

The major part of the book so far has been concerned with the important management functions of planning and control, where the costing information generated in Part I has been used to design the planning and control systems discussed in Part II. Inevitably, this has involved some decision making, for example on the normal price to charge, and in this final part we are going to concentrate on the use of costing information for decision making in a wide variety of contexts.

Some decisions are concerned with making the best use of existing resources and can therefore be described as short-term in nature. Examples of short-term decisions are:

- The price to charge for a special order
- Closure of an unprofitable product/department
- The most profitable product mix
- The best use of limited resources
- Whether to make or buy-in

All of these short-term decisions are based on the technique of marginal costing and require us to examine how costs and/or revenue will change as a result of any decision we make. Essentially, we choose the course of action which will increase our present profit (or minimize a loss), either by reducing operating costs or by selecting more profitable business.

Other decisions are concerned more with the acquisition of new resources and lead to an examination of the costs and benefits that will accrue from such investments. These are decisions with long-term consequences because the resources may be used for many years to come. What they have in common with short-term decisions is that both are based on the same marginal costing technique.

The appraisal of a long-term investment again requires us to identify the costs and revenue resulting solely from that action. Examples of long-term investments are:

- New products requiring additional fixed/current assets
- Cost saving investments in new equipment
- Lease or buy decisions

All investment situations demand the identification of yearly cash flows which lend themselves both to the application of discounting techniques and to further financial modelling to take account of risk. We start first, however, with a look at short-term decision making.

10 Short-term decisions

The basis for all short-term decision making is the technique of marginal costing. This is the name given to a method of costing which looks at costs in terms of whether they change in sympathy with the level of output, or remain a constant total sum – in other words, whether they are variable costs, or fixed costs, respectively. We are going to concentrate on the financial aspects of decision making, but very often human and qualitative factors also come into play.

Decision making is about the future and involves a choice between alternative courses of action, of which one choice may simply be the *status quo*. To reach a decision we must concentrate on relevant information about costs and revenue, rather than past data, unless these are used as a guide to the future. Any sunk costs are ignored as irrelevant.

When making decisions within existing capacity limits we are trying to ensure that resources are used to the best advantage. The assumption is usually made that only variable costs need to be taken into account because, by definition, fixed costs will remain constant whatever action is taken. Situations where fixed costs may also change are examined later in the chapter when segment margins and differential costing are introduced.

We start by looking at the not-uncommon situation of being asked to price a one-off order below the normal rate charged.

Pricing Special Orders	If we can make the assumption that fixed costs will remain unchanged when we use spare capacity for a special order, then we need only consider the effects of such an order on sales revenue and variable costs. These two items make up what has previously been referred to as 'contribution'. Therefore we look at the change in contribution that results from accepting a special order to decide if it is worthwhile.

Example

A manufacturer has been offered a special contract to make equipment for which a valued customer is willing to pay £25,000 providing certain delivery requirements can be met. The following provisional costing has been made:

	£
Material	3,000
Labour (1,600 hours)	8,000
Variable overhead	4,000
Allocated fixed overhead	8,000
Estimated cost	£23,000

(Certified Diploma)

Comparing the estimated cost of £23,000 with the offered price of £25,000 yields a profit figure of £2,000, but it is incorrect to think that total profits will increase by only this amount. The existing fixed costs will not change if this order is accepted, as the allocation of £8,000 to the new order will be offset by a reduction of £8,000 in the fixed costs being allocated to existing work. The correct way to examine the situation is to present the data in a marginal costing format as follows:

	£	£
Sales value		25,000
Less: Variable costs:		
Material	3,000	
Labour	8,000	
Variable overhead	4,000	15,000
Contribution		£10,000

The conclusion we draw is that the firm will increase profit by £10,000 as the extra cost of this contract amounts to £15,000 and the price offered was £25,000.

If the firm had sufficient spare capacity to undertake the contract then our advice would be to go ahead as this will increase profits by £10,000. It would also need to be sure that taking a one-off order at a specially low price does not harm existing customers, nor lead to requests for permanently low prices on regular work.

The situation is somewhat different when spare capacity does not exist and resources have to be switched from other work.

Example

Consider the above example again if we are now told that it will be necessary to divert labour from casual work which takes 1,600 hours and yields a contribution of £6.50 per hour.

Instead of charging labour to this contract at a cost price of £8,000 we need to charge it at the cost of the alternative foregone. The casual work would yield 1,600 x £6.50 = £10,400 and this is the 'opportunity cost' of labour for this special contract. The situation now looks like this:

	£	£
Sales value		25,000
Less: Variable costs:		
Material	3,000	
Labour	10,400	
Variable overhead	4,000	17,400
Contribution		£7,600

Still keeping to the premise that the £8,000 allocated fixed costs are merely a reallocation of existing fixed costs from other work, then the total profit of the firm should increase by £7,600 if the order is accepted. However, if additional fixed costs of £8,000 happened to be incurred on this contract then it would not be a viable proposition.

Let us now consider an extreme case of over-capacity in an industry where competing firms are struggling to survive and new business is fought for most fiercely. This could apply to many cyclical industries like construction, shipbuilding, and ship-repairing, or in other industries where technological change makes existing operations uncompetitive.

Example

Imagine a ship repair yard which is short of work with many men idle but receiving a guaranteed wage. Tenders are invited for an immediate repair to a damaged ship which will take a few weeks to complete. Rumours on the grapevine suggest that another firm is tendering on the basis of direct labour and material costs plus only half of the normal fixed overhead charge. Is it still worth competing?

The approach to take in this situation is to consider the extra costs which will be incurred if the tender is accepted. These extra costs will include all direct materials, any wage payments in excess of the guaranteed amount, direct expenses and variable overheads. A tender price in excess of these costs but below that of the other firm will be worthwhile. If, say, only a quarter of fixed overheads were recovered in addition to all the above costs, then a positive contribution will be made towards the fixed overheads and guaranteed wages. Both these latter costs have to be paid, so that a smaller loss will be incurred taking on the repair job than going without it.

Obviously neither firm can continue very long tendering for work well below total costs, but in the short-term this situation can exist from time to time in certain industries. If demand does not pick up, then such firms must find new product lines or leave the industry.

A further possibilty is that spare capacity does not exist to take on a special order without foregoing existing work. In this case we compare the contribution earned from the special order with the contribution foregone on the existing work that must be displaced. In both cases the fixed costs are ignored as they remain constant and are incurred irrespective of which work is undertaken.

Even if the contribution from the special order is potentially higher, we may not necessarily proceed with it. Giving up regular work, for a more profitable one-off opportunity that may never be repeated, is not necessarily good business.

Maximizing Profit from Scarce Resources

If firms are short of work, then the allocation of scarce resources to the most profitable product lines is never a problem. By definiton, there are always enough resources to go round. By scarce resources we mean the particular factor(s) of production that limit the firm's growth at this moment in time, in much the same way as the key or limiting factor mentioned in the context of budgeting.

Scarce resources can be one or more of the following:

- Space
- Equipment
- Skilled labour
- Raw material
- Working capital

When resources are insufficient we need to know how best to allocate them to product lines. Where there is only one scarce resource at any one moment in time, then products should be placed in rank order by the amount of contribution they earn for every unit of that scarce resource.

Example

A firm makes only three products and has no space to expand further. Its management wish to know which products are the most profitable so that they can concentrate their sales promotion accordingly. The following information is available:

	A £000	B £000	C £000	Total £000
Sales	300	150	400	850
Less:				
Direct labour	20	20	30	70
Direct materials	100	60	100	260
Variable overheads	30	10	30	70
Allocated fixed overheads	75	25	155	255
Total costs	225	115	315	655
Profit	£75	£35	£85	£195
Space occupied (sq.m.)	3,000	1,000	6,000	10,000

In this situation the scarce resource is space and, therefore, the firm should aim to make the most profitable use of that space. This will be achieved, not by calculating the profit per square metre, but by calculating the contribution per square metre. The reasoning here is that fixed overheads are always somewhat arbitrarily apportioned to product lines. It is also the case that as soon as the volumes in the product mix change, then the profit does not change pro rata because of the very nature of fixed costs.

The information should therefore be presented in a marginal costing format to arrive at the contribution per square metre on each product:

	A £000	B £000	C £000	Total £000
Sales	300	150	400	850
Less: Variable costs	150	90	160	400
Contribution	£150	£60	£240	£450
Contribution ratio	50%	40%	60%	53%
Space occupied (sq.m.)	3,000	1,000	6,000	10,000
Contribution per sq.m.	£50	£60	£40	£45

Without any scarce resource we should rank the three products in order of their contribution ratio, which is the order CAB. When we take the scarce resource of space into account, and aim to maximize the contribution earned in that space, the contribution per square metre ranks the products in the different order of BAC.

A firm facing this situation should endeavour to switch productive resources away from Product C to Product B primarily, or, failing that, from C to A . Sales promotion and marketing effort should be biased to this end, but obviously there is no point in producing products, however profitable they may seem on paper, if there is no demand for them.

Another point to bear in mind is whether the individual products comprise a product range where demand is not discrete, but is either competitive or complementary. In the former case, the promotion of the most profitable product will reduce demand for the other less profitable products in the range, to the benefit of the firm overall. In the latter case demand for all three products may move in step with each other, so that one product should not be promoted in isolation.

Multiple Scarce Resources

The above analysis was based on the premise that only one scarce resource existed at the time. It is perfectly feasible for more than one limiting factor to exist concurrently, say when both space and skilled labour-hours were insufficient for potential demand. When we consider also machine capacity and working capital requirements, it could be possible to have two, three or more scarce resources to consider at any one time.

Faced with this resource allocation problem we still proceed by identifying the contribution from each product line for each scarce resource separately. The operational research technique of linear programming is then used to decide how many of each product to make.

When only two scarce resources exist this is done by expressing mathematical equations in a graphical form and interpreting the graph to find the optimum solution. Should more than two limiting factors exist concurrently, then a computer program will rapidly find the optimum solution. Reference should be made to a suitable book on operational research techniques for managers if you need to pursue this topic further.

Closing Down a Department/ Product

Another situation which is often confusing to management is when consideration is being given to the closure of a segment of the total operation. This decision epitomizes the difference between the absorption costing and marginal costing approaches and, as we shall see, it is the latter which we apply in this context.

Example

Imet Ltd manufactures three products A, B and C, of which the first two are making acceptable profits but C has been losing money for some time. The most recent results for last month were:

	A £000	B £000	C £000	Total £000
Sales	60	120	90	270
Less: Total costs	42	99	93	234
Profit/(Loss)	18	21	(3)	36

The directors have considered a number of possible courses of future action but meanwhile have no new products available. Nor can they sell more of products A or B without drastically reducing the selling price. The immediate decision is whether to drop product C and apparently save £3,000 per month.

On investigation the accountant has found that the total costs of all products include £54,000 of common fixed costs apportioned £12,000, £24,000 and £18,000 to A, B and C respectively. The fixed costs of £18,000 presently borne by product C will continue, irrespective of whether that product is made or discontinued.

A more helpful analysis of the situation is to set out the contribution made by each product to the total fixed costs incurred by the firm and the overall profit achieved:

	A £000	B £000	C £000	Total £000
Sales	60	120	90	270
Less: Variable costs	30	75	75	180
Contribution	30	45	15	90
Less: Fixed costs				54
Profit				£36

The directors of Imet Ltd can now conclude that it is better to continue selling product C for the moment because it is making a contribution of £15,000 towards fixed costs. If product C is discontinued the contributions from the remaining two products will not change, neither will the fixed costs incurred by the firm. Discontinuing product C immediately is not advisable as profits will fall by £15,000 to only £21,000 as follows:

	A £000	B £000	Total £000
Sales	60	120	180
Less: Variable costs	30	75	105
Contribution	30	45	75
Less: Fixed costs			54
Profit			£21

Having identified the basic approach to product closures let us make it more realistic by now assuming that all fixed costs are not common to all products, but that some of the £54,000 is specific to individual products. These specific fixed costs are known as direct fixed costs and we will take them to be £5,000, £13,000 and £6,000 respectively, leaving £30,000 of common fixed costs. When specific fixed costs are deducted from the product contribution we get what is referred to as the 'segment margin':

	A £000	B £000	C £000	Total £000
Sales	60	120	90	270
Less: Variable costs	30	75	75	180
Contribution	30	45	15	90
Less: Direct fixed costs	5	13	6	24
Segment margin	25	32	9	66
Less: Common fixed costs				30
Profit				£36

When considering a product or department closure it is not usually the products' total contribution which is lost when the activity ceases, but the segment margin, which takes into account the saving of direct fixed costs.

If we consider product C in the above example, then its contribution of £15,000 will cease when it is dropped. Also the direct fixed costs of £6,000 applicable solely to that one product line will be saved. The combined effect is the loss of the segment margin amounting to £9,000, which means a drop in overall profits of that amount. Such action is not advisable until such times as other products can be introduced which would yield a greater segment margin from the use of the same capacity.

Leaving aside this drastic surgery, let us look at some management decisions that are concerned with changing the existing product mix.

Product Mix

Very often managers need to make decisions regarding possible changes in the sales volume of their firm's products. To do this effectively they need information on the profitability of the present mix of products to compare with the profitability of any proposed mix.

Our measure of profitability is the concept of contribution which leaves fixed costs to one side, on the grounds that such costs are common to all possible sales mixes and will not vary in total. Consider the following.

Example

The following data relate to the three products of the Alpha Marketing Company:

	Products		
	A	B	C
Selling price per unit	£40	£52	£50
Variable cost per unit	£32	£46	£35
Unit sales	30,000	50,000	20,000

Alpha's management have wondered whether the present sales mix results in the best possible profit. They are considering what would happen to profits if the following revised sales mix were adopted: A 30,000, B 30,000 and C 40,000.

We can advise them of the consequences of such a change by comparing the total contribution earned by each of the two alternative product mixes, as follows:

	A	B	C	Total
Contribution per unit	£8	£6	£15	—
Original mix:				
Volume (units)	30,000	50,000	20,000	—
Total contribution	£240,000	£300,000	£300,000	£840,000
New mix:				
Volume (units)	30,000	30,000	40,000	—
Total contribution	£240,000	£180,000	£600,000	£1,020,000

The increase in the total contribution of £180,000 is 21% better than before. Whatever the level of fixed costs, Alpha will be this £180,000 better off in increased profits or reduced losses.

Sometimes management are faced with various options when considering a change in the product mix so that each option has to be evaluated in terms of its contribution to profit. The following example again illustrates the point that some fixed costs may be specific to one product line, as opposed to other fixed costs which are common to all products. As explained earlier, when specific fixed costs are deducted from a product's contribution we get what is known as its segment margin.

Example

The Robbit Plating Company has the following budgeted figures for its various processes next year:

	Process		
	A £000	B £000	C £000
Sales value	480	480	160
Variable costs	432	384	120
Fixed costs (allocated)	24	36	50

The company is concerned about process C and several alternatives are being considered:

Alternative 1
Cut C's selling price by 10%. It is estimated that this will increase C's unit sales by 40%.

Alternative 2
Substitute a new process D for C. Estimated sales are £140,000 in the first year. Variable costs are estimated at 55% of sales. Fixed costs directly attributable to C of £10,000 will be eliminated but £16,000 additional fixed costs directly attributable to D will be incurred.

Alternative 3
Eliminate C entirely. This will reduce the fixed costs attributable to C by £10,000.

Alternative 4
Convert C into a special finish by adding additional treatments, which will secure a price increase of 20%. The additional costs incurred will be 10% of the new increased price.

Management wants to know the effect of each alternative on the profit of the company and their ranking in order of preference. (Certified Diploma)

None of the four options concerns process A or B so these two can be ignored in the sense that whatever contribution they currently make will continue at the same level. We shall therefore examine each alternative course of action in turn.

Alternative 1

A cut of 10% in the unit sales price will reduce current sales from £160,000 to £144,000 with variable costs remaining at £120,000 to give a revised contribution of £24,000. A 40% increase in volume will yield a 40% increase in the contribution, i.e. an extra £9,600 profit.

Alternative 2

The original contribution from C of £40,000 will be lost but the direct fixed costs of £10,000 will be saved giving a segment loss of £30,000 on C. The new process D will yield a contribution of 45% of the £140,000 sales amounting to £63,000. This is reduced by the direct fixed costs of £16,000 to leave a segment margin of £47,000. Overall this gain of £47,000, less the lost £30,000 on process C, leaves an extra £17,000 profit. This information is presented again under the heading of 'Differential Costing' later in the chapter.

Alternative 3

The elimination of process C entirely without a replacement loses the segment margin of £30,000.

Alternative 4

The original sales value of process C will rise from £160,000 to £192,000 with the special finish. Variable costs will amount to the original £120,000 plus the additional £19,200, making £139,200 in total. This yields a contribution of £52,800, which is £12,800 more than the original contribution from process C.

To summarize and rank the four alternatives in order of attractiveness we can say:

Rank 1	Alternative 2	Increases profit by £17,000
Rank 2	Alternative 4	Increases profit by £12,800
Rank 3	Alternative 1	Increases profit by £9,600
Rank 4	Alternative 3	Reduces profit by £30,000

Differential Costing

When alternative courses of action are being compared it is useful to set the alternatives side by side and examine the difference between them. It is not surprising that this approach is referred to as 'differential costing' for the obvious reason. It is, however, a wider approach than pure marginal costing because it takes all costs and revenues into account.

Example

We will use the same information in the Robbit Plating Company example above for the second alternative mentioned. This proposal replaces their existing process C by a new process D. Using a differential costing approach now, we can set out the information as follows:

	Process C £000	Process D £000	Difference £000
Sales	160	140	20
Variable costs	120	77	43
Contribution	40	63	23
Direct fixed costs	10	16	6
Segment margin	30	47	17

Our conclusion from this differential cost analysis is that the new Process D will yield £17,000 more profit for the Robbit Plating Company than the existing Process C. This is of course the same conclusion that we reached previously.

Make or Buy Decisions

The question whether to manufacture a component or to buy it in from another firm is one often faced by manufacturing firms. Other sectors may face the same decision regarding a particular service, for example the choice between in-house or specialist market research. The answer may not be decided just on financial grounds but obviously the effect on profits is of major importance.

Assuming first that a firm is already making the component and has spare capacity, then the buying-in costs should be compared with the costs that would be saved if production ceased. These costs would normally include the variable costs plus any direct fixed costs. Any common fixed costs allocated to this component's manufacture will continue irrespective of make or buy.

Example

An offer has been made by another company to supply your firm on an annual contract with a certain component for the sum of £40,000 per annum.

The annual cost of your production of components has been budgeted as follows for the coming year:

	£
Materials	14,000
Labour	12,000
Variable overheads	3,000
Direct fixed overheads	6,000
Fixed overheads (common)	12,000
Total cost	£47,000

We should never make the comparison of the £47,000 total cost of manufacturing with the buying-in cost of £40,000. This is because the allocation of £12,000 common fixed costs will not be saved should production cease. All other costs, totalling £35,000, might be saved depending on whether labour can be deployed elsewhere. A comparison of this £35,000 avoidable cost with the offer of £40,000 is the correct one to make, so we should conclude that it is cheaper to make the component ourselves.

This conclusion may well be different if we are working to full capacity, when buying-in the component would release capacity to do other work. Let us assume now that the same labour could be used to do other work that would earn us a contribution of £19,000.

This becomes the opportunity cost for labour and increases our avoidable costs to £42,000, which is now in excess of the £40,000 offered by the other firm. Whether this £2,000 saving is sufficient to warrant buying-in is debatable, when security of supply, labour relations and other factors are taken into account.

If we assume now that your firm has not previously used the component, then the buying-in cost should be compared with the costs of own manufacture in a similar way. In the above example the additional costs incurred by manufacturing are £35,000, which is cheaper than the buying-in alternative costing £40,000.

Summary

Marginal costing is probably the most useful technique for managers to appreciate. This chapter has examined a wide variety of essentially short-term decisions of a one-off nature. Such decisions have been concerned primarily with the best use of a firm's existing resources in terms of their profit outcome.

At the heart of the marginal costing technique lies the concept of 'contribution', which takes only sales revenue and variable costs into account. In some circumstances direct fixed costs specific to an individual product are considered to identify the segment margin.

Common fixed costs are never relevant in decisions concerning special prices; the best use of scarce resources; the closure of a product/department; or changes in the product mix.

In the next chapter we examine decisions with a longer outlook, where capital is invested in equipment or projects that have an expected life of many years.

Further reading

Books
Arnold, J. & Hope, T. *Accounting for Management Decisions* (PHI).
Drury, C. *Management and Cost Accounting*, 2nd edn (VNR).
Lucey, T. *Costing,* 3rd edn (DPP).

Work-based assignment

Choose any commodity or service that is currently bought-in from outside, but which could be provided in-house. Identify the incremental costs which would be incurred by in-house provision and conduct a 'make or buy' type of appraisal.

Questions with answers (see Appendix 4)

1 Vexed Ltd is facing a short-term problem of insufficient raw materials to meet next months budgeted production of its three products A, B and C.

The original budgets for next month were:

	Product A £000	Product B £000	Product C £000	Total £000
Variable costs:				
Raw materials	34	18	26	78
Direct labour	40	31	58	129
Variable overheads	16	11	12	39
Fixed cost apportionment	60	44	56	160
Total costs	150	104	152	406
Profit	44	28	36	108
Sales	194	132	188	514

The amount of raw materials available for next month's total production of all three products is unlikely to exceed £50,000.

You are required:
(a) to calculate the most profitable sales mix possible in this case, assuming that Vexed Ltd want to produce a minimum of 50% of budget for all three products.
(b) to state your conclusions and the reasoning behind your approach.   (DMS)

2 Your company manufactures three products, the Alpha, the Beta and the Gamma. The following information has been given to you from the sales forecast for the month of August:

	Alpha	Beta	Gamma
Forecast demand	50	150	200
Raw materials per unit	£100	£150	£80
Direct labour-hours	5	8	2
(at £3 per hour)			

Variable overhead: 10% of total cost of materials and labour.

Fixed overhead is to be allocated to the products at 150% of total direct labour cost.

Selling price is calculated by adding 50% of total cost.

(a) Calculate: (i) the unit selling prices
(ii) the contribution per direct labour hour.
(b) Prepare a forecast of the profit for the month of August in sufficient detail to measure the performance of each product.
(c) If the direct labour available in August falls below that required to produce at the forecast level, how would you allocate it in order to maximize your profit, assuming that each product may be sold independently and that the labour force can be transferred from one product to another? (IOM)

3 An offer has been made by a company to supply on an annual contract all the requirements for components in a section of your business, for the sum of £32,000 per annum. The annual costs of your own production of components have been budgeted as follows for the coming year:

	£
Materials	12,000
Labour	10,000
Overheads	15,000
	£37,000

Required: A report showing the information which you would take into account when considering such a proposition. (Certified Diploma)

4 Flanges Ltd fabricate equipment to specific orders from customers. They have received an enquiry from a new customer and have priced it at £30,000 on a full cost basis including £3,500 profit. The customer has declined to pay this much and has counter-offered £26,000.

What do you advise Flanges Ltd to do, and on what assumptions is your answer based?

(DMS)

Questions for class use

1 A company manufactures four products. The following information has been provided for the last accounting period:

Product	Sales value £000	Contribution/Sales ratio
Q	240	15%
R	300	17%
S	160	(–) 6.25%
T	140	5%

Total fixed costs are £60,000

(a) Required:
(i) total variable costs for all products,
(ii) the net profit or loss of the company,
(iii) the total contribution/sales ratio.
(b) 5,000 units of product S were sold. Certain modifications have been proposed which would increase variable costs by £4 per unit, but the selling price could be increased to £40 per unit. It is forecast that 3,000 units could be sold in the next accounting period. Required: Your recommendation for this proposal.
(c) Define 'differential costing'. Your explanation should refer to calculations you have made in (b) above. (AAT)

2 You are the manager of a small factory making a number of products, all of which are in healthy demand. Your production space is limited and there is no room for expansion.

Construct a simple example to explain how you would attempt to maximize the profit of your firm in this situation. (DMS)

3 Explain why absorption costing is a dangerous tool to use when examining the effects of a change in the level of activity. (DMS)

4 Compare and contrast 'profit' with 'contribution' as measures of product profitability. Illustrate your answer with situations where each may be appropriate. (DMS)

11 Investment appraisal

Capital is not free. The owners of firms and financial institutions require a return on their investment in the company. In its turn the company must earn a return on assets at least equal to the cost of capital. To do otherwise will not satisfy the providers of that capital and will make the raising of future capital more difficult, if not impossible.

Firms need to set a minimum required rate of return against which the profitability of proposed new investments is measured. This required rate must be at least equal to the cost of the different types of capital used in the business.

There are two main sources of new capital for new investments. Either firms can borrow the money, usually from a financial institution, or they can obtain it from the owners, either through share issues or by retaining profits. Most firms use a mix of owners' and borrowed capital and the relationship between the two is known as 'capital gearing'.

A company is said to be highly geared when it has a large amount of borrowed capital relative to owners' capital. It is lowly geared when the proportion of borrowed capital is small. The relationship between these two sources of capital can be expressed by calculating each source as a proportion of the total capital, as the following example shows.

Example

	Low gearing	High gearing
Owners' capital (share capital + retained profits)	90%	50%
Borrowed capital	10%	50%
Total capital	100%	100%

New projects must be financed by new capital. We therefore need to look at the cost and mix of new capital to calculate the minimum required rate of return on any new investment. Also we must bear in mind the effects of taxation on each type of capital, as they differ in this respect. We will first examine the cost of borrowed capital, then the cost of equity, and weight the different proportions to get an overall cost.

Cost of Borrowed Capital

The cost of borrowed capital can be regarded as the effective rate of interest which has to be paid on new loans to get them taken up by investors at par. Such rates of interest vary over time in sympathy with interest rates obtainable on alternative investments. They also vary slightly according to the size of the loan and the degree of risk attached to the particular firm.

Because interest is an allowable expense for tax purposes, a 35% rate of corporation tax reduces the rate of interest by about one-third. For example, a rate of interest of 10% would only cost a firm 6.5% after tax relief.

Cost of Equity

The equity of a company is its risk capital, embracing ordinary share capital and retained profits, both of which can be regarded as having the same cost. Companies retain profits to short-circuit paying out all profits with one hand, while asking shareholders to buy new shares with the other.

Put simply, the cost of equity is the return shareholders expect the company to earn on their money, which will vary from industry to industry and from one company to another. It is their estimation, often not scientifically calculated, of the rate of return which will be obtained both from future dividends and an increased share value. Unfortunately, simple concepts are not always so easy to apply in practice. The cost of capital is a favourite battlefield for academics with no one agreed practical solution. One common approach to calculate the cost of equity is:

$$\text{Cost of equity} = \frac{\text{Current net dividend}}{\text{Current market price}} \times 100\% + \text{Average annual growth rate } \%$$

Example

If, say, the annual dividend is 20p and the market price £2 per share, with a growth in profits averaging 10% per annum, this gives:

$$\text{Cost of equity} = \frac{20\text{p}}{£2} \times 100\% + 10\%$$

$$= 20\%$$

As new projects are financed by a mix of borrowed capital and equity capital, we now need to combine them together to calculate the weighted average cost of capital at the desired level of capital gearing.

Weighted Average Cost of Capital

Let us assume Canny Ltd attempt to keep their gearing ratio of borrowed capital to shareholders' funds in the proportion of 30:70 when measured in terms of their current market value. The nominal cost of new capital from these sources has been assessed at, say, 10% and 20% respectively. We now need to take account of the 35% tax relief on interest, the cost of each type of new capital, and the mix of types to calculate the overall cost as follows:

Type of capital	Proportion		After-tax cost		Weighted cost
10% Loan capital	0.3	×	6.5%	=	1.95%
Shareholders' funds	0.7	×	20.0%	=	14.00%
Total	1.0				15.95%

The resulting weighted average cost of about 16% is the minimum rate which Canny Ltd will accept on proposed investments. Any investment which is not expected to achieve a 16% return is not a viable proposition for this firm. We now want to link this concept of the cost of capital to the decision of whether a new investment is worthwhile or not.

Investment Appraisal Investment appraisal is concerned with decisions now which will have long-term effects. It concerns whether, when and how to spend money on capital projects. Such decisions are important ones for the companies involved because often large sums of money are committed in an irreversible decision, with no certain knowledge of the size of future benefits. If this measurement is done badly, it can hamper a firm's growth and employment prospects for years to come, and may lead to an inability to attract new investors.

Types of Investment Situation

There are a number of basic situations where an appraisal takes place :

- Expansion – where we assess the worthwhileness of expanding existing product lines by acquiring more fixed assets and supporting working capital.
- New product/diversification – where we assess the viability of the more risky investment in totally new products.
- Cost saving – where we assess the profitability of a cost-saving scheme, e.g. when an investment in a new machine automates an existing manual process.
- Alternative choice – where we decide between alternative investments to achieve the same ends, e.g. choosing between two or more models of a machine we wish to acquire where their financial characteristics differ.

- Financing – where we compare the cost of purchasing an asset outright with the alternative cost of leasing.

All the above investment situations have the same common approach. In each case we must decide whether the benefits we get from the initial investment are sufficient to justify the original capital outlay.

Example

Suppose a printing firm is considering buying a binding machine for £9,000 which will reduce labour costs on this activity by £3,000 every year, for each of the five years the machine is expected to last. What the management of this firm have to consider – and this is no easy task – is whether a return of £3,000 every year for five years justifies the initial investment of £9,000. Later in this chapter we shall consider the risk that the savings may not amount to £3,000 per annum and/or the machine may not last five years. For the moment we will assume that we do know these values with certainty.

We measure the worthwhileness of investment proposals by building simple financial models of the expected events. Using the binding machine example above we can set out the expected events as cash inflows (+) or outflows (–) at the end of each year of the machine's life, starting at Year 0 which is now.

Financial model of the binding machine project

	£
Year 0	– 9,000
Year 1	+ 3,000
Year 2	+ 3,000
Year 3	+ 3,000
Year 4	+ 3,000
Year 5	+ 3,000
Total profit	+£6,000

There may be some investment situations where no benefits are quantifiable in money terms. For example, the government may require firms to invest in fire detection and alarm systems in all their premises. In this case firms have no choice, and although there will be benefits in employee welfare these are not readily quantifiable in cash terms.

Even in this kind of situation an appraisal technique could be used to help us make the choice between competing systems which have different financial characteristics. In the case of the fire detection and alarm systems, one supplier's equipment may have a high capital cost but a low maintenance cost over a long life. An alternative supplier's equipment may have a low capital cost but high maintenance costs over a short life. We need to formalize this information to make a rational judgement.

Cash Flows

All appraisal methods require an estimate of the yearly cash flows attributable solely to the project under review. Typically there will be an initial cash outflow on a project, being cash spent on the physical assets such as buildings, plant, vehicles, machinery and the like. If any of these items needs replacing before the project ends, then a cash outflow will also occur in that later year.

Other cash outflows may occur through the firm building up stocks or giving credit to its customers. These working capital items will be cash outflows at the beginning of the project or at some subsequent date if increased in amount. At the end of a project the working capital is released and becomes a cash inflow at that time.

Cash inflows occur, for example, from sales revenue less their wage and material costs. No deduction from such income is made for depreciation as the total asset cost is shown as a cash outflow at the time of purchase. Where cost-saving projects are concerned, the cash inflow each year is the value of these cost savings, again without charging any depreciation. It is worth emphasizing at this point that profits which accrue from cost-saving investments are just as valuable as profits from investments which extend the firm's output.

At this stage all cash flows are expressed in £s of Year 0 purchasing power, and inflation is ignored. An explanation of how to deal with inflation follows in a later section, but first we need to review the four main methods used to appraise investment projects.

Appraisal Methods

Two of the methods we cover are relatively crude measures of the worthwhileness of any investment and this sums up their weakness. The remaining methods are much more precise as they are both based on yearly interest calculations. They are easy techniques to understand and, with the help of modern calculators or computers, are not difficult to implement. The advantage of interest-based methods of appraisal is that only these methods can adequately incorporate working capital requirements, tax payments and allowances, inflation and risk.

Payback Method

Simplicity is the keynote of this investment appraisal method. Payback measures the number of years it is expected to take to recover the cost of the original investment.

As an illustration, let us assume that the board of directors of the printing firm mentioned earlier set a maximum period of two years within which any investment must be paid back. Payback in the binding machine example will take exactly three years to complete and the investment will be rejected:

Financial model of the binding machine project

	Yearly cash flow £	Cumulative cash flow £
Year 0	− 9,000	− 9,000
Year 1	+ 3,000	− 6,000
Year 2	+ 3,000	− 3,000
(Maximum payback period allowed: 2 years)		
Year 3	+ 3,000	Nil
Year 4	+ 3,000	+ 3,000
Year 5	+ 3,000	+ 6,000
Total profit	+£6,000	+£6,000

One disadvantage of this method is that cash received after payback is completed is totally ignored. Nor does the payback method attempt to measure this total profitability over the whole life of the investment and other methods have to be introduced to do this. However, payback is still used and can yield useful information as an indicator of risk, but it is best used in conjunction with another method.

Rate of Return Method

The rate of return used to be the main method of investment appraisal as it purports to measure exactly what is required, namely the annual profit as a percentage of the capital invested.

An average profit is calculated by taking the total profits earned on the investment over the whole of its life and dividing by the expected life of the project in years. 'Profit' in this context is reached after charging the total cost of the investment, or wholly depreciating it (in accountants' terminology). This total profit is more easily understood as the total cash inflows less the total cash outflows over the whole life. Referring back to the binding machine example we get:

$$\text{Average profit} = \frac{\pounds 6,000}{5 \text{ years}} = \pounds 1,200 \text{ p.a.}$$

The average investment is normally regarded as half the original investment on the grounds that if it will be wholly depreciated by the end of its useful life; halfway through its life the investment will be half-depreciated. Referring again to the binding machine example:

$$\text{Average investment} = \frac{£9,000}{2} = £4,500$$

Combining the average profit of £1,200 and the average investment of £4,500 gives a rate of return of 27% per annum for each of the five years.

A disadvantage of this method is that the calculation can give misleading results. Provided total profits were £6,000 over the five years, the return will be 27% irrespective of whether the pattern of cash flows increased, decreased or just stayed constant, as in the example. The method does not take the yearly incidence into account. Nor will this method help rank projects whose lives vary as, say, when a project giving a 27% return for five years is compared with another project giving a 20% return for seven years.

True Rate of Return The profitability of an investment should be measured by the size of the profit earned on the capital invested. This is what the rate of return method attempts to do without perfect success. An ideal method will not rely on averages but will relate these two factors of profit and capital employed to each other in every individual year of the investment's life.

A useful analogy can be made with a building society mortgage. In this situation the borrower pays to the society a sum of money each year. Part of this sum is taken as interest to service the capital outstanding, leaving the remainder as a capital repayment to reduce the capital balance. The profitability of the investment from the society's viewpoint can be measured by the rate of the interest payment, assuming that the yearly capital repayments have paid off all the mortgage.

The example overleaf sets out the yearly cash flows of £3,540 required on a repayment mortgage of £20,000 over 10 years, with interest at 12% per annum on the reducing balance. The small surplus remaining at the end of 10 years is negligible, given the size of the annual cash flows.

Example

£20,000 mortgage at 12% p.a. repayable over 10 years

Year	Annual cash flow	Interest payment at 12% p.a.	Capital repayment	Capital balance outstanding
	£	£	£	£
0	−20,000			20,000
1	+ 3,540	2,400	1,140	18,860
2	+ 3,540	2,263	1,277	17,583
3	+ 3,540	2,110	1,430	16,153
4	+ 3,540	1,938	1,602	14,551
5	+ 3,540	1,746	1,794	12,757
6	+ 3,540	1,531	2,009	10,748
7	+ 3,540	1,290	2,250	8,498
8	+ 3,540	1,020	2,520	5,978
9	+ 3,540	717	2,823	3,155
10	+ 3,540	379	3,155	+ 6

This building society is getting a true return of 12% p.a. on the reducing capital balance of the mortgage.

Present Value

The calculations involved on proving the building society's return on investment to be 12% are somewhat laborious. A simpler method is used in practice, based on the principles of compound interest. Suppose £1 had been invested one year ago at interest of 10% per annum. After one year the sum has grown to £1.10. If the £1 had been invested two years ago it would have grown to £1.21 with the first year's interest reinvested for a second year. Compound interest measures the future value of money invested some time in the past.

It is equally possible to look at money in the reverse direction, i.e. at the present value of money receivable at a future point in time. The present value of a future sum of money is the equivalent sum now that would leave the recipient indifferent between the two amounts. The present value of £1 receivable in one year's time is that amount which, if invested for one year, would accumulate to £1 in one year's time. Using a 10% rate of interest, £1 receivable in one year's time has an equivalent value now of £0.909 because £0.909 invested for one year at 10% will accumulate to £1.

The following is an extract from the present value table shown in Appendix 1, alongside the compound interest factors at the same rate of interest:

Year	Present value of £1 receivable in a future year with interest at 10%	Future value of £1 with compound interest at 10%
	£	£
0 (now)	1.000	1.000
1	0.909	1.100
2	0.826	1.210
3	0.751	1.331
4	0.683	1.464

The relationship between the factors is that one is the reciprocal of the other for the same year. For example:

$$\text{In Year 4, } 1.464 = \frac{1}{0.683}$$

Returning to the building society mortgage example, this was shown to have a true rate of profitability of 12%. This can now be proved using the simpler present value approach shown below.

Example

Calculation of the rate of profitability of a £20,000 mortgage repayable over 10 years with interest at 12% p.a. using present value factors:

Year	Annual cash flow	Present value factors at 12%	Present value	Present value
	£		£	£
0	− 20,000	1.000		−20,000
1	+ 3,540	0.893	+ 3,161	
2	+ 3,540	0.797	+ 2,821	
3	+ 3,540	0.712	+ 2,520	
4	+ 3,540	0.636	+ 2,251	
5	+ 3,540	0.567	+ 2,007	
6	+ 3,540	0.507	+ 1,795	
7	+ 3,540	0.452	+ 1,600	
8	+ 3,540	0.404	+ 1,430	
9	+ 3,540	0.361	+ 1,278	
10	+ 3,540	0.322	+ 1,140	+20,003
				+ £3

(negligible)

To do this the cash flows are tabulated yearly and brought back (discounted) to their present value by the use of present value factors. In effect, interest is deducted for the waiting time involved. The remaining cash is therefore available to repay the original investment.

The profitability of the investment is measured by the maximum rate of interest which can be deducted, while leaving just enough cash to repay the investment. This rate of interest is the same 12% as we found when we calculated the interest and capital repayments previously. We can still say that the true rate of profitability on the investment is 12%.

The effect of using present value (PV) factors on the future cash flows is to take compound interest off for the waiting time involved. If a higher rate of interest than 12% had been applied, then not all the capital would be repaid over the 10-year life. If a lower rate of interest than 12% had been used, the capital repayments would be larger each year as the present values would be larger. This would result in the mortgage being repaid in less than the 10 years stipulated.

Both the methods of calculation explained above arrive at the same conclusion, although at first sight they may not appear related. That they are related can be seen by comparing the capital repayments in the former with the inverted present values of the latter, which are almost identical apart from rounding off differences. This will always be the case in examples with constant annual cash flows. The present value approach will also give correct results with any fluctuating pattern of annual cash flows.

Net Present Value Method

We can now use this present value approach to assess the profitability of investment projects.

Example

The directors of E Ltd are considering investing £150,000 on a press to make and sell an industrial fastener. Profits before charging depreciation (i.e. cash inflows) are expected to be £60,000 for each of the first four years tapering off to £40,000 in Year 5 and only £20,000 in Year 6, when the press will be scrapped. E Ltd normally require a minimum rate of return of 20%.

The cash flows can now be set out and multiplied by the present value factors at 20% to discover whether this project is viable or not:

Calculation of the net present value at 20%

Year	Annual cash flow £	PV factors at 20%	Present value £	£
0	− 150,000	1.000		− 150,000
1	+ 60,000	0.833	+ 49,980	
2	+ 60,000	0.694	+ 41,640	
3	+ 60,000	0.579	+ 34,740	
4	+ 60,000	0.482	+ 28,920	
5	+ 40,000	0.402	+ 16,080	
6	+ 20,000	0.335	+ 6,700	+ 178,060
			NPV	+ £28,060

The net present value (NPV) surplus of £28,060 means that the annual cash flows are big enough to allow more interest to be deducted and still repay the original investment. This investment is therefore worthwhile as it more than fulfils the requirement of a 20% return.

The 'net' in net present value means the sum of the negative and positive present values and this method of investment appraisal is widely known as the net present value method, or 'NPV method' for short.

Discounted Cash Flow Yield Method

The NPV method answers the question of a project's viability when tested against the minimum required rate of return for that particular company. This required rate is alternatively referred to as the criterion rate, or cut-off rate, being 20% in the above example. But sometimes managers want to know not just whether a project is viable, but what rate of return they can expect to earn on a project.

To answer this question the NPV method is taken a stage further. The annual cash flows are discounted again at a higher trial rate of interest. Such a trial is an educated guess, but a higher rate rather than a lower rate is chosen because of the NPV surplus which previously occurred. Assuming a trial rate of 30% was chosen, then the annual cash flows can be discounted by the present value factors at 30% :

Calculation of the net present value at 30%

Year	Annual cash flows £	PV factors at 30%	Present value £	£
0	− 150,000	1.000		− 150,000
1	+ 60,000	0.769	+ 46,140	
2	+ 60,000	0.592	+ 35,520	
3	+ 60,000	0.455	+ 27,300	
4	+ 60,000	0.350	+ 21,000	
5	+ 40,000	0.269	+ 10,760	
6	+ 20,000	0.207	+ 4,140	+ 144,860
			NPV	− £5,140

As there is a deficit net present value of £5,140, the rate of return is less than 30%. This is because too much interest has been deducted to allow all the capital to be repaid.

If, instead of going to an estimated trial rate of 30%, the annual cash flows had been repeatedly discounted at 1% intervals from the 20% required rate, then a zero net present value would have been found at approximately 28%. This is the true rate of return on the project and is known as the discounted cash flow yield. In other words the DCF yield is the solution rate of interest which results in an NPV of zero. Economists refer to this DCF yield as the 'internal rate of return', but both names mean the same thing.

Interpolation

It would be a tedious task to adopt the above suggestion of successive discounting at 1% intervals, but fortunately this is not required. The NPV calculations at 20% and 30% yielded a surplus of £28,060 and a deficit of £5,140, respectively. This provides sufficient information to estimate the DCF yield reasonably accurately by interpolation, which can then be proved by calculation.

A quick way to interpolate is to calculate the change in the NPV that equates to a 1% change in the discount rate, as follows:

$$\text{Change in NPV of } 1\% = \frac{\text{Total change in NPV}}{\text{Total change in interest rate}}$$

$$1\% = \frac{£28,060 + £5,140}{10\%}$$

$$1\% = £3,320$$

The discount rate of 30% resulted in a deficit NPV of £5,140. A reduction of 1% in the discount rate will reduce this deficit by £3,320, so a reduction of about 1.5% will be required to give an NPV of zero. The DCF yield can therefore be estimated at 28.5%, which should then be tested for accuracy, after which a more precise interpolation can be made if necessary.

Another interpolation method takes the form of a simple graph with the rate of interest on the vertical axis and the net present value on the horizontal axis. The NPVs from the trial at the company's required rate and the further guesstimate are then plotted against their respective interest rates and the two plots joined by a straight line, as in Figure 19.

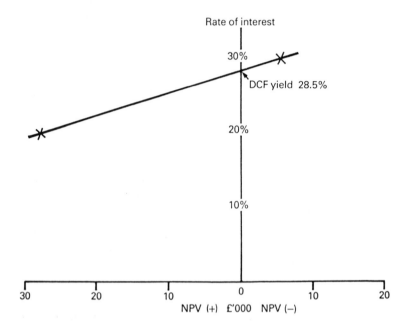

Figure 19 Interpolation chart

The approximate DCF yield is where the straight line intersects the vertical axis at a zero NPV. If the two plots are far removed from the actual rate of return, the interpolation may not be quite accurate and again it should be proved by a final calculation.

It is mathematically possible to calculate the DCF yield to more than one decimal place. Although one decimal place may be justifiable, there is usually no case for further precision. This is because the basic data on which the calculations are performed are only estimates of future events. To calculate the DCF yield to, say, three decimal places gives an impression of precision which is illusory.

Other Short Cuts

The interpolation techniques described earlier are obvious short cuts in the search for the solution rate of interest. Some managers may have access to calculators or computers which can rapidly answer the question of a project's rate of profitability.

Another short cut is applicable where there is a constant annual cash flow in every year of a project's life. This method is based on the principle that if a constant cash flow is multiplied by individual PV factors, the total present value will be the same as if the constant annual cash flow had been multiplied by the sum of the individual PV factors. This will always apply if we ignore the rounding-off differences on individual PV factors.

Example

$$£1,000 \times 0.870 = \quad £870$$
$$£1,000 \times 0.756 = \quad £756$$
$$£1,000 \times 1.626 = £1,626$$

If the sum of the individual PV factors had to be arrived at by literally adding up the individual factors, this might be thought to be a long short cut! Fortunately a table exists with all the adding up done for the reader, and the total of any number of separate yearly factors can be read off at a glance. Such a table is shown in full in Appendix 2 as the cumulative present value of £1 per annum.

A cumulative PV table can be used as a short cut to both the NPV and the DCF yield. Because the cumulative table applies only to constant annual cash flows, this technique is usually used for rule-of-thumb calculations on a project's profitability.

Very often managers or industrial engineers want a quick guide as to whether it is profitable to pursue a certain course of action. This can easily be done using a cumulative PV table when the cash flows are constant. A more comprehensive evaluation incorporating taxation, grants, working capital changes, etc., can be done later.

Example

Take a proposal to introduce a fork-lift truck costing £50,000 to handle palletized stock in a warehouse. This can be expected to yield an annual saving in labour costs of £18,500 after deducting truck running costs. The equipment is expected to last six years and the company regards a 25% return before tax as a minimum requirement.

Calculation of the NPV on a fork-lift truck project

Year	Annual cash flow	Cumulative factor at 25%	PV
	£		£
0	− 50,000	1.000	− 50,000
1–6	+ 18,500	2.951	+ 54,594
		NPV	+ £4,594

Because there is a NPV surplus we conclude that the project will satisfy the required rate of return of 25%.

The above method quickly calculates the NPV but can be used to even greater effect in finding the DCF yield. Here we require the cumulative PV factor to be calculated first, and then looked up on the line of the relevant year of the cumulative PV table.

$$\text{Cumulative PV factor} = \frac{\text{Cost of investment}}{\text{Constant annual return}}$$

$$= \frac{£50,000}{£18,500}$$

$$= 2.703$$

Looking along the Year 6 line of the cumulative PV table for 2.703, we find 2.700 at 29% which is therefore the size of the DCF yield.

Comparison of Appraisal Methods

Four methods of investment appraisal have been discussed so far and useful conclusions can be drawn by examining the ranking of three sample projects by these four methods:

Appraisal methods compared

Year	Project A		Project B		Project C	
	£	£	£	£	£	£
0		− 200,000		− 200,000		− 200,000
1	+ 20,000		+ 80,000		+ 60,000	
2	+ 40,000		+ 60,000		+ 60,000	
3	+ 60,000		+ 60,000		+ 60,000	
4	+ 60,000		+ 40,000	+ 240,000	+ 60,000	
5	+ 60,000		−		+ 40,000	
6	+ 68,000	+ 308,000	−		+ 20,000	+ 300,000
Total profit		+ 108,000		+ 40,000		+ 100,000

Payback period (ranking BCA)	4.33 years	3 years	3.33 years
Rate of return (ranking ACB)	18%	10%	16.7%

NPV at 12%	– £884	– £12,580	+ £15,100
(ranking CAB)			
DCF yield	12%	8.5%	15%
(ranking CAB)			

The payback method selects project B as the most attractive investment but ignores the short life remaining after payback is completed. This is taken into account, however, by the DCF yield method which shows up project B in its true light as the least profitable of all three projects.

The rate of return method selects project A as the most profitable simply because the average profit per year is more than in the other two projects. When the timing of those profits is taken into account, then project A is shown to give a DCF yield, or true return, of only 12% compared with its undiscounted rate of return of 18%.

When project A is compared with project C on the DCF yield method, the extra £8,000 profit on project A does not compensate for the slow build-up of the project. Even though total profit is £8,000 less on project C, the project is more profitable than project A because discounting emphasizes the value of earlier high returns.

In short, payback can yield useful information about risk and cash returns but should not be used as a sole criterion. Either of the two discounting methods will give more accurate results than the rate of return method when assessing the profitability of an investment over its whole life. However, firms may sometimes calculate the rate of return expected in the first year of operation and compare this with the actual return earned for monitoring purposes. This monitoring or post-audit of a project is an important part of investment appraisal.

So far we have described the basic appraisal techniques which can be used to decide whether long-term investments are viable or not. The situations described were based on a number of limiting assumptions, namely that:

- Unlimited capital was available
- Investments were not mutually exclusive
- Company tax payments/allowances did not apply
- Inflation did not exist
- All data could be estimated precisely

We now want to relax these limiting assumptions one by one to see what happens in the real world that firms inhabit. The virtues of discounted cash flow appraisal methods were emphasized, notwithstanding that empirical evidence points to payback remaining the most popular criterion.

These virtues of discounting techniques are now enhanced as we relax each of the above assumptions, because only yearly cash flow models can cope with the complexities.

Capital Rationing

Care must be taken when ranking in the situation where capital is insufficient to undertake all projects and has to be allocated to the most profitable ones. The selection of projects should be based on the profitability index of the competing projects for those scarce funds. This will ensure that the maximum £ inflow is earned for every £1 outflow.

Example

A firm has £200,000 capital to invest in some of the following projects:

Project	Cost	Profitability index
A	£36,000	1.27
B	£73,000	1.08
C	£120,000	1.52 *
D	£48,000	1.36 *
E	£36,000	1.15
F	£25,000	1.78 *

The projects selected (*) will be F, C and D ranked in order of their profitability index and using £193,000 of the £200,000 capital available. The remaining projects are rejected as they earn less present value inflow for every £1 initially invested than do the projects selected. If capital was not the only scarce resource at this time, then resort must be made to linear programming in a similar way to that described in Chapter 10.

Mutually Exclusive Projects

In certain situations a choice has to be made between alternative projects. By 'alternative', we mean that the selection of one investment automatically rules out the other, as in the case of a choice between two machines to perform the same function.

Such projects are called mutually exclusive investments and the choice should be based on the one which gives the highest NPV surplus, or lowest NPV deficit if the appraisal considers only costs.

Example

A decision has been made to install a machine to automate a manual process. Two possible machines have been identified with differing purchase costs and estimated savings over a 10-year life:

	Purchase cost	Annual saving	NPV at 15%
Machine A	£25,000	£6,000	+ £5,114
Machine B	£35,000	£7,500	+ £2,642

In this case machine A will be selected as it yields the highest NPV surplus over and above the 15% cost of capital used in the present value calculations.

In some situations we may be examining costs only, with a view to minimizing the overall cost of fixed assets like machines or buildings over their whole life. This accords with the ideas of terotechnology which aims to pursue economic life cycle costs.

In cases where we are trying to identify the most economic asset to use from a number of choices, we base our selection on the one with the lowest total present value cost. This entails discounting all future operating and maintenance costs back to their present value at the firm's cost of capital, and adding this sum to the original capital cost.

Example

You are advising a company which proposes to erect a new factory building. Two types of construction are being considered, the costs of which are detailed below. The company's cost of capital is 10% and the life of each type of construction is estimated at 20 years with no residual value at the end of that period. Which type of building would have the lowest cost over its life?

	Construction	
	Type A	Type C
Cost of building	£700,000	£944,000
Maintenance costs (net of tax) at each period	£100,000	£110,000
Maintenance period	Every 3 years	Every 8 years

(RICS)

The approach to this problem is to bring the periodic maintenance costs back to their present value by discounting at the appropriate 10% PV factors. When the original cost is also included we get a total PV for the whole 20 years and the design with the lowest overall PV should be selected:

		Type A				Type C		
Year	Cash flow	PV factor	PV £	Year	Cash flow	PV factor	PV £
0	−700,000	1.000	−700,000	0	−944,000	1.000	−944,000
3	−100,000	0.751	− 75,100	8	−110,000	0.467	− 51,370
6	−100,000	0.564	− 56,400	16	−110,000	0.218	− 23,980
9	−100,000	0.424	− 42,400				
12	−100,000	0.319	− 31,900				
15	−100,000	0.239	− 23,900				
18	−100,000	0.180	− 18,000				
		NPV	−£945,700			NPV	−£1,019,350

The lower total PV of the two alternatives considered is that of the Type A building and this will be the preferred choice. Any number of alternative designs can be considered in this way.

Where the expected lives of alternative assets are not equal, resort can be made to the annual equivalent cost technique described in *Investment Appraisal* by Mott and listed under 'Further reading' at the end of the chapter.

Taxation

Cash flows on any project will be incomplete if we do not build the tax effects into the yearly figures. There are two aspects to taxation, one negative and the other positive. The negative side is the payment of tax on profits whilst the positive side is the receipt of tax allowances on certain new assets which effectively reduce the tax payments.

Corporation tax is the system of taxation which applies to profits of all limited companies and nationalized industries, as opposed to income tax which applies to the profits of the self-employed and partnerships. Differences between the two systems are confined mainly to the tax rates and the timing of the tax payments, as the tax allowances are the same in both cases. We shall concentrate our attention on the former.

The profit on which corporation tax is levied is not identical with the profit disclosed in the firm's profit and loss account, but it is an adjusted figure after some costs have been disallowed and allowances inserted. The main difference is that the Inland Revenue disallow any depreciation that a company has charged to its profit and loss account and substitute capital allowances instead.

Example

	£
Profit as per profit and loss account	1,900,000
Add back: Depreciation	400,000
	2,300,000
Deduct: Capital allowances	440,000
Taxable profit	£1,860,000

Corporation tax payable then becomes £1,860,000 multiplied by the current rate(s) of tax.

It is therefore never possible to reduce the size of the company tax bill by increasing the depreciation charge, because whatever figure is charged, the Inland Revenue will add it back. However, it would be manifestly unfair if companies were disallowed depreciation and given nothing in its place: hence the system of writing-down, or capital allowances.

Capital Allowances

The Inland Revenue have their own system of depreciation allowances which are called capital allowances or writing-down allowances. These are generally available to firms which buy new fixed assets of the specified categories, although some allowances are restricted to specific industries only.

Rates of capital allowances at April 1990 are:

- Industrial buildings (qualifying industries only)   4% p.a. on a straight-line basis
- Plant and machinery, office equipment, all motor vehicles (all industries)   25% p.a. on a reducing-balance basis

We shall take the 25% capital allowance on plant and machinery as an example as this applies to all fixed assets other than buildings and to all industries. The effect of the reducing-balance method is that an asset is never fully depreciated at any moment in time, and when it is sold or scrapped any unclaimed allowances are claimed later.

The amount of tax actually saved by getting an allowance is the capital allowance for the year multiplied by the rate of tax. This tax saving becomes a cash inflow for that particular year.

Example

A firm buys a computer installation for £80,000 and claims 25% capital allowance. The rate of corporation tax is 35%.

Calculation of tax saved

	£	Rate of tax		Tax saved £
Purchase cost of computer	80,000			
Year 1: 25% allowance	20,000	× 35%	=	£7,000
Balance at end Year 1	60,000			
Year 2: 25% allowance	15,000	× 35%	=	£5,250
Balance at end Year 2	45,000			
Year 3: 25% allowance	11,250	× 35%	=	£3,937
Balance at end Year 3	33,750			
	etc.			

Tax Payments

Unlike income tax on our salaries which is collected monthly at source under the PAYE system, companies make tax payments on their yearly net income (profit) on only two or three occasions, which fall mainly in the following year. Although the total corporation tax liability is based on the profit for the year when that is finally calculated, some tax is collected in stages before that time by reference to the size of the interim and final dividend payments.

These timings differ from one company to another and it is a generally agreed convention that tax payments are included in the yearly cash flow following the year the profit was made.

The taxable profit in any year is the profit from sales before charging either interest or depreciation. Interest is not deducted because the discounting process performs this function, and as we have seen, capital allowances take the place of depreciation. If the investment was of a cost-saving nature, then these cost savings increase profit and are therefore still taxable. Again no charge for either interest or depreciation should be offset against the cost savings.

We now want to see how tax savings from capital allowances and tax payments on the profit arising from the new investment are built into the yearly cash flows. We then proceed with the discounting process, using present value factors as before.

Example

A firm is considering buying a machine which costs £80,000 and is expected to last five years, when its scrap value will be about £2,000 only. Taxable profits are estimated to be £40,000 each year and the rate of corporation tax is 35%. Capital allowances of 25% on the reducing balance can be claimed but no allowances are available on the £30,000 working capital required. The cost of capital is 18% and this is regarded as the minimum requirement to be earned on any new investment.

Year	Capital cost £	Taxable profit £	Tax payment on profit £	Tax saved by C.A. £	Annual net cash flow £	18% PV factors	PV £
0	−80,000 −30,000				−110,000	1.000	−110,000
1		+40,000		+7,000	+47,000	0.847	+39,809
2		+40,000	−14,000	+5,250	+31,250	0.718	+22,438
3		+40,000	−14,000	+3,937	+29,937	0.609	+18,232
4		+40,000	−14,000	+2,953	+28,953	0.516	+14,940
5	+30,000 +2,000	+40,000	−14,000	+2,215	+60,215	0.437	+26,314
6			−14,000	+1,661	−12,339	0.370	−4,565
						NPV	+£7,168

Our conclusion is that this project is viable as it results in a surplus NPV after discounting at the required rate of 18%. This surplus is understated slightly as there are unclaimed tax allowances to come later, which are not included in the above appraisal.

You will have noticed how working capital has been included in the above cash flows. Firms need to earn a return on this capital just as much as on the capital tied up in fixed assets. By subjecting the initial outflow of working capital and its eventual release to the discounting process, we ensure that the firm earns sufficient cash to service the capital tied up in stocks and debtors.

Inflation

Up to this point we have ignored inflation and its effects on the future cash flows of projects being appraised. Inflation brings two additional problems to project appraisals. It increases the uncertainty surrounding the value of future costs and revenue and it also influences the required rate of return through its effects on the cost of capital.

When describing how to incorporate both of these aspects in appraisals it is useful first to distinguish between the real rate of return on a project and its nominal rate of return. A simple example may clarify this difference between real and nominal rates of return.

Example

Suppose an investor receives an income of £100 per annum on an investment of £1,000, then this is a nominal or apparent rate of return of 10%. If inflation is zero then the real rate of return will also be 10%, as the investor can spend the £100 interest each year and still keep the spending power of the original £1,000 capital intact. If, however, inflation is running at 6% per annum the investor needs to reinvest £60 of the interest to keep the value of capital intact and can only spend the remaining £40. This £40 can be described as a real return of 4% on the investment. In approximate terms we can therefore say:

Real return = Nominal return − Rate of inflation

4% = 10% − 6%

At high rates of return/inflation this approximate relationship may need refining and the more accurate relationship is now shown using decimal notation:

$$\text{Real return} = \frac{(\text{Nominal return } 1.10)}{(\text{Rate of inflation } 1.06)} - 1$$

$$= (1.038 - 1) = 0.038 \times \frac{100}{1} \% = 3.8\%$$

Turning now to individual project appraisals, we need to know whether the yearly cash flows have been inflated year by year or not. If they have been inflated year by year, then the DCF yield is the nominal return expected from that investment. The real return will be the nominal DCF yield minus the general rate of inflation.

When the yearly cash flows are not inflated year by year but are expressed in the constant terms of Year 0 £s, then the DCF yield is the real return expected from the investment.

At appraisal time we are therefore faced with a choice. We can express future cash flows at their inflated values and find the nominal rate of return. Alternatively, we can express the future cash flows in Year 0 £s and find the real rate of return.

Our choice is influenced by the way management express the target rate of return and whether we see the future cash flows keeping pace with inflation or not. Firms are tempted to express their cost of capital in nominal terms because interest rates and the cost of equity are expressed in nominal terms also. This means we should inflate the yearly cash flows, possibly at different rates for different items, and find the nominal DCF yield.

An alternative approach, if we expect the yearly cash flows to more-or-less keep pace with inflation, is to find the real DCF yield on the cash flows expressed in constant Year 0 £ values. We then convert this real DCF yield to a nominal DCF yield by adding the estimated rate of inflation.

Risk and Uncertainty

It would be unrealistic for us to assume that the future events expressed in yearly cash flows will occur exactly as predicted. The nature of investment appraisal is such that we are dealing with an uncertain future with the risk that one or more of income, costs, tax, inflation or project life may vary from our estimate. Some writers differentiate between risk and uncertainty along the lines that risk can be quantified but uncertainty cannot. It is intended here to use the terms synonymously.

When projects are overwhelmingly profitable it does not matter which appraisal techniques are used as they are viable on any test we care to apply. Most projects, however, are more marginal and subject to a greater degree of uncertainty.

It is here that discounting techniques come into their own by taking into account each year's cash flow over the whole life of the project. This allows us to manipulate the data to answer 'what if' questions and generally apply financial modelling techniques. Computers have an obvious role here when we are dealing with reiterative calculations on raw data.

The more substantial a project is, relative to the size of the firm, the more sifting should be done before approval is given. We are now going to examine various approaches to risk and uncertainty, ranging from a crude payback criterion at one extreme to portfolio theory at the other.

Payback was described earlier in this chapter as a relatively crude technique used to test the viability of projects. This is performed by counting the number of years it takes to recover the original investment using either undiscounted or discounted cash flows.

Sometimes firms use payback in a slightly different context to reduce the risk element in a project by setting a maximum allowable payback period. When this is applied to cash flows discounted at the firm's cost of capital, it ensures that the minimum required return is always achieved and that cash is quickly generated for reinvestment in a new project.

If we can assume that events in the coming year or two are more capable of being forecast with a high degree of certainty, then this also reduces the risk element. This is because distant cash flows are multiplied by relatively small present value factors and, conversely, a higher weighting is given to more immediate cash flows.

These advantages are sufficient for many firms and payback remains one of the most popular appraisal techniques. We should be aware, however, of its potential weakness in selecting less profitable projects by its concentration on quick returns.

Example

Year	Project A £	Project B £
0	− 10,000	− 10,000
1	+ 4,000	0
2	+ 4,000	+ 4,000
3	+ 4,000	+ 4,000
4	+ 4,000	+ 4,000
5	0	+ 4,000
6	0	+ 4,000
7	0	+ 4,000
8	0	+ 4,000
Payback period	2.5 years	3.5 years
DCF yield	22%	25%

If the maximum payback period was set at three years then project A would be selected rather than the more profitable, but slow-starting, project B.

Instead of pinning all their faith on the DCF yield resulting from the expected cash flows, firms sometimes calculate two further sets of cash flows based on pessimistic and optimistic assumptions respectively.

At one extreme will be the combination of the pessimistic assumptions. This will assume highest capital cost, shortest life, lowest sales volume and price, highest operating cost and the like. The DCF yield prepared from these data will be the lowest return envisaged.

At the other extreme will be the cash flows resulting from everything being favourable at the same time. This situation will incorporate the lowest possible capital cost, longest life, highest sales volume and price, lowest running cost and so on. The resultant DCF yield will be the highest possible return that could be achieved.

In effect the pessimistic and optimistic forecasts set the outer limits, or parameters, within which we would expect to find the actual DCF yield. They therefore give a better perspective of the range within which the return on investment will fall.

Example

DCF yields on different sets of cash flows

	Pessimistic	Expected	Optimistic
Project A	22%	27%	40%
Project B	− 12%	12%	21%
Project C	− 3%	20%	40%

If this company required a return of, say, 20%, then project A will be approved as it satisfies the 20% required return in all conceivable circumstances. It is very unlikely project B will be approved, however, as only in the most optimistic circumstances will the 20% criterion just be satisfied. Project C is more difficult to evaluate as the possibilty of a small loss has to be balanced against the possibility of a very high rate of return of 40%.

If either of the two extreme conditions are very unlikely to occur, managers should not pay them too much attention in their decision taking. The main drawback of this method is now apparent. It does not quantify the degree of optimism or pessimism assumed in the sets of cash flows. A statistical technique that can be applied to overcome this weakness is contained in probability theory.

Example

A firm is considering buying new equipment costing £80,000 which has an expected life of ten years and is also expected to save £17,600 in operating costs each year when compared with existing methods. It is thought that at worst these savings would not fall below £11,600 per annum and at best that they would not exceed £23,600 per annum. The project manager has assigned subjective probability factors to various estimates of savings which are used to calculate the expected or weighted average DCF yield:

Annual saving £	Probability factor	DCF yield	DCF yield × probability
11,600	0.05	7%	0.35%
13,600	0.15	11%	1.65%
15,600	0.25	15%	3.75%
17,600	0.33	18%	5.94%
19,600	0.15	21%	3.15%
21,600	0.05	24%	1.20%
23,600	0.02	27%	0.54%
	1.00		16.58%

The weighted average or expected DCF yield turns out to be 16.6%, which would be satisfactory if the required return was set at a lower level. If the required return was, say, 20%, this project would not be satisfactory as the expected DCF yield at 16.6% is significantly less. Only the last three sets of possible cash flows yield a return in excess of 20% and their combined probabilities or level of confidence in a satisfactory outcome is only 0.22, which is 22%.

On a more complex project, such as an expansion scheme to sell a new product, we can apply probability factors to each constituent item making up the cash flows. In this case we would use computers to perform the hundreds of reiterative calculations and there are appropriate programs dedicated to this task.

Another approach to risk is to recognize that different kinds of investment carry different degrees of risk and should therefore be set different target rates of return. A simple approach to this idea is to add an extra discount rate, called a 'risk premium', to the basic cost of capital, so setting different target rates of return for different risk categories of investment. The risk premium may vary according to the risk category of the investment under review and is based on a subjective assessment of the risks involved, as the following example illustrates.

Example

Risk category	Type of project	Cost of capital	Risk premium	Target rate of return
No risk	Financing decision	15%	—	15%
Low risk	Cost saving – existing technology	15%	3%	18%
Medium risk	Expansion – new markets, existing technology	15%	10%	25%
High risk	Expansion – new markets, new technology	15%	20%	35%

In practice investors demand a higher return on more risky investments than on less risky ones. By using the risk premium approach firms are giving recognition in their individual investment appraisals to what investors themselves practise when investing in individual companies.

An extension of this idea is found in what is referred to as 'portfolio theory', where a collection of investments is described as a portfolio. Many portfolios can be constructed from different combinations of investments.

The risk level of each portfolio is measured by the variability of possible returns about the mean, expressed in standard deviations. Investors' attitudes to 'risk versus return' can be expressed on indifference curves. In Figure 20, any point on indifference curve IC_1 gives a higher return, or lower risk, than its equivalent point on IC_2, which itself is preferred to IC_3.

When we add various alternative portfolios assigned the letters A–H to the same graph, the selected portfolio will be the one which reaches the highest possible indifference curve. This is indicated on Figure 20 as portfolio E, which is the closest to IC_2, with no portfolio reaching IC_1.

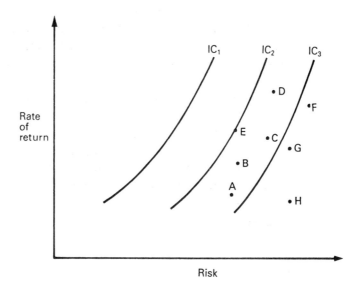

Figure 20 Portfolio selection

Portfolio theory goes on to say that it is not the individual project risk that matters, but its effect on the overall portfolio's risk. Therefore, when we evaluate a risky project we need to correlate the individual project risk with that of the existing portfolio it would join if accepted.

A branch of portfolio theory called the 'capital asset pricing model' states that we should calculate the net present value on a new project at a composite discount rate, comprising:

(a) the rate of interest representing the risk-free cost of capital, plus
(b) a risk premium or discount determined by the correlation of the risk on the individual project with the risk on the whole existing portfolio it would join. The size of this correlation is referred to as the 'beta factor', and can vary from −1.0 to +1.0.

One further approach to risk in the context of investment appraisal is that of sensitivity testing. This takes the form of recalculating the NPV or DCF yield assuming a different value for any one variable in the cash flows.

Example

A firm requires a minimum return of 15% on any new investment and is proposing to buy a new machine costing £20,000 which is expected to save £5,000 each year of its 10-year life. This project may be sensitive to any reduction in the expected life or annual saving.

First the DCF yield is calculated on the expected events: it turns out to be 21%. Next an arbitrary percentage change in one variable is taken and the DCF yield is recalculated to get an estimate of sensitivity. If, say, the estimated life was 10% less at only nine years, the DCF yield is still as high as 20% and therefore this project is relatively insensitive to variations in the length of life. This would not be true, however, in the case of short-life projects of only a few years.

The sensitivity test is then repeated for a 10% reduction in the annual savings, reverting to the original expected life of 10 years. This reduces the DCF yield from the original 21% to only 18%, so we conclude that this project is more sensitive to inaccuracies in the savings estimate than to those in its estimated life.

Many other techniques are available to deal with risk, including the 'minimax criterion' and decision tree analysis coupled with probability theory.

Summary

This chapter started with the premise that the cost of capital employed in any business sets the minimum required rate of return needed to be earned on any new investment it undertakes.

The profile of any investment can be expressed in terms of money flowing in and out of the organization year by year. These yearly cash flows form the basis for a number of techniques aimed at deciding the worthiness of any planned investment.

These techniques range from the simple idea of a payback period to measures of the rate of profitability using discounted cash flow, when the individual yearly timings of cash flows are given full recognition.

One discounting technique is the net present value method, which tells us if a certain minimum level of profitability is expected to be achieved. The DCF yield method goes a stage further and measures the expected rate of profitability on the proposed investment.

It is unrealistic to assume that there will be one certain set of net cash flows on a project, apart from exceptional cases. Consequently we should allow for the possibility of different values of cash flows when assessing the profitability of an investment. Relatively crude techniques such as payback, risk premium and optimistic/pessimistic forecasts can be used, but projects absorbing a significant amount of a firm's capital demand more sophisticated treatment.

Both the DCF yield or NPV methods can be used to find out how sensitive they are to variations in any one key variable in the cash flows. Having identified the items of cash flow which are most significant, these can be given maximum management attention at the design, operation and post-audit stages.

An alternative, or perhaps additional, technique is to construct various sets of net cash flows based on different assumptions. The likelihood of each occurring is subjectively assessed and a probability factor allocated accordingly. The profitability of a project can then be assessed as a weighted average of all the possible events.

In case this sounds like too much work, the existence of computer programs reduces the analysis to a matter of minutes at most. The compilation of the cash flows and the assignment of probability factors will obviously take much longer but will be time well spent compared with the consequences of a bad decision.

A further approach is based on portfolio theory, taking the view that an investment should not be regarded in isolation but as an addition to existing investments. When the risk category of the new investment differs from that of the existing portfolio, this affects the required return used in the discounting process.

We must guard against the possible danger of being mesmerized by a numerical answer of great mathematical precision built on weak foundations. Within all these scientific approaches there is still a place for management art and subjective judgement. It is when these are reinforced by a quantitative assessment of the costs and benefits that the outcome is surely improved.

Having examined a plethora of techniques in this chapter, it is appropriate to see which appraisal techniques are actually used in real life. Pike's article 'The capital budgeting revolution', listed below under 'Further reading', draws on a survey by Pike & Wolfe of investment appraisal practices of 100 large UK companies.

In 1986, 75% used the DCF yield, with 68% using a NPV; both percentages are considerably higher than in the first survey of 1975. Over half the companies used an average accounting rate of return, whilst a massive 92% used a payback period in 1986. These figures show that multiple techniques are in use. Some formal assessment of risk on all projects was carried out by 86% of the companies, and nearly two-thirds had a post-audit procedure for major projects at the later date.

Further reading

Books

Levy, H. & Sarnat, M. *Capital Investment and Financial Decisions* (Prentice Hall) 1986.

Mott, G. *Investment Appraisal* (M & E Handbook) 1989.

Pike, R. & Robbins, R. *Investment Decisions and Financial Strategy* (Philip Allan) 1985.

Articles

Mills, R. W. Capital budgeting techniques used in the UK and the USA. In *Management Accounting* (Jan. 1988).

Pike, R. The capital budgeting revolution. In *Management Accounting* (Oct. 1988).

(a) Identify a piece of equipment that could be used by your organization as a cost-saving investment. Estimate the yearly costs and benefits and the expected life of the investment. Appraise using the payback, return on capital and DCF yield methods.

(b) Ascertain which appraisal methods are employed by your organization and how taxation, inflation and risk are incorporated in them.

Questions with answers (see Appendix 4)

1 The board of Pilmar Plastics Ltd is considering whether or not to replace equipment used in the manufacture of a particular type of television case. It is estimated that the remaining life of this product is five years and that at the end of that time any equipment held will be valueless. The selling price of the case is £5.00 and sales of 20,000 units per annum are expected over the next five years. Three alternatives have been suggested by the Chief Production Engineer:

A   Persisting with the existing equipment which originally cost £60,000 five years ago and which is being depreciated at 10% per year on a straight-line basis. The total annual cost of this method including depreciation is £95,000. This method has a continuing investment in working capital of £20,000.

B   Purchase of new equipment which would cost £300,000. In this case there would be a trade-in allowance of £50,000 on the old equipment. This method requires a total investment in working capital of £40,000 and the total annual cost, including depreciation, would be £82,000.

C   Sale of the existing equipment to Biret (Gloucester) Ltd for £20,000 plus a royalty of 25p on each case sold over the next five years. Biret expects to sell 20,000 units per annum. The cost of capital used by Pilmar Plastics Ltd for appraising capital proposals is 15%.

Required:
(a) Show, by computation, which of the three alternatives A, B or C offers the most attractive financial proposition for Pilmar Plastics Ltd. (Ignore taxation.)
(b) Comment on the implications of the information produced in your answer to (a).   (Certified Diploma)

2 (a) Assuming that a plc was wholly financed by equity capital, what is the cost of equity implied in the following information?

Market price per ordinary share		£1.56
Dividend per share for:	1990	12.0p
	1989	11.0p
	1988	9.9p
	1987	9.0p

(b) Another company is solely financed by equity and estimates its cost of capital to be 22%. It now decides to raise 20% more capital by way of a 10% loan. What is its new overall cost of capital if Corporation Tax is at 35%?
(c) For what purposes does a company need to know its own cost of capital?
                                                                (DMS)

3   You are considering purchasing a word processor for £10,000 to improve office efficiency. Part of the justification is that it will save approximately 20 hours' labour per week which is normally paid at £3 per hour. Additionally there will be an improvement in quality and flexibility which is not immediately measurable.

Your company is in the private sector where the rate of Corporation Tax is 35% and Capital Allowances are 25% on the reducing balance. The processor is expected to last at least five years and have negligible value when scrapped.

You are required:
(a) To calculate whether the investment is worthwhile, based on the above data, assuming the company requires a DCF yield of 12%.
(b) To draw conclusions from your calculations in (a) and from the other information given.   (DMS)

Questions for class use 1 (a) Why do the Inland Revenue not allow a company's own depreciation charge to be used when calculating the taxable profit?
(b) Explain how taxation is incorporated into the yearly cash flows in discounted cash flow appraisals.   (DMS)

2   The directors of Milnthorpe Engineering plc are considering the feasibility of issuing 12% debentures at par to raise £1m for an investment to broaden their product range. The new plant is expected to produce a return of £240,000 per year indefinitely, before tax and interest charges.

The company's existing capital structure is:

	£
Issued ordinary shares (£0.50 nominal value)	3,000,000
Issued 5% preference shares (£1 nominal value)	6,000,000
Reserves	6,000,000
	£15,000,000

The current market values of ordinary and preference shares are £2.00 and £0.80 respectively, and the company's current maintainable earnings before meeting Corporation Tax at an effective rate of 50% are £3,840,000 per year.

Required:
(a) Calculate the weighted average cost of capital before the issue of the debentures.
(b) If there is no change in the cost of either equity or preference capital, what would you expect the market value for ordinary shares to be immediately after the issue of the debentures, and what would the weighted average cost of capital be at that time?
(c) Discuss the effect of issuing debentures on the weighted average cost of capital of a company.   (Certified Diploma)

3   The DCF yield method of investment appraisal has been criticized on the grounds:
   (i) that inflation is not always allowed for in the cash flows and in the cost of capital;
   (ii) that the cash flows are just estimates and therefore subject to uncertainty;
   (iii) that discounting based on year-end factors ignores the continuous flow of cash in and out.

How valid are these criticisms and how do you answer them?   (DMS)

Appendix 1: Present value of £1

n Year	5%	6%	7%	8%	9%	10%	11%	12%	13%	14%	15%	16%	17%	18%	19%	20%	21%	22%	23%	24%	25%	26%	27%	28%	29%	30%	35%	40%
0	1.000	1.000	1.000	1.000	1.000	1.000	1.000	1.000	1.000	1.000	1.000	1.000	1.000	1.000	1.000	1.000	1.000	1.000	1.000	1.000	1.000	1.000	1.000	1.000	1.000	1.000	1.000	1.000
1	.952	.943	.935	.926	.917	.909	.901	.893	.885	.877	.870	.862	.855	.847	.840	.833	.826	.820	.813	.807	.800	.794	.787	.781	.775	.769	.741	.714
2	.907	.890	.873	.857	.842	.826	.812	.797	.783	.769	.756	.743	.731	.718	.706	.694	.683	.672	.661	.650	.640	.630	.620	.610	.601	.592	.549	.510
3	.864	.840	.816	.794	.772	.751	.731	.712	.693	.675	.658	.641	.624	.609	.593	.579	.564	.551	.537	.524	.512	.500	.488	.477	.466	.455	.406	.364
4	.823	.792	.763	.735	.708	.683	.659	.636	.613	.592	.572	.552	.534	.516	.499	.482	.467	.451	.437	.423	.410	.397	.384	.373	.361	.350	.301	.260
5	.784	.747	.713	.681	.650	.621	.593	.567	.543	.519	.497	.476	.456	.437	.419	.402	.386	.370	.355	.341	.328	.315	.303	.291	.280	.269	.223	.186
6	.746	.705	.666	.630	.596	.564	.535	.507	.480	.456	.432	.410	.390	.370	.352	.335	.319	.303	.289	.275	.262	.250	.238	.227	.217	.207	.165	.133
7	.711	.665	.623	.583	.547	.513	.482	.452	.425	.400	.376	.354	.333	.314	.296	.279	.263	.249	.235	.222	.210	.198	.188	.178	.168	.159	.122	.095
8	.677	.627	.582	.540	.502	.467	.434	.404	.376	.351	.327	.305	.285	.266	.249	.233	.218	.204	.191	.179	.168	.157	.148	.139	.130	.123	.091	.068
9	.645	.592	.544	.500	.460	.424	.391	.361	.333	.308	.284	.263	.243	.225	.209	.194	.180	.167	.155	.144	.134	.125	.116	.108	.101	.094	.067	.048
10	.614	.558	.508	.463	.422	.386	.352	.322	.295	.270	.247	.227	.208	.191	.176	.162	.149	.137	.126	.116	.107	.099	.092	.085	.078	.073	.050	.035
11	.585	.527	.475	.429	.388	.350	.317	.287	.261	.237	.215	.195	.178	.162	.148	.135	.123	.112	.103	.094	.086	.079	.072	.066	.061	.056	.037	.025
12	.557	.497	.444	.397	.356	.319	.286	.257	.231	.208	.187	.168	.152	.137	.124	.112	.102	.092	.083	.076	.069	.062	.057	.052	.047	.043	.027	.018
13	.530	.469	.415	.368	.326	.290	.258	.229	.204	.182	.163	.145	.130	.116	.104	.093	.084	.075	.068	.061	.055	.050	.045	.040	.037	.033	.020	.013
14	.505	.442	.388	.340	.299	.263	.232	.205	.181	.160	.141	.125	.111	.099	.088	.078	.069	.062	.055	.049	.044	.039	.035	.032	.028	.025	.015	.009
15	.481	.417	.362	.315	.275	.239	.209	.183	.160	.140	.123	.108	.095	.084	.074	.065	.057	.051	.045	.040	.035	.031	.028	.025	.022	.020	.011	.006
16	.458	.394	.339	.292	.252	.218	.188	.163	.141	.123	.107	.093	.081	.071	.062	.054	.047	.042	.036	.032	.028	.025	.022	.019	.017	.015	.008	.005
17	.436	.371	.317	.270	.231	.198	.170	.146	.125	.108	.093	.080	.069	.060	.052	.045	.039	.034	.030	.026	.023	.020	.017	.015	.013	.012	.006	.003
18	.416	.350	.296	.250	.212	.180	.153	.130	.111	.095	.081	.069	.059	.051	.044	.038	.032	.028	.024	.021	.018	.016	.014	.012	.010	.009	.005	.002
19	.396	.331	.277	.232	.194	.164	.138	.116	.098	.083	.070	.060	.051	.043	.037	.031	.027	.023	.020	.017	.014	.012	.011	.009	.008	.007	.003	.002
20	.377	.312	.258	.215	.178	.149	.124	.104	.087	.073	.061	.051	.043	.037	.031	.026	.022	.019	.016	.014	.012	.010	.008	.007	.006	.005	.002	.001
25	.295	.233	.184	.146	.116	.092	.074	.059	.047	.038	.030	.025	.020	.016	.013	.011	.009	.007	.006	.005	.004	.003	.003	.002	.002	.001	.001	.000
30	.231	.174	.131	.099	.075	.057	.044	.033	.026	.020	.015	.012	.009	.007	.005	.004	.003	.003	.002	.002	.001	.001	.001	.001	.000	.000	.000	.000
35	.181	.130	.094	.068	.049	.036	.026	.019	.014	.010	.008	.006	.004	.003	.002	.002	.001	.001	.001	.001	.000	.000	.000	.000	.000	.000	.000	.000
40	.142	.097	.067	.046	.032	.022	.015	.011	.008	.005	.004	.003	.002	.001	.001	.001	.000	.000	.000	.000	.000	.000	.000	.000	.000	.000	.000	.000
45	.111	.073	.048	.031	.021	.014	.009	.006	.004	.003	.002	.001	.001	.001	.000	.000	.000	.000	.000	.000	.000	.000	.000	.000	.000	.000	.000	.000
50	.087	.054	.034	.021	.013	.009	.005	.003	.002	.001	.001	.001	.000	.000	.000	.000	.000	.000	.000	.000	.000	.000	.000	.000	.000	.000	.000	.000

Note: The above present value factors are based on year-end interest calculations.

Appendix 2: Cumulative present value of £1 per annum

n Year	5%	6%	7%	8%	9%	10%	11%	12%	13%	14%	15%	16%	17%	18%	19%	20%	21%	22%	23%	24%	25%	26%	27%	28%	29%	30%	35%	40%
1	.952	.943	.935	.926	.917	.909	.901	.893	.885	.877	.870	.862	.855	.847	.840	.833	.826	.820	.813	.807	.800	.794	.787	.781	.775	.769	.741	.714
2	1.859	1.833	1.808	1.783	1.759	1.736	1.713	1.690	1.668	1.647	1.626	1.605	1.585	1.566	1.546	1.528	1.510	1.492	1.474	1.457	1.440	1.424	1.407	1.392	1.376	1.361	1.289	1.224
3	2.723	2.673	2.624	2.577	2.531	2.487	2.444	2.402	2.361	2.322	2.283	2.246	2.210	2.174	2.140	2.106	2.074	2.042	2.011	1.981	1.952	1.923	1.896	1.868	1.842	1.816	1.696	1.589
4	3.546	3.465	3.387	3.312	3.240	3.170	3.102	3.037	2.974	2.914	2.855	2.798	2.743	2.690	2.639	2.589	2.540	2.494	2.448	2.404	2.362	2.320	2.280	2.241	2.203	2.166	1.997	1.849
5	4.329	4.212	4.100	3.993	3.890	3.791	3.696	3.605	3.517	3.433	3.352	3.274	3.199	3.127	3.058	2.991	2.926	2.864	2.804	2.745	2.689	2.635	2.583	2.532	2.483	2.436	2.220	2.035
6	5.076	4.917	4.767	4.623	4.486	4.355	4.231	4.111	3.998	3.889	3.784	3.685	3.589	3.498	3.410	3.326	3.245	3.167	3.092	3.021	2.951	2.885	2.821	2.759	2.700	2.643	2.385	2.168
7	5.786	5.582	5.389	5.206	5.033	4.868	4.712	4.564	4.423	4.288	4.160	4.039	3.922	3.812	3.706	3.605	3.508	3.416	3.327	3.242	3.161	3.083	3.009	2.937	2.868	2.802	2.508	2.263
8	6.463	6.210	5.971	5.747	5.535	5.335	5.146	4.968	4.799	4.639	4.487	4.344	4.207	4.078	3.954	3.837	3.726	3.619	3.518	3.421	3.329	3.241	3.156	3.076	2.999	2.925	2.598	2.331
9	7.108	6.802	6.515	6.247	5.995	5.759	5.537	5.328	5.132	4.946	4.772	4.607	4.451	4.303	4.163	4.031	3.905	3.786	3.673	3.566	3.463	3.366	3.273	3.184	3.100	3.019	2.665	2.379
10	7.772	7.360	7.024	6.710	6.418	6.145	5.889	5.650	5.426	5.216	5.019	4.833	4.659	4.494	4.339	4.192	4.054	3.923	3.799	3.682	3.571	3.465	3.366	3.269	3.178	3.092	2.715	2.414
11	8.306	7.887	7.499	7.139	6.805	6.495	6.207	5.938	5.687	5.453	5.234	5.029	4.836	4.656	4.486	4.327	4.177	4.035	3.902	3.776	3.656	3.544	3.437	3.335	3.239	3.147	2.752	2.438
12	8.863	8.384	7.943	7.536	7.161	6.814	6.492	6.194	5.918	5.660	5.421	5.197	4.988	4.793	4.610	4.439	4.278	4.127	3.985	3.851	3.725	3.606	3.493	3.387	3.286	3.190	2.779	2.456
13	9.394	8.853	8.358	7.904	7.487	7.103	6.750	6.424	6.122	5.842	5.583	5.342	5.118	4.910	4.715	4.533	4.362	4.203	4.053	3.912	3.780	3.656	3.538	3.427	3.322	3.223	2.799	2.469
14	9.899	9.295	8.745	8.244	7.786	7.367	6.982	6.628	6.302	6.002	5.724	5.468	5.229	5.008	4.802	4.611	4.432	4.265	4.108	3.962	3.824	3.695	3.573	3.459	3.351	3.249	2.814	2.478
15	10.380	9.712	9.108	8.559	8.061	7.606	7.191	6.811	6.462	6.142	5.847	5.575	5.324	5.092	4.876	4.675	4.490	4.315	4.153	4.001	3.859	3.726	3.601	3.483	3.373	3.268	2.825	2.484
16	10.838	10.106	9.447	8.851	8.313	7.824	7.379	6.974	6.604	6.265	5.954	5.669	5.405	5.162	4.938	4.730	4.536	4.357	4.190	4.033	3.887	3.751	3.623	3.503	3.390	3.283	2.834	2.489
17	11.274	10.477	9.763	9.122	8.544	8.022	7.549	7.120	6.729	6.373	6.047	5.749	5.475	5.222	4.990	4.775	4.576	4.391	4.219	4.059	3.910	3.771	3.640	3.518	3.403	3.295	2.840	2.492
18	11.690	10.828	10.059	9.372	8.756	8.201	7.702	7.250	6.840	6.467	6.128	5.818	5.534	5.273	5.033	4.812	4.608	4.419	4.243	4.080	3.928	3.786	3.654	3.529	3.413	3.304	2.844	2.494
19	12.085	11.158	10.336	9.604	8.950	8.365	7.839	7.366	6.938	6.550	6.198	5.877	5.584	5.316	5.070	4.844	4.635	4.442	4.263	4.097	3.942	3.799	3.666	3.539	3.421	3.311	2.848	2.496
20	12.462	11.470	10.594	9.818	9.129	8.514	7.963	7.469	7.025	6.623	6.259	5.929	5.628	5.353	5.101	4.870	4.657	4.460	4.279	4.110	3.954	3.808	3.673	3.546	3.427	3.316	2.850	2.497
25	14.094	12.783	11.654	10.675	9.823	9.077	8.422	7.843	7.330	6.873	6.464	6.097	5.766	5.467	5.195	4.948	4.721	4.514	4.323	4.147	3.985	3.834	3.694	3.564	3.442	3.329	2.856	2.499
30	15.372	13.765	12.409	11.258	10.274	9.427	8.694	8.055	7.496	7.003	6.566	6.177	5.829	5.517	5.235	4.979	4.746	4.534	4.339	4.160	3.995	3.842	3.701	3.569	3.447	3.332	2.857	2.500
35	16.374	14.498	12.948	11.655	10.567	9.644	8.855	8.176	7.586	7.070	6.617	6.215	5.858	5.539	5.251	4.992	4.756	4.541	4.345	4.164	3.998	3.845	3.703	3.571	3.448	3.333	2.857	2.500
40	17.159	15.046	13.332	11.925	10.757	9.779	8.951	8.244	7.634	7.105	6.642	6.234	5.871	5.548	5.258	4.997	4.760	4.544	4.347	4.166	3.999	3.846	3.703	3.571	3.448	3.333	2.857	2.500
45	17.774	15.456	13.606	12.108	10.881	9.863	9.008	8.283	7.661	7.123	6.654	6.242	5.877	5.552	5.261	4.999	4.761	4.545	4.347	4.166	4.000	3.846	3.704	3.571	3.448	3.333	2.857	2.500
50	18.256	15.762	13.801	12.234	10.962	9.915	9.042	8.305	7.675	7.133	6.661	6.246	5.880	5.554	5.262	5.000	4.762	4.545	4.348	4.167	4.000	3.846	3.704	3.571	3.448	3.333	2.857	2.500

Note: The above present value factors are based on year-end interest calculations.

Appendix 3: Glossary of terms

Absorption costing A system of costing where cost units (i.e. products) absorb indirect costs in addition to the allocated direct costs.

Acid test See **Liquidity ratio**

Activity-based costing The identification of activities as a basis for charging overhead costs to products.

Activity ratio Used in standard costing to express the actual work produced as a percentage of the budgeted work for the same period when both are expressed in standard hours.

Apportionment The process of splitting an indirect cost into smaller parts to charge to various cost centres.

Asset Any possession or claim on others which is of value to a firm. See also **Fixed assets** and **Current assets**.

Balance sheet A statement of the financial position of a firm at a point in time showing the assets owned and the sources of finance.

Batch costing A type of job costing where a batch of identical products is treated as an individual job for costing purposes. The unit cost is found by dividing the total batch cost by the number of units produced.

Break-even chart A graph showing the break-even point where the total cost line intersects the sales revenue line.

Break-even point The level of output, or sales value, at which total cost equals total revenue.

Budgetary control A system of detailed financial plans to meet corporate objectives over a future period of time, not exceeding one year.

Capacity ratio Used in standard costing to express the actual hours worked as a percentage of the budgeted standard hours.

Capital allowance The Inland Revenue's equivalent of a company's depreciation charge. Allowances are granted on purchases of certain new fixed assets and reduce taxable profits.

Capital employed All sources of finance excluding current liabilities. Sometimes called net capital employed.

Capital expenditure Expenditure on fixed assets with a life expectancy of more than one accounting period.

Capital gearing The relationship of borrowed capital to either shareholders' funds or total capital employed.

Cash budget A monthly plan of future cash receipts and payments showing the cumulative balance.

Common fixed cost A fixed cost which does not relate to any one cost unit but is incurred on behalf of multiple cost units.

Contract costing A type of job costing where all costs are accumulated on an individual contract, e.g. for a building or engineering construction.

Contribution The difference between sales and the variable cost of goods sold, before charging any fixed costs.

Contribution price variance Used in standard marginal costing to evaluate any difference in actual sales price from the standard sales price for the actual quantity sold. Identical with the sales price variance in standard absorption costing.

Contribution ratio or profit/volume ratio Contribution expressed as a percentage of sales revenue.

Contribution volume variance Used in standard marginal costing to evaluate the total contribution gained or lost through actual sales volume varying from the budgeted sales volume.

Controllable cost A cost which is the direct responsibility of, and influenced by, the manager concerned.

Corporation tax Tax levied on a limited company's profit after capital allowances have been deducted.

Cost centre A physical location within an organization where costs are accumulated.

Cost classification The analysis of costs into homogeneous groups according to source, nature and ultimate destination in the costing system.

Cost code A numbering system used to describe the type, source and purpose of all costs and income.

Cost element Labour or material or expense.

Cost-plus pricing Where a percentage mark-up is added to the total cost of a product to calculate the selling price.

Cost unit Any product or service to which costs can be charged.

Cost/volume/profit (CVP) analysis A study of the effect of changing levels of output on profit.

Creditor Any third party to whom a firm owes money. Trade creditors are purchases bought on credit and awaiting payment in due course.

Current assets Stocks, work-in-progress, debtors and cash/bank balances.

Current liabilities Short-term sources of finance from trade creditors, bank overdraft, dividend and tax provisions awaiting payment within the next twelve months.

Current ratio A measure of liquidity obtained by dividing current assets by current liabilities.

Debt ratio Total debts expressed as a percentage of total assets.

Debtor A credit customer or other party who owes money to the firm.

Depreciation A proportion of the original (or current) cost of a fixed asset which is charged as an expense in the profit and loss account.

Differential costing The costs and/or revenues of alternative courses of action which are compared to identify the difference between them.

Direct cost A cost which can be specifically allocated to a cost unit (product), say, for example, any raw materials used or labour expended.

Direct fixed cost A fixed cost which can be specifically identified with a product line or segment of activity.

Discounted cash flow (DCF) yield A measure of the true rate of profitability expected on a project. It represents the maximum rate of interest which could be allowed, leaving a net present value of zero.

Dividend cover A measure of the security of the dividend payment obtained by dividing the profit after tax by the total dividend for the year.

Earnings Profit attributable to the ordinary shareholders after interest, tax and any preference dividends have been deducted, irrespective of whether that profit is distributed or retained in the company.

Earnings per share Earnings for the year divided by the number of ordinary shares issued.

Efficiency ratio Used in standard costing to measure efficiency by expressing the standard hours equivalent of the work produced as a percentage of the actual hours taken.

Financial accounting The recording of financial transactions leading to the preparation of global financial statements, for example profit and loss account or balance sheet. Although used by top management, these statements are also used for external reporting.

Fixed assets Physical assets kept by the firm to carry on its business, for example buildings, plant and vehicles.

Fixed budget A budget which remains unchanged irrespective of the actual level of output.

Fixed costs Costs which do not vary in total when the level of activity varies. Rent and rates are typical examples.

Fixed overhead expenditure variance The difference between the actual cost and the budgeted cost of fixed overheads.

Fixed overhead volume variance The under- or over-recovery of fixed overheads caused by the actual level of activity varying from the budgeted level used to set the standard absorption rate.

Flexible budget A budget which is designed to change in accordance with the actual level of activity achieved.

Funds flow see **Sources and applications of funds statement**

Gearing see **Capital gearing** or **Operational** or **operating gearing**

Goal congruence When the objectives of an individual manager coincide with those of the organization.

Gross profit The difference between sales and the cost of sales before charging general overhead expenses.

Income gearing The annual interest charge expressed as a percentage of the annual operating profit. The larger this percentage is, the higher the level of financial risk.

Incremental expenditure The additional expenditure incurred in pursuing a new project.

Indirect costs or **Overheads** Costs which cannot be identified with specific cost units.

Inter-firm comparison The comparison of accounting ratios of different firms to measure relative performance.

Interest cover the number of times the annual operating profit covers the interest charge.

Internal rate of return (IRR) see **Discounted cash flow (DCF) yield**

Investment appraisal The use of accounting and statistical techniques to determine the worthwhileness of new investment projects.

Investment centre A type of responsibility centre where the manager is responsible for revenues, costs, profit and investment culminating in either a residual profit or return on capital objective.

Irrelevant costs Costs which remain unaffected by the decision under review and can therefore be ignored.

Job costing A system of costing which accumulates costs for each job separately.

Labour efficiency variance The difference between the hours taken and the standard hours allowed for the actual level of production, evaluated at the standard rate per hour.

Liabilities Money owing and repayable at some future time to shareholders or third parties, for example banks and suppliers.

Liquid assets Cash, bank balances and customer debts which will be converted into cash in a few weeks. Essentially, liquid assets are all current assets excluding stocks and work-in-progress.

Liquidity The ability of a company to pay its short-term debts when they become due.

Liquidity ratio A measure of liquidity obtained by dividing liquid assets by current liabilities.

Machine-hour rate A method of charging overheads to cost centres obtained by dividing the budgeted overheads by the budgeted number of hours.

Managed cost see **Controllable cost**

Managed cost centre A responsibility centre where the manager is responsible for giving the best level of service whilst keeping within his budget.

Management accounting The provision of detailed cost and income data to facilitate the role of managers in financial planning, controlling and decision making.

Management by exception The reporting to managers of only the significant variances from standard or budget.

Management information system Any planned system of collecting, storing, processing and presenting information to management so that effective decision making and control can take place.

Margin Either gross or net profit as a percentage of sales value.

Margin of safety The difference between the current level of activity and that needed to break-even, expressed as a percentage of the current level.

Marginal costing A system of costing used for decision making which is based on the analysis of costs into fixed and variable categories.

Mark-up A percentage addition to costs to cover overheads and/or profit.

Master budget The overall budget built up from the detailed functional budgets and expressed in a budgeted profit and loss account, a budgeted balance sheet and a budgeted funds flow statement.

Material mix variance The cost difference arising from the combination of materials in non-standard proportions.

Material price variance The difference in cost between actual and standard unit purchase prices, multiplied by the actual quantity purchased.

Material usage variance The difference in cost arising when the actual quantity of material is compared with the standard quantity for the actual level of production. Both quantities are evaluated at the standard price.

Material yield variance The value of the abnormal gain or loss in process, in excess of the standard allowance.

Net capital employed see **Capital employed**

Net cash flow A comparison of total cash in with total cash out for each year, being part of an investment appraisal.

Net current assets see **Working capital**

Net present value (NPV) The value obtained by discounting all yearly net cash flows back to Year 0 value at either the cost of capital or another target rate.

Operational or **operating gearing** A measure of the effect a given change in sales will have on profit, obtained by dividing contribution by net profit.

Opportunity cost The cost of a resource in an alternative use to the one being considered.

Overhead absorption rate A basis on which indirect costs are charged to individual product lines, for example £x per direct labour-hour.

Overhead efficiency variance This variance arises in standard costing when overheads are recovered on the basis of time as opposed to units of product. It is the difference between the standard overhead cost allowed for the actual production level achieved, and the standard overhead cost for the actual time taken.

Overhead expenditure variance The difference between the actual cost and the budgeted cost of overheads.

Overhead recovery rate see **Overhead absorption rate**

Overheads see **Indirect costs**

Payback period The number of years taken to recoup the original investment.

Portfolio theory A branch of investment appraisal concerned with risk and the discounting rate to apply to present value calculations.

Present value The value now of a future sum of money after interest has been deducted by discounting at an appropriate rate.

Price/earnings ratio A stockmarket yardstick used to assess the market rating of ordinary shares. It is calculated by dividing the market price by the earnings per share.

Prime costs The total of all direct labour, direct material and direct expenses.

Process costing The system of costing used when production is of a continuous nature rather than in discrete units.

Profit and loss account A statement of trading performance, typically for a month or a year, in which sales income is compared with total expenditure, which comprises the cost of sales and overheads relating to the period under review. Once the profit is computed, the statement concludes by showing its appropriation in tax and dividend payments with any balance being retained.

Profit centre A type of responsibility centre where the manager is responsible for costs and revenues and therefore profit. Managers have no authority over the level of investment in this case.

Profit margin A ratio used to measure performance, calculated by expressing gross or net profit as a percentage of sales value.

Profit/volume ratio see **Contribution ratio**

Profit/volume chart A chart or graph depicting profit or loss at all levels of activity.

Profitability A relative measure of performance found by expressing profit as a percentage of capital employed and/or turnover.

Profitability index A measure of the attractiveness of an investment, found by dividing the NPV of the inflows by the NPV of the outflow. It is also used in capital rationing situations to ensure the maximum £ inflow for every scarce £1 outflow.

Quick ratio see **Liquidity ratio**

Rate of return A rather arbitrary method of investment appraisal which relates average annual profit to the capital employed.

Rate of return pricing A method of pricing where the total cost of products is enhanced by the amount of profit required to yield the desired return on capital.

Ratio A pair of figures, usually taken from a profit and loss account and/or a balance sheet, which are related together and used as an indicator of performance. A typical example is the return on capital.

Relevant costs Costs which are affected by the decision under review and which therefore must be taken into account.

Relevant range The range of activity level within which costs behave in a linear fashion.

Residual profit or **Residual income** Used in responsibility accounting as a performance target for managers. It is calculated as a money figure of profit after interest has been charged on the capital invested.

Responsibility accounting A system of accounting used in decentralized organizations to identify costs, income, profit and investment with individual managers for the purpose of assessing their performance.

Responsibility centre A part of a decentralized organization for which a manager has responsibility. It can be a managed cost centre, or a revenue centre, or a profit centre, or an investment centre.

Return on capital A key ratio used to measure overall performance, calculated by expressing annual profit as a percentage of the closing (or average) capital employed.

Revenue see **Turnover**

Revenue centre A type of responsibility centre where the manager is responsible for the income generated from sales.

Sales price variance The total gain or loss caused by selling the actual level of sales at a non-standard price. It is calculated by multiplying the actual sales quantity by the difference between standard and actual selling prices.

Sales volume variance The total value of the profit margins gained or lost on the difference in quantity between actual sales and budgeted sales.

Segment margin The contribution of a product line, or other segment of a business, after any direct (specific) fixed costs have been taken into account.

Semi-variable or **Semi-fixed costs** Costs which include both fixed and variable elements and therefore neither stays constant nor moves *pro rata* with the level of activity.

Sensitivity analysis Used in investment appraisal as a risk technique where any component in the net cash flows can be examined for its effect on the NPV or DCF yield when its value is varied from the original estimate.

Sources and applications of funds statement A financial statement for a period of time showing both internal and external sources of cash and where that cash has been applied.

Standard cost A predetermined cost which is compared with the actual cost to highlight any significant variances for investigation and analysis.

Standard cost centre A type of responsibility centre where the managers' performance is judged by their ability to operate within the standard costs allowed for their products.

Standard hour A measure of the volume of work achievable in one hour.

Standard marginal cost A type of standard cost where only variable costs are included in the standard cost specification. Fixed costs are excluded for control by budgets or other means.

Stock turnover rate A ratio used to measure the time in weeks over which any kind of stock is used up.

Sunk costs Costs which were previously incurred and are now irrelevant to the decision under review, other than any opportunity cost they may possess.

Transfer pricing The basis for pricing goods or services transferred between different segments of an organization. It is a critical issue when the performance of the individual segments is monitored, as is usually the case.

Turnover or **Revenue** Alternative terms for the value of sales within a period of time.

Turnover of capital employed A ratio used as a performance indicator to measure the number of £ sales achieved within a year for every £1 of capital employed in the business.

Uniform costing A system of cost comparisons between similar organizations operating in service industries so that relative performance can be measured.

Variable costs Costs which vary in total when the level of activity varies. For example, the total cost of direct materials will move *pro rata* to the level of activity.

Variance The difference between a budget/standard and the actual cost.

Variance analysis The analysis of differences between standard costs and actual costs into their causes.

Working capital or **Net current assets** The part of a firm's total capital which is tied up in stocks, work-in-progress and debtors and not financed by short-term debts. It is equal to current assets less current liabilities.

Z score A measure based on weighted ratios used to assess a company's viability or to predict its possible failure

Zero-based budget A budget compiled without reference to the prior year's budget.

Appendix 4: Suggested answers

These are intended as a guide to the main points which should be included in an answer. Reference is made to an appropriate part of the text if the answer is contained therein. I am grateful to the Association of Accounting Technicians for permission to reproduce their suggested answers, which are denoted (AAT) at the foot. All other answers are the author's own responsibility and do not necessarily reflect the views of the examining bodies concerned.

Chapter 1 Cost analysis and classification

1

(a) The classification of costs is the grouping of costs in a systematic way according to their nature or purpose. A subjective classification is when, say, all wages costs are grouped together for the different kinds of tasks performed within the organization. Objective classifications, however, are when costs are grouped by the cost centres where they were incurred or by the cost units on which they were incurred.

(b) Coding is the use of a numbering system to describe fully any cost (subject) and its destination in the costing system (object). All prime documents are coded before entry into the accounting system. Most cost codes are composite codes, being compiled of separate series of numbers relating to both subject and object.

There are many advantages derived from the use of coding. Financial data, when coded, are unambiguous and can be easily input into computerized accounting systems. Management can then obtain all the information they require about the costs of products and the cost of running cost centres. This greatly helps them carry out their planning, controlling and decision making roles. Additionally, coding allows a company to produce detailed financial statements such as the profit and loss account and balance sheet.

Chapter 2 Costing labour, materials and overheads

1

(a) Stock valuation at 30 June based on LIFO valuation: 2,000 units valued at £4,000 (1,500 at £2.50 + 500 at £0.50). Stock valuation at 30 June based on FIFO valuation: 2,000 units at £2.70 valued at £5,400 in total.

(b)

	LIFO		FIFO	
	£	£	£	£
Sales		124,000		124,000
Opening stock	3,750		5,000	
Purchases	81,550		81,550	
	85,300		86,550	
Less: Closing stock	4,000	81,300	5,400	81,150
Trading profit		£42,700		£42,850

(c) Mr Wood's suggestion must not be adopted since a consistent policy is demanded in accounting in financial statements. If it was adopted, the company's profit and loss account would disclose a distorted profit figure. Mr Wood should be advised to disclose the information shown in (b) FIFO above, a profit of £42,850, as his main account, but also an accompanying note indicating that the change in stock valuation has been made and that under the basis previously adopted the trading profit would be £42,700.

(d) Accounting practice relating to stock valuation on the historical basis has been spelled out in SSAP 9 'Stocks and WIP' which implies that stock should be valued on the lower of cost or net realizable value. This may be construed as meaning that LIFO is not acceptable, and no doubt the company has been informed to this effect by its accountant. Generally acceptable methods are FIFO, weighted average, and adjusted standard price. Other reasonable explanations would also be accepted.

(e) Advantages of FIFO method. The technique is based on the logical assumption that materials are consumed in the order in which they are purchased. This means that it is:

(i) Reasonably easy to administer and charge issues to production.
(ii) Simple to explain to managers responsible for costs.
(iii) Generally acceptable for closing stock purposes.

Disadvantages:

(i) In times of inflation, production is charged at outdated prices.
(ii) Managers may be confused by being charged with different prices for identical materials.
(iii) It is held that the method overstates profit, and undercharges current production. (AAT adapted)

2

(a) (i) $\dfrac{£100,800}{24,000 \text{ h}} = £4.20/\text{h}$ $\qquad \dfrac{£94,500}{21,000 \text{ h}} = £4.50/\text{h}$

(ii) $\dfrac{£100,800}{42,000 \text{ h}} = £2.40/\text{h}$ $\qquad \dfrac{£94,500}{9,000 \text{ h}} = £10.50/\text{h}$

(b) **Total cost per product**

(i) *Labour-hour rate*	P	Q	R
	£	£	£
Direct costs	34.50	24.00	40.50
Overheads – machining	8.40	4.20	8.40
– finishing	6.75	4.50	9.00
	£49.65	£32.70	£57.90

(ii) *Machine-hour rate*	£	£	£
Direct costs	34.50	24.00	40.50
Overheads – machining	9.60	3.60	7.20
– finishing	5.25	5.25	10.50
	£49.35	£32.85	£58.20

(c) The factory manager has looked at the above figures and has seen that the answers are only marginally different. By combining the labour- or machine-hour rates, the total costs are still about the same as in the statement. A more realistic cost would be using a machine-hour rate for the machining area, and a labour rate for finishing. Departmental rates are normally used in costing practice.

(d) Hi–Lo, least squares, scattergraph, etc., are acceptable methods to find the fixed cost and the variable rate of overhead cost. Using the Hi–Lo method gives a fixed cost of £50,000 and a variable rate of £2 per hour. (AAT adapted)

3

(a) Overhead rate $= \dfrac{£165,000}{50,000\ h} = £3.30\ /h$

(b) Overheads will be over-recovered by 5,000 hours, which at £3.30 per hour, amounts to £16,500.

Chapter 3 Job, batch, contract and process costing

1 The charge for the job amounts to £193.16 made up as follows:

	£	£
Direct material		91.20
Direct labour	12.00	
	2.50	
	1.00	15.50
Overheads 2 h at £20	40.00	
0.5 h at £6.67	3.33	
0.25 h at £18	4.50	47.83
Sub-total		154.53
Profit and general overhead (25%)		38.63
Total charge		£193.16

2		*Job A*		*Job B*		*Job C*
		£		£		£
Direct materials		524		671		382
Labour – direct	158 h	790	170 h	850	16 h	80
– indirect	316 h	1,264	190 h	760	30 h	120
Site expenses		118		170		25
Administration*		237		180		23
Total costs 100%		2,933	Material	671	Material	382
80%			Other	1,960		
25%					Other	248

	Job A £	Job B £	Job C £
Selling price	3,318		
Contract profit	385		
Staff bonus 20%	77		
Profit to company	308		
Projected costs:			
B – 20%		490	
C – 75%			744
Projected total costs		3,121	1,374
Selling price		2,750	1,950
Contract profit (loss)		(371)	576
Projected staff bonus		Nil	115
Projected profit to company		£(371)	£461

* Hourly rate for recovery = £440/880 h = 50p

(a) Profit to company on Job A = £308
(b) Projected loss on Job B = £371. Projected profit on Job C = £461
(c) Job B should be subject to careful scrutiny. It may be revealed that costs have escalated since the contract price was agreed. Possibly a negotiated adjustment to the selling price may be feasible. Material costs are 27% of selling price compared with 18–20% for Jobs A and C. The ratio of direct/indirect hours is abnormally high on Job B. Similarly site expenses appear to be excessive.

(d)

		Job D
	£	£
Selling price 2,750 + 10%		3,025
Less: Variable costs:		
Material	671.00	
Labour – Skilled 212.5 h at £5	1,062.50	
– Semi-skilled 237.5 h at £4	950.00	
Site expenses	212.50	
		2,896
Contribution		£129

Accept order if sufficient labour available in June.

		Hours			Hours
Skilled	A	158	Semi-skilled	A	316
	B	170		B	190
	C	16		C	30
Hours available		344			536
Required:	B	42.5	20%		47.5
	C	48	75%		90
	D	212.5	100%		237.5
Hours required		303			375
Surplus hours		41 h			161 h

This confirms that the order must be accepted as there is sufficient skilled and semi-skilled labour available to complete it in June. (AAT)

211

Chapter 4 Pricing

1

(a)

	Betascope	
	per unit	*1,000 units*
	£	*£*
Raw material $17 \times £7.50$	127.50	127,500
Direct labour $125 \times £2.50$	312.50	312,500
Variable overheads	125.00	125,000
Total variable costs	£565.00	£565,000
Fixed overheads	56.50	56,500
Total cost	£621.50	£621,500
Profit mark-up	310.75	310,750
Sales	£932.25	£932,250

Unit selling price = £932.25

(b) The total contribution required = Fixed costs + Profit

= 56,500 + 310,750

= £367,250

The new unit contribution $= \dfrac{£367,250}{800 \text{ units}}$

= £459.06 per unit

The new unit selling price:

Raw material	146.62
Direct labour	343.75
Variable overheads	131.25
Contribution	459.06
Selling price	£1080.68

2

(a) The charge for the job amounts to £268.25 made up as follows:

	£	£
Direct material		42.00
Direct expenses		36.50
Direct labour	10.00	
	4.00	
	0.60	14.60
Variable overheads	40.00	
	10.00	
	2.50	52.50
Fixed overheads	60.00	
	5.00	
	4.00	69.00
Sub-total		214.60
Profit and administrative overheads	25%	53.65
Total charge for the job		£268.25

(b) If a price of £200 were accepted, this would incur a loss of £68.25 on a full cost basis. However, this reduced price would give a positive contribution of £54.40 after deducting all variable costs, i.e. direct costs plus variable overheads. Accepting the order at this price would be sensible only if there is spare capacity not likely to be used with more profitable work. If this new customer is encouraged to return with further orders this 'loss leader' approach may also be worthwhile, provided new work is at full prices. There could be problems if other existing customers find out.

Chapter 5 Profit/volume planning

1

(i)

	£	£
Selling price per sledge		6.50
Variable costs – raw material	2.20	
– packing material	0.25	
– machine time	0.60	
– packing time	0.40	3.45
Contribution		3.05
Fixed costs per sledge		0.39
Profit		£2.66

(ii) The break-even point is reached when sufficient unit contributions amount to the total fixed costs per week. Therefore:

$$\text{Break-even point} = \frac{£300}{£3.05} = 98 \text{ sledges}$$

(iii) If raw materials rise in price by £1.10 then the unit contribution falls to £1.95.

$$\text{New break-even point} = \frac{£300}{£1.95} = 154 \text{ sledges}$$

2 See text of Chapter 5 under headings 'Planning for Change' and 'Operating Gearing' for a full discussion of this question.

3

(a) $$\text{Break-even point} = \frac{\text{Fixed cost}}{\text{Contribution per unit}} = \frac{£201,600}{£6 \text{ (i.e. } 20-14)} = 33,600 \text{ units}$$

The break-even chart should show the total cost and sales curves intersecting at approximately 34,000 units.

(b)

Profit and Loss Account

	£	£
Sales 36,000 × £20		720,000
Less: Wages	£2.00	
Materials	£8.00	
Variable o/h	£4.00	
	36,000 × £14.00	504,000
Contribution		216,000
Less: Fixed costs		201,600
Budgeted profit		£14,400

(c) Return on investment
$= 15\% \times £330,000$
$= £49,500$

Total contribution required
$=$ Fixed cost + Profit requirement
$= £201,600 + £49,500$
$= £251,100$

Required volume
$= \dfrac{\text{Total contribution required}}{\text{Contribution per unit}}$

$= \dfrac{£251,100}{£6}$

$= 41,850$ units

(d) The company is not achieving the required rate of return as it is only selling 36,000 units at a profit of £14,400. To achieve a return of 15% on capital invested requires sales of 41,850 at the present selling price and cost structure. This is beyond normal capacity. Other ways to achieve a 15% return include cost reduction; increased selling price if possible with market research on effects; introduction of new products. (AAT adapted)

Chapter 6 Standard costing

1

(a)

		Period 1	*Period 2*
(i)	Efficiency Ratio	$\dfrac{1750}{1800} \times 100\% = 97.2\%$	$\dfrac{2250}{2400} \times 100\% = 93.7\%$
(ii)	Activity Ratio	$\dfrac{1750}{2000} \times 100\% = 87.5\%$	$\dfrac{2250}{2250} \times 100\% = 100\%$
(iii)	Capacity Ratio	$\dfrac{1800}{2000} \times 100\% = 90\%$	$\dfrac{2400}{2250} \times 100\% = 106.6\%$

(b) The activity ratio shows that the production level was exactly in line with that budgeted in period 2, a significant improvement from only 87.5% in period 1. However, the capacity ratio exceeding 100% shows that this was achieved by working more hours than those budgeted whilst there was also a drop in the efficiency level during those hours from 97.2% in period 1 to 93.7% in period 2.

2

(a) Total material cost variance:

		£
Standard cost	3,150 units $\times$ 1.5 kg $\times$ £0.60	3,159.00
Actual cost	2,740 kg $\times$ £0.58 = £1,589.20	
	2,315 kg $\times$ £0.62 = £1,435.30	3,024.50
		£ 134.50 (F)

Material price variance:

	£
Standard cost of purchases 5,055 kg x £0.60	3,033.00
Actual cost of purchases	3,024.50
	£ 8.50 (F)

Material usage variance:
(Standard quantity – Actual quantity) × £0.60
(5,265   –   5,055) × £0.60   £ 126.00 (F)

Total wages variance:
Standard cost   3,510 × £3.80 × £0.60   8,002.80
Actual cost   880 × £3.90 = £3,432 }
           1,300 × £3.65 = £4,745 }   8,177.00
                                £ 174.20 (A)

Wages rate variance:
Standard cost of hours worked 2,180 × £3.80   8,284.00
Actual cost of hours worked   8,177.00
        £ 107.00 (F)

Labour efficiency variance:
(Standard hours required – Actual hours worked) × £3.80
(2,106   –   2,180) × £3.80   £281.20 (A)

(b) **Cost Statement – May 1983**

	£
Sales, at standard selling price 3,510 x £3.50	12,285.00
Factory cost of sales 3,510 x £3.18	11,161.80
Gross profit at standard	£1,123.20

Add: Favourable variances: £
    Material price   8.50
    Material usage   126.00
    Wages rate   107.00   241.50
                             1,364.70

Deduct: Adverse variances:
        Labour efficiency   281.20
Gross profit, actual   £1,083.50

(c) Past performance is a method sometimes adopted in fixing standard prices, but it is not necessarily a good guide and could be misleading. It should only be used in the event of no other information with regard to expected performance being available.

Past performance includes past prices, past inefficiencies, previous conditions and methods of work. It is a concept of good management that efforts should always be made to improve past performance and, therefore, future activity should be influenced by determined and objective efforts to control cost.

Standards should be based on known future prices and efficient methods of work. Conditions should be anticipated and control features designed to enable corrections to be made where necessary. The statement is not to be accepted.

(AAT)

Chapter 7 Budgetary control

1

(a) (i) Controllable costs, also known as managed costs, are those which can be influenced by the actions of the person in whom control of a cost centre is vested.

(ii) Non-controllable costs are those charges which are beyond the control of the manager of a cost centre. Generally these tend to be fixed costs, whereas controllables are usually variable.

(b)

Budget Statement   Date.....

Workshop or Department no. .....

	This month			Cumulative to date		
	Budget	*Actual*	*Gain/ Loss*	*Budget*	*Actual*	*Gain/ Loss*
Controllable costs:						
Basic wages						
Overtime premium						
Direct materials						
Power						
Total controllables						
Non-controllables:						
Rent						
Rates						
Depreciation						
Insurance						
Total non-controllables						
Total costs						

(c) (i) Preparation of budgets is primarily the main task and duty of the budget committee.

(ii) Generally one of the committee's members, usually the Cost Accountant, prepares and distributes a timetable for each stage of the budgeting process.

(iii) Information must be made available to the committee and to executives and managers in the form of their functional and financial objectives.

(iv) Functional managers' co-operation is encouraged so that all objectives are capable of being summarized into master budgets.

(v) Budgets are consolidated, prepared and issued before any budget year (or other period) is started.

(vi) Actual results are compared with budget on a regular basis.

(vii) Action is taken by the committee to motivate managers to achieve budget where results are varying from targets.   (AAT)

2

(a)   A Manpower Budget details the number of persons required to meet the Production/Operations Budget, classified by skills and by departments, from which the cost of labour can be calculated. This feeds into Production Cost Budgets, the Cash Budget and the Budgeted Profit and Loss Account. Additionally, the Manpower Budget allows the Personnel and Training function time to recruit/train/retrain as necessary.

(b)   (i) Machining centre:

Component	Quantity	Hours	Total Hours
xa	53,000	2	106,000
xb	52,500	4	210,000
ya	39,000	1	39,000
yb	39,500	3	118,500
			473,500

Assembly centre:

Product	Quantity	Hours	Total Hours
X	52,000	3	156,000
Y	39,000	4	156,000
			312,000

Effective hours per employee p.a. = $(40 \times 52) - (25 \times 8)$ = 1,880 hours p.a.
Machining centre: 473,500/1,880 = 251.86 employees
Assembly centre: 312,000/1,880 = 165.96 employees

(ii)   It would pay the firm to 'round up' the above numbers, because overtime would be more expensive than the lost fractions. So the final numbers are: Machining 252 employees; Assembly 166 employees

3

(a)   (i)   The purpose of a cash budget is to provide information relating to future cash movements, giving sufficient notice of any surplus or deficiency of cash so that action may be taken to the benefit of the company.

(ii)   The principal source of information is the operating and capital expenditure budgets of the business which are prepared in advance of the cash budget.

(b)   (i)

Cash Budget for three months ending 31st March 1985

	January £	February £	March £
Receipts:			
Sales: Credit	3,750	3,750	4,500
Cash	3,500	1,250	3,000
Equipment		2,000	
	7,250	7,000	7,500
Payments:			
Purchases: Credit	5,000	6,000	5,750
Cash	500	250	250

	January	February	March
Wages	250	250	250
Postage & packing	750	900	1,000
Dividends			375
Equipment		2,000	2,000
	6,500	9,400	9,625
Cash flow	750	(2,400)	(2,125)
Opening balance	2,250	3,000	600
Closing balance	3,000	600	(1,525)

(ii)   **Forecast Trading and Profit & Loss Account**
for three months ending 31st March 1985

	£	£
Sales (credit 13,250 + cash 7,750)		21,000
Less: Stock at 1st January		6,000
Add: Purchases (18,500 + 1,000)	19,500	
		25,500
Less: Stock at 31 March		11,500
		14,000
Gross profit (33.3% on sales)		7,000
Less: Wages	750	
Postage and packing	2,650	
Loss on sale of equipment	1,750	
Depreciation	150	
		5,300
Net profit		£1,700

(iii)   **Forecast Balance Sheet as at 31st March 1985**

	£	£	£
Fixed assets:			
Equipment, at cost		6,000	
Less: Depreciation		150	
			5,850
Current assets:			
Stock		11,500	
Debtors		5,000	
		16,500	
Less: Current liabilities:			
Creditors	8,750		
Bank overdraft	1,525		
Dividends due	375	10,650	
			5,850
			11,700
Represented by:			
Capital		10,000	
Net profit		1,700	11,700

(c)   A cash budget projects movements of cash only, whereas the profit and
loss account displays both cash and credit transactions, as it is assumed
that credit will be realized in the course of time. Non-cash movements are

also necessary in order to obtain distributable profits, so depreciation and loss on sale of assets have been recorded. (AAT)

Chapter 8 Ratio analysis

1

(i)   Gross profit percentage $= \dfrac{1725}{3100} \times 100\% = 55.6\%$

(ii)   Net profit percentage $= \dfrac{670}{3100} \times 100\% = 21.6\%$

(iii) Return on total assets $= \dfrac{670}{2055} \times 100\% = 32.6\%$

(iv)   Quick ratio $= \dfrac{870}{665} = 1.3 : 1$

(v)   Debtors collection period $= \dfrac{770}{3100} \times 365 = 91$ days

(vi)   Stock : turnover $= \dfrac{3100}{310} = 10$ times

(vii) Fixed assets : turnover $= \dfrac{3100}{875} = 3.5$ times

(viii) Return on shareholders' funds $= \dfrac{586}{690} \times 100\% = 84.9\%$

(ix)   Current ratio $= \dfrac{1180}{665} = 1.8 : 1$

(x)   Debt ratio $= \dfrac{1365}{2055} \times 100\% = 66.4\%$

Very few ratios have an absolute value but they are used in a relative way in intra- and inter-firm comparisons. Both gross and net margins are calculated using the profit before tax and interest to identify the trading profit, irrespective of the capital structure in force. Both these figures seem satisfactory but knowledge of the industry is necessary. Also the returns on shareholders' funds and on total assets both appear quite satisfactory.

The quick ratio exceeds the 1:1 norm and the current ratio is near the 2:1 norm, but this requirement varies widely. On the other hand the debt ratio seems high, as two-thirds of all assets are financed by debt.

Asset turnover rates also need comparisons to make any judgement but the debtors collection period of 91 days would seem too long for most industries, especially if credit is granted on a net monthly basis.

2

The return on capital is low at 6.7% compared with firm X at 21.7%. This is primarily due to the profit margin being only 5% compared with 13%. Both direct labour and materials are relatively higher than those of firm X but perhaps too little is being spent on selling and distribution expenses.

Fixed asset turnover is either very good, or denotes either old or under-provision of equipment, which might be the cause of the high direct labour, etc.

Stock turnover is too low and this partly reflects in much too high a current ratio, although the acid test ratio also suggests too many liquid assets.

Borrowings are on the low side so there is no sign of overgearing.

Chapter 9 Responsibility accounting

1
(a) See pp. 135–6 for descriptions of the principal types of financial responsibility centre.
(b) The choice of appropriate centres will depend on the corporate strategy employed in the organization with regard to decentralization; the organization structure which reflects the degree of decentralization; and the management philosophy. There are many behavioural implications in responsibility accounting. Authority must go with the responsibility to achieve corporate objectives.
(c) The prime criterion is the promotion of 'goal congruence', so that managers, in pursuing their individual objectives, do not conflict with other managers' or corporate objectives. Other criteria are the need for clear and fair financial measurements to be employed which are appropriate to the authority and responsibility of the manager concerned. Different types of responsibility centre may be appropriate for different parts of an organization.

2
(a) This division is likely to be an investment centre and be judged by the return on capital achieved as a result of its own management decisions. This could be expressed as a percentage return on capital, or as a residual profit after allowing for interest on that capital.
(b) The social services department will be a managed cost centre, probably broken down into a number of smaller managed cost centres. Here, managers are charged with the responsibility of providing the best level of service while keeping within agreed cost budgets.
(c) The branch may be regarded as a revenue centre if sales are all at nationally agreed prices and local costs are constrained by an imposed budget. In the absence of these two constraints the branch would be a profit centre.

Chapter 10 Short-term decisions

1
50% of budgeted levels will use up £39,000 of raw materials being 50% of the £78,000 total. The remaining £11,000 of raw materials should be allocated to the product(s) with the highest contribution per £1 of raw material used on that product. We therefore need to calculate the contribution on individual product lines and then the contribution per £1 of raw material used in the process, as follows:

	Product A £000	Product B £000	Product C £000	Total D £000
Sales	194	132	188	514
Less: Variable costs	90	60	96	246
Contribution	104	72	92	268
Raw material used	34	18	26	78
Contribution per £1 of raw material	£3.06	£4.00	£3.54	

Therefore more raw material should be allocated to product B up to its maximum budget potential. This will use up £9,000 of the £11,000 available. The remaining £2,000 of raw material should then be allocated to product C. The revised budget will now be:

	Product A £000	Product B £000	Product C £000	Total D £000
Sales	97	132	108.5	337.5
Variable costs:				
Raw materials	17	18	15	50.0
Direct labour	20	31	33.5	84.5
Variable overheads	8	11	6.9	25.9
Total variable costs	45	60	55.4	160.4
Contribution	52	72	53.1	177.1
Fixed costs				160.0
Profit				17.1

2

(a) Unit selling prices £223.50; £341.10; £155.40 respectively. Unit contributions £97.00; £149.70; £60.80 respectively. Contribution per D.L. hour £19.40; £18.71; £30.40 respectively.

(b)
Forecast Profit for August

	Alpha £	Beta £	Gamma £	Total £
Sales	11,175	51,165	31,080	93,420
Less:Variable costs	6,325	28,710	18,920	53,955
Contribution	£4,850	£22,455	£12,160	39,465
Less: Fixed costs				8,325
Net Profit				£31,140
Contribution ratio	43.4%	43.9%	39.1%	42.2%

Ranking of products by contribution ratio in order of preference is B; A; G.

(c) With insufficient labour to produce at the forecast levels, the products will be ranked in order of their contribution per direct labour-hour. Gamma contributes £30.40 per hour and will be produced first up to the maximum forecast demand. Any labour remaining will be used to produce Alpha which contributes £19.40 per hour. Once forecast demand of that is met, any labour remaining will be used to produce Beta which is the least profitable, contributing only £18.71 per labour-hour.

3   This is a 'make or buy' decision which hinges on the behaviour of the £37,000 total annual costs (i.e. whether variable or fixed). Also required is information on whether the capacity released when components are bought-in can be utilized in an alternative way to make a contribution to fixed costs. See Chapter 10 under 'Make or Buy Decisions', for full discussion of these points.

4   The total costs for this order were estimated at £26,500 which is £500 more than the new customer's offer of £26,000, hence a small loss would result. However, if Flanges Ltd were short of work, this order would result in a substantial contribution to fixed overheads. Provided there are no knock-on effects with existing customers, Flanges Ltd would be advised to take the order and increase capacity working. The customer should be advised that this is a one-off step and that similar low prices cannot be guaranteed in the future.

Chapter 11 Investment appraisal

1

(a)   The basis of choice between these three alternatives is to select the one offering the highest NPV surplus after the yearly cash flows have been discounted at the 15% cost of capital for Pilmar.

Both the original cost of the equipment and the existing working capital are ignored as they are 'sunk costs' common to all situations. Any new investment in equipment or working capital must be taken into account, as must the sale or release of any investment at the appropriate time.

Depreciation must be excluded from costs as it is not a cash transaction.

The calculations are:

Alternative A:
Net present value + £46,812.
Based on sales £100,000 less costs £89,000 ignoring depreciation.
£11,000 × 3.352 cum pv factor + £20,000 × 0.497 re release of working capital at end of year 5.

Alternative B:
Net present value + £11,336.
Based on sales £100,000 less costs £22,000, ignoring depreciation.
£78,000 × 3.352 + £40,000 × 0.497 re release of working capital. Initial investment at year 0 is £270,000 (£300,000 − £50,000 + £20,000).

Alternative C:
Net present value + £56,760.
Based on £5,000 × 3.352 re royalties plus £40,000 released at year 0 from working capital and sale of old equipment.

(b)   The NPV calculations in (a) suggest that the highest return will be found from ceasing manufacture now and selling out to Biret Ltd, taking royalties on future sales. This alternative C yields £10,000 more present value than continuing to manufacture with the old equipment (A) and £45,000 more than would result from buying new equipment (B). A further advantage of alternative C is that the risk element is minimized. The royalty payment is based on unit sales irrespective of changes in costs and selling prices and will vary only with demand, as it would on all alternatives.

2

(a)   The cost of equity can be found from Gordon's dividend growth model, which combines the dividend yield with the average growth in dividends in recent years, when both are expressed as percentages:

$$\frac{12p}{156p} \times 100\% = 7.7\% + 10\% \text{ Average growth rate} = 17.7\%$$

(b)   A weighted average cost of capital calculation is required, allowing for 35% tax relief on the interest payment.

Type	Proportion	Net cost	Weighted cost
Equity	5/6	22%	18.32%
10% Loan	1/6	6.5%	1.08%
		WACC	19.40%

(c)   The cost of capital is primarily used in investment decisions, when the weighted average cost of capital is used as the discount rate when calculating NPVs. It is also regarded as the minimum acceptable return on any new investment. Finally, it is used as a comparative cost when considering leasing or invoice discounting as methods of financing.

3

(a)

Year	Cash flow £	Tax paid £	Tax saved £	Net cash flow £	12% PV factors	PV £
0	−10,000			−10,000	1.000	−10,000
1	+3,120		+875	+3,995	0.893	+3,568
2	+3,120	−1,092	+656	+2,684	0.797	+2,139
3	+3,120	−1,092	+492	+2,520	0.712	+1,794
4	+3,120	−1,092	+369	+2,397	0.636	+1,524
5	+3,120	−1,092	+277	+2,305	0.567	+1,307
6	—	−1,092	+831	−261	0.507	−132
					NPV	+£200

(b)   This appears to be a marginally viable project with the NPV so close to zero. However, when allowance is made for the possibly extended life, the increased quality and flexibility, then a case can probably be made for going ahead with the investment. Inflation has been ignored as it is assumed the 12% discount rate is a real rate, as opposed to a nominal rate.

Index

Index